Duncan Leitch

# ASSISTING REFORM IN POST-COMMUNIST UKRAINE 2000–2012

The Illusions of Donors and the Disillusion of Beneficiaries

With a foreword by by Kataryna Wolczuk

*ibidem*-Verlag
Stuttgart

**Bibliografische Information der Deutschen Nationalbibliothek**
Die Deutsche Nationalbibliothek verzeichnet diese Publikation in der Deutschen Nationalbibliografie; detaillierte bibliografische Daten sind im Internet über http://dnb.d-nb.de abrufbar.

**Bibliographic information published by the Deutsche Nationalbibliothek**
Die Deutsche Nationalbibliothek lists this publication in the Deutsche Nationalbibliografie; detailed bibliographic data are available in the Internet at http://dnb.d-nb.de.

Cover picture: © V. Karamushka, reprint with kind permission.

∞

Gedruckt auf alterungsbeständigem, säurefreien Papier
Printed on acid-free paper

ISSN: 1614-3515

ISBN-13: 978-3-8382-0844-2

© *ibidem*-Verlag

Stuttgart 2016

Alle Rechte vorbehalten

Das Werk einschließlich aller seiner Teile ist urheberrechtlich geschützt. Jede Verwertung außerhalb der engen Grenzen des Urheberrechtsgesetzes ist ohne Zustimmung des Verlages unzulässig und strafbar. Dies gilt insbesondere für Vervielfältigungen, Übersetzungen, Mikroverfilmungen und elektronische Speicherformen sowie die Einspeicherung und Verarbeitung in elektronischen Systemen.

All rights reserved. No part of this publication may be reproduced, stored in or introduced into a retrieval system, or transmitted, in any form, or by any means (electronical, mechanical, photocopying, recording or otherwise) without the prior written permission of the publisher. Any person who does any unauthorized act in relation to this publication may be liable to criminal prosecution and civil claims for damages.

Printed in the EU

*This book is dedicated to the memory of my late wife Julia Burdett whose idea it was that I should write it.*

# CONTENTS

Foreword by Dr Kataryna Wolczuk ..................................................................11
Glossary of Acronyms ........................................................................................12
Acknowledgements ............................................................................................13
**CHAPTER I: INTRODUCTION AND THEORETICAL FRAMEWORK** .15
**Part I: Background to the Study and Key Research Questions** ...................15
Context and Rationale for the Research: the Current Crisis in Ukraine. ......15
Bridging a Gap in the Literature .....................................................................16
International Technical Assistance and the Blame Game ............................18
Research Questions ......................................................................................... 20
The Argument ...................................................................................................21
The Researcher as Participant .........................................................................23
Overview of Chapters ......................................................................................25

**Part II: External Assistance and Domestic Reform
– What the Literature Tells Us** ........................................................................27
Introduction .......................................................................................................27
Theorising External Influence (i): the EU and the Accession States ...............27
Theorising External Influence (ii) : the EU and its Neighbourhood ............28
Theorising External Influence (iii):Transnational Policy Transfer ................31
Theorising External Influence (iv):
the Political Economy Analysis of International Aid ......................................32
Conclusions ......................................................................................................35

**CHAPTER II: THE HISTORICAL CONTEXT - INTERGOVERN-
MENTAL RELATIONS IN THE NEWLY INDEPENDENT UKRAINE** ....39
Introduction .....................................................................................................39
**Part I: The Ukrainian State in The First Decade After Independence** .......41
The Challenge of State Building and the Threat of Disintegration ...............41
Regional Policy and Intergovernmental Finance in the
Decade after Independence .............................................................................50
Institutions under Pressure .............................................................................55
Conclusions to Part I ........................................................................................59

**Part II: Post-Soviet Transition and The Sharing of International Know How** ..................................................................60

Introduction ..................................................................60

The Challenge of State Building and the Response of International Donors..................................................................61

Conclusions..................................................................68

**CHAPTER III: CASE STUDY I - FISCAL DECENTRALISATION AND THE BUDGET CODE REFORM OF 2000/1** ..................................71

Introduction ..................................................................71

**Part I: Preparing the Reform** ..................................................................74

Fatal Flaws Appear in the *Matryoshka* ..................................................................74

The Emergence of Personal and Institutional Networks..................................................................81

International Technical Assistance in the Preparation of Budget Reform ....92

Conclusions to Part I..................................................................103

**Part II: Reform Adoption and Implementation**..................................................................105

Introduction ..................................................................105

The Passing of the Law on the State Budget for 2001 ..................................................................106

Budget Code Reform and the Challenge of Implementation..................................................................113

Conclusions..................................................................122

**CHAPTER IV: CASE STUDY II - REGIONAL POLICY REFORM IN UKRAINE 2000-2012** ..................................................................125

Introduction ..................................................................125

**Part I: The Struggle for Settled Legislation**..................................................................129

Regional Policy Reform in Ukraine in a National and International Context..................................................................129

The Emergence of a Pro-Reform Enclave in the Ministry of Economy .......132

Conclusions to Part I..................................................................146

**Part II: International Advice and Regional Policy Reform** ..................................................................148

Introduction ..................................................................148

Institution Building: the New Priority for International Assistance to Ukraine ..................................................................149

Establishing a Stable Legislative Framework for Regional Policy ..................152

Conclusions ..................................................................173

**CHAPTER V: ANALYSIS AND DISCUSSION - LINKING THE CASE STUDY EVIDENCE TO THEORY** ................................................................ 175

Introduction .............................................................................................. 175

**Part I: Theorising International Technical Assistance** ............................. 178

Normative Institutional Isomorphism and Policy Transfer ......................... 178

Pro-Reform Enclaves and Informal Coalitions ............................................. 179

Shared Features of the Case Studies ............................................................ 181

Distinguishing Features of the Case Studies ................................................ 185

The Policy Transfer Network ........................................................................ 191

Conclusions to Part I .................................................................................... 193

**Part II: Reform Failure and the Political Economy Analysis of Development Theory** ................................................................ 195

Introduction .................................................................................................. 195

From Know How Sharing to the Mainstream of International Development ................................................................................................. 196

Experts Bringing Solutions (i): Developing Countries & the Political Economy Analysis ........................................................................................ 198

Internal Contradictions in Donor Policy towards Public Administrative Reform in Ukraine ........................................................................................ 201

Institutional Development and the Project Cycle of Technical Assistance ..................................................................................... 202

Experts Bringing Solutions (ii): Ukraine & the Output Culture of Technical Assistance ..................................................................................... 204

Behind the Façade of Ukraine's Formal Institutions: the Political Intelligence Deficit ....................................................................................... 206

Ukraine as a Neo-Patrimonial State ............................................................. 210

Conclusions .................................................................................................. 213

**CHAPTER VI: CONCLUSIONS** .................................................................... 216

Bibliography ................................................................................................. 223

List of Interviewees ...................................................................................... 248

# Foreword

Ukraine shot to international attention in late 2013. And with this attention has come a greater focus on Ukraine as a state and the realisation of how little we know about a crucial aspect of this large and complex country's journey since independence – relations between the centre and the periphery. This book helps fill that gap. For sure, it has long been known that reforms were essential if the country was to endure, let alone prosper, but so far little academic attention was paid to the one issue which threatened Ukraine's very survival: mismanaged relations between centre and the regions. Amidst the war in the Donbas, reforms became an imperative not only for overcoming the profound economic crisis but for the survival of the state as a whole. Decentralisation is seen as a particularly urgent political instrument to bring peace, stability and prosperity to Ukraine.

But Ukraine is not starting from scratch. The country has been independent for over two decades and has witnessed waves of international assistance with the shifting agenda of international donors. By its very nature, international assistance relies on the paradigm that change is possible. However, this is not the first time that decentralisation has been attempted in Ukraine and it would be a mistake to ignore the lessons emerging from the reform process so far. By offering a sophisticated and nuanced insight into the decentralisation reforms that took place in Ukraine during 2000-12, the book gives the reader a vista of not only what is possible, but also, the causes of failure in this regard. As such, the book provides a sobering read for anyone prepared to scrutinise the process and learn from the misconceptions and shortcomings of the past efforts. Most importantly it documents the sheer intricacy of reforming the stalled and opaque centre-periphery relations which are permeated with vested interests. All this is not to say that reforms are not possible but that they are difficult and require an inter-twinning of domestic and external factors. There is much to be learnt from this thoroughly researched book and I hope it will become required reading for experts and scholars promoting decentralisation in Ukraine and elsewhere.

Dr Kataryna Wolczuk  
Centre for Russian, European and Eurasian Studies  
University of Birmingham

## Glossary of Acronyms

| | |
|---|---|
| CIDA | Canadian International Development Agency |
| DFID | Department for International Development |
| EBRD | European Bank for Reconstruction and Development |
| ENP | European Neighbourhood Policy |
| ENPI | European Neighbourhood Policy Instrument |
| EU | European Union |
| FAO | Fiscal Analysis Office of the Verkhovna Rada |
| GBP | British Pound Sterling |
| IMF | International Monetary Fund |
| LARGIS | Local and Regional Government Institutional Strengthening |
| LGAP | Local Government Assistance Programme (Poland) |
| LGI | Local Government and Public Service Initiative |
| MoE | Ministry of Economy |
| MoF | Ministry of Finance |
| MRDC | Ministry of Regional Development and Construction |
| OECD | Organisation for Economic Cooperation and Development |
| PCA | Partnership and Cooperation Agreement |
| SIGMA | Support for Improvement in Governance and Management |
| SME | Small or Medium Sized Enterprise |
| TACIS | Technical Assistance to the Commonwealth of Independent States |
| UAH | Ukrainian Hryvnia |
| UK | United Kingdom of Great Britain and Northern Ireland |
| USAID | United States Agency for International Development |
| USD | United States Dollar |
| USSR | Union of Soviet Socialist Republics |

# Acknowledgements

I am deeply indebted to my two academic supervisors: Dr Kataryna Wolczuk of the Centre for Russian, European and Eurasian Studies in the University of Birmingham for her insightful advice and guidance and her constant encouragement to me to make the transition from practitioner to academic researcher; and Dr Adrian Campbell of the International Development Department for his critical eye and unerring ability to look at a problem from an original perspective. I am also very grateful to Professor Julian Cooper and Professor Hilary Pilkington for encouraging me to undertake this study and to Marea Arries and Tricia Carr for all their administrative and personal support over the years.

I would like to thank the 40 Ukrainian and other interviewees who patiently and unhesitatingly gave up their time and allowed me to ask them endless questions. What is recorded here is only a small reflection of the enormously rich background detail and understanding which they were happy to share with me, some on several occasions. I would particularly like to mention Serhiy Romaniuk, Anatoliy Maksiuta, Olena Nyzhnyk, Svetlana Kruglyak, Irina Lekh, Kataryna Maynzyuk, Yuriy Dzhygyr, Professor Kenneth Davey and Dr Wayne Thirsk. I would also like to thank my family and good friends in the UK for their tolerance and understanding of my often obsessive behaviour, particularly in the latter months of the study.

I am grateful to the Economic and Social Research Council for the funding provided through the Centre for East European Language-Based Area Studies (CEELBAS) scheme, without which I could not have completed this research.

# CHAPTER I: INTRODUCTION AND THEORETICAL FRAMEWORK

## Part I: Background to the Study and Key Research Questions

Context and Rationale for the Research: the Current Crisis in Ukraine

The origins of the current crisis in Ukraine lie not so much in domestic conflict over its future identity as an eastward or westward looking state as in the comprehensive failure to reform its system of government in the generation that has passed since independence. The spontaneous eruption of mass protest on Kyiv's Maidan in December 2013, like that of the Orange Revolution nine years earlier, was not about the abstract and unwanted question of whether Ukraine's destiny lies with the European Union or with the Russian Federation. It was above all an outcry of collective anger at the way the country has been misgoverned for the last 20 years, an issue which has touched on the everyday lives of all Ukrainians and every region.

The reform of public administration, involving a top-to-bottom re-imagining and re-structuring of the machinery of the post-Soviet state, was arguably the single most important reform task facing Ukraine's first post-independence governments of the early 1990s and was regarded by many as the key to the country's democratic consolidation (Youngs 2009: 905). As such, if anything should have been a priority for international assistance and expert advice, this was surely it. Instead the international community, intent on securing Ukraine's speedy transition to a liberal market economy, followed the accepted paradigm of the period that the role of the state should be curtailed as far as possible, and that any reduction in the overblown size of post-communist government and administration was to be welcomed. Accordingly the substantial European and North American resources invested in advising on Ukraine's programme of reform were focused on deregulation and on securing the speedy transfer of state and communal assets into private ownership.

It was only on the eve of the new millennium that the attention of the international community turned to the quality of Ukraine's public institutions, apparently in the belated realisation that a functioning liberal market democracy is dependent on effective regulation by a transparent and accountable system of government administration. By now however an increasing scepticism about the commitment of Ukraine's new political and business elite to serious reform had entered the discourse of international assistance programmes. Alongside this was an all too clear ambivalence on the part of the European Union to the aspiration to future membership which had been a central policy of the Ukrainian leadership since the late 1990s. This was most evident in the failure to engage more positively with pro-reform forces in the aftermath of the Orange Revolution in 2005.

These broad attitudes found particular expression in the ill-coordinated and frequently tokenistic efforts of donor technical assistance programmes in the area of public administrative reform which are the subject of this study. The research is the first in-depth examination of what Wedel (1998: 9) describes as the 'relationships of aid' and their consequences for reform outcomes in a post-communist state. Furthermore, the study analyses the influence of international advice on an aspect of administrative reform which has particular resonance in the light of the events of 2013-14, the relationship between Kyiv and the regions of Ukraine. The research is necessarily academic in nature, setting out to understand and explain how external assistance has impacted on the course of reform rather than to produce a set of policy recommendations. Nevertheless the author hopes that the study includes observations and insights regarding the provision of expert advice which will be of interest to policy-makers at a time when external assistance to reform in Ukraine has once again forced itself to the top of the international agenda.

Bridging a Gap in the Literature

As recently as 2010 an independent expert commission set up to advise the incoming president, Viktor Yanukovych, concluded that Ukraine's fundamental problem was the dysfunctionality of its state and in particular the failure of its administrative system to be endowed with an ethos of public service (Aslund and Paskhaver 2010: 17). Given the importance of the reform of public administration to Ukraine's post-communist transformation, it is surprising there has been almost no academic research into the efforts of the international community to advise the government of Ukraine on this central issue.

Scholars from both Comparative Politics and EU Studies have debated extensively the impact of external influence on reform in post-communist states since the early 1990s, some at the broad level of relations between western governments and the countries of Central and Eastern Europe and the former Soviet Union, and many more on the influence of the European Union (EU) on the accession states of 2004 and 2007 and in the countries of the EU's post-enlargement Neighbourhood Policy. Only a few of these studies (for example Fritz 2007) have addressed the question of public administrative reform specifically, and almost invariably research design has been at a macro-level rather than focusing on the interaction between external and domestic actors on the ground. Exceptions to the latter observation include Brown 2001, Ivanova & Evans 2004, Linden 2002, Swain 2006, 2007.

One might expect this omission to have been made good in studies of the delivery of international aid in the literature of Development Studies, where as Sakwa observes the object of analysis is the 'gulf....between promise and achievement' and insights from research into external advice to developing countries might well have something useful to offer to students of post-communist states also (1996: 178). However a search of this literature proves disappointing as there has been a conscious distancing of the international development community, academically and professionally, from the analysis of external assistance to post-communist states. The origins of this appear to lie in disagreements in the 1990s over the purpose of international aid to these countries, with scholars of Development Studies regarding assistance to the newly independent states of Central and Eastern Europe and the former Soviet Union as short-term and driven by foreign policy rather than development objectives, in particular the priority attached to the eradication of poverty (UK DFID: 1997; White 1998).

In summary there is little in the existing scholarly literature on post-communist states which examines the influence of external advice on the course of public sector reform in Ukraine, or which provides a bottom-up, micro-level perspective on the 'agendas, interests and interactions' of international donors and the recipients of their advice, and how these may or may not shape the reform choices of domestic actors (Wedel 1998: 8; Grabbe 2006: 74). The present study aims to bridge this gap.

International Technical Assistance and the Blame Game

In the twenty or so years since the dissolution of the Soviet Union in 1991 the international community has been very active in supporting and shaping what was regarded as the economic and political 'transition' of Ukraine and other post-communist states to a western-style market economy and liberal democracy. The principal instrument used by all countries has been expert-led programmes of 'technical assistance', usually defined as a process of providing countries with the skills required to promote development (DFID 1997: 38) or as a mechanism for improving the organisational capacities of government institutions in 'transitioning contexts' (Brown 2001: 738).

Financially this has involved the allocation of substantial resources on the part of the international community. Between 1991 and 2011 an estimated USD 6.5 billion was spent on technical assistance to Ukraine by the major donor countries, prominent among which were the USA (USD 3 billion) and the European Union (EUR 1.5 billion). In the first decade of the new millennium the EU alone allocated in excess of EUR 200m (IBRD 2012: 10). Other significant donors providing technical assistance have included the United Nations Development Programme and, on a bilateral basis, the governments of Denmark, Germany, the Netherlands, Sweden, Switzerland and the United Kingdom. Generally speaking programmes have been agreed on a government to government basis but delivered by non-government institutions such as universities and consultancy companies. One commentator has characterised the result somewhat cynically as an international 'transition industry' (Swain 2006).

In the area of public administration at least, the results of this major investment of time, money and expertise have been disappointing. In common with other aspects of Ukraine's 'stuttering domestic transformation' (Wolczuk 2004: 22), progress with reforming the machinery of the state has been minimal. In its 2006 Ukraine Governance Assessment SIGMA ('Support for Improvement in Governance and Management', a joint initiative of the OECD and EU) noted that despite advances in many areas since independence it was apparent that the 'command paradigm' of the Soviet period was still very much in evidence in the field of public administration. Accountability for the actions of state servants at all levels was weak and inadequately underpinned by legislation, and public administration overall was not fulfilling its primary responsibility, that of providing continuity in the functioning of the state and protecting its legality (SIGMA 2006: 11).

In spite of initially promising steps to devolve power to sub-national government, including the signing of the European Charter of Local Self-Government in 1997, and a new State Law on Local Self-Government in the same year, at the end of 2014 the 3-tier vertical system of Ukrainian public administration remains broadly similar to that of the Soviet period. Numerous attempts have been made to introduce a more decentralised and locally accountable structure, most notably in an ill-fated initiative early in the presidency of Viktor Yushchenko,[1] but none has yet been realised. The balance of authority between Kyiv, the regions and the localities remains much as it was in the late 1990s, heavily weighted towards the centre (Wolczuk 2002: 86).

It has been customary to lay the blame for the lack of progress squarely with Ukraine's political class, calling into question not only its commitment to adopt the European standards of public administration to which it formally aspires, but also the capacity of Ukraine's institutions to undertake the necessary reforms, even assuming consensus can be reached on what needs to be done (SIGMA 2006: 31; Solonenko 2008: 32). The terms of reference for the EU's most recent programme in support of the Ukrainian government's

---

[1] The 2005 'Reform for People' programme, led by Vice-Premier Roman Bezsmertniy, which recommended self-governing status for all levels of subnational government.

policy towards the regions are unequivocal about where the problem lies, remarking that when it comes to external assistance the 'institutional and absorption capacities' of its partners are 'generally very low' (EU ENPI SURDP 2011: 4). Donors' opinions are not disinterested of course and a preoccupation with defending an aid budget or a consultancy contract can lead to past achievements being overstated and failures downplayed (Grabbe 2006: 74).

Ukrainian opinions on the issue may also be less than impartial, though these at least are usually influenced by direct experience of technical assistance on the ground. A report from a Kyiv non-governmental institution with wide experience of donor interventions writes that the EU, in the 'carrying out of numberless aid programs has only substituted for the idea of reform and imitated lively reformist activity, presenting results that are mostly wishful thinking. Ineffective aid is actually damaging to Ukraine, as it fills in the vacuum created by the lack of reforms with a pointless process of executing aid programs that cannot possibly reach their declared goals' (Granovsky & Nanivska 2010: 15).

The major purpose of the present study is to provide an analysis of the outcome of donors' interaction with their Ukrainian partners which is supported by empirical evidence. Success in this endeavour will be dependent on asking the appropriate research questions and establishing the most suitable methodological framework for answering them.

Research Questions

The research sets out to answer the following questions:

*Main Research Question*

- What influence have programmes of international technical assistance had on the course of public administrative reform in Ukraine in the period 2000-2012, in particular with regard to the relationship between national and sub-national government?

*Subordinate Research Questions*

- What reforms in the relationship between Kyiv and the regions over this period are attributable to the influence of external advice through technical assistance?

- What are the conditions under which external advice through technical assistance has been successful in influencing the course of reform?

- What are the principal constraints on the influence of external advice through programmes of technical assistance?

- How does a study of the influence of international technical assistance in the field of public administrative reform add to an understanding of the broader influence of external actors on the course of reform in Ukraine, in particular that of the European Union?

The Argument

The study argues that international assistance to the promotion of reform in Ukraine's system of public administration has had a negligible impact in the decade or more covered by the research. The reasons for this are to be found as much in the institutional arrangements of donor organisations as in any institutional inertia or absence of political will on the Ukrainian side.

Having largely ignored the question of institutional reform in the machinery of the state for the first decade after Ukraine's independence in 1991, focusing their assistance instead on the privatisation of the economy and a reduction in the role of government, international donors eventually agreed to give priority to the issue as the new millennium began. However, the intervening period had seen increasing institutional fragmentation and erosion at all levels of administration in Ukraine and the emergence of a new network of political, bureaucratic and business elites with powers of patronage extending deep into all public institutions. The task international donors had set themselves was thus even more challenging than it had been a decade earlier.

Nevertheless it was apparent that there were active pro-reform constituencies in Ukraine, including isolated pockets within the state apparatus itself, with ambitions to overcome the corrosive effects of these opaque and shadowy relationships and to bring the machinery of the state into closer alignment with international practice. Many of these activists were motivated by an aspiration to see Ukraine become a member of the European Union at some point in the future, however distant the prospect might currently seem.

The international community's strategy for supporting pro-reform activism in Ukraine, two examples of which are examined in detail in the case studies, was profoundly compromised by weaknesses in the mechanisms employed to provide advice and assistance. For while there was an appreciation at an intellectual and policy level that the re-building of state institutions requires a coordinated and long-term commitment on the part of donors, in practice the instruments used were unchanged from those of the one-off know how and skills sharing exchanges of the heady days of the early post-independence period.

The limited time horizons of project-based technical assistance - in the case of support to the reform of Ukraine's regional policy five major and virtually unrelated interventions from three donors over a period of ten years – have led inevitably to inconsistencies and discontinuities on the part of donors and to the disappointment and disillusion of their partners, whose default position has nevertheless remained one of good will, generous expectation and patient perseverance. Meanwhile the dysfunctionality of Ukraine's state institutions has persisted and even, as recent events have shown, increased.

The short-termism and superficiality of international donor assistance, combined with the absence of external incentives in the shape of a credible offer of future membership from the European Union, has left Ukraine's pro-reform constituencies as unsupported as they were a decade or more ago and still without the domestic and external alliances needed to overcome the powerful vested interests who continue to oppose reform.

## The Researcher as Participant

From 2000 to 2009 I worked for approximately six months a year in Ukraine and was a participant in a number of the international projects discussed in the study. I was Project Manager of UK DFID's LARGIS programme from 2000 to 2002, which worked on both the Budget Code reform and the first drafts of the State Law on the Stimulation of Regional Development, processes which are the centrepieces of the case studies in chapters III and IV. I was also a senior expert from 2003 to 2007 in DFID's two regional programmes which followed LARGIS, Action Donbas and the Lviv Development Project. Finally in 2008/9 I was Lead International Adviser in the Canadian Governments's Regional Governance and Development project which is discussed in chapter IV.

The idea for this research did not emerge until 2008 before which my role in Ukraine had been solely that of practitioner, and the empirical stage of the research, which forms the basis of the two case studies, took place between 2012 and 2014[2] when I was no longer working as an expert adviser to the Ukrainian authorities. Nevertheless my extensive previous involvement as a practitioner clearly presented both opportunities and challenges for the research design and methodology.

It was my first-hand experience of work on fiscal decentralisation and regional policy which led me to select these as the topics for empirical research and which provided me with ready access to the principal pro-reform actors in both areas on the Ukrainian side and to a number of the leading international specialists who advised them. I was very fortunate in this respect and even more so because our aquaintance over a number of years meant that interviewees were prepared to talk informally and frankly in a way which might otherwise not have been possible. I only had one refusal to my requests for interview and several key informants were happy to answer my questions on a number of occasions over the two years of data collection. This was especially useful since my thinking on various issues was itself developing over time.

---

[2] Work was started on the study in 2009 but for family reasons the author took leave of absence in 2010 and 2011.

While I did not embark on the research with any clear theoretical propositions about the influence of international assistance on reform processes, I did feel a personal commitment to giving voice to the opinions of Ukrainian actors in particular. This stemmed from my own suspicion, which had gathered strength over the period of my working in Ukraine, that as many of the obstacles to effective technical assistance lie on the donor side as on that of the recipient. Yet this is hardly reflected in the professional literature about reform advice to Ukraine, much of which is written by donors themselves and from a donor perspective only. If there is a bias in my selection of informants, towards the Ukrainian partner rather than the international donor, it results from this attempt to achieve a better overall balance of view on the influence and usefulness of external advice.

As the previous paragraph implies, the challenge for the practitioner turned researcher is to recognise and deal with the methodological problem that being a participant in certain events will inevitably influence one's interpretation of them. For example I was an active participant in some of the early discussions of the Budget Code reform (chapter III), when the conflicting positions of pro-reform voices on the Ukrainian side were at their most apparent. These were to have important implications for the role subsequently played by external advice. My approach in this and other similar contexts was always to check or triangulate my own analysis of events with the accounts of leading Ukrainian actors and international advisers who were also present, and whose expert knowledge and understanding of the issue in question were invariably greater than my own. While the starting point of an interview may have been questions based on my own recollection or analysis of a particular situation, the case study findings rest largely on the wealth of insights and new material, some of it written, provided by respondents, much of which was previously unknown to me.

The outcome is that the critique of international assistance to the reform of public administration in Ukraine, which is set out in chapter V following the case studies, is some distance away from my thinking when I embarked on my first interviews in the autumn of 2012. Furthermore, my own appreciation of the limitations of external advice was incomparably richer than it had been when I was working as a practitioner. As a result I feel that the conduct of the research has not only been robustly inductive in approach, but has also been a highly significant process of learning and discovery for me personally.

Overview of Chapters

The book is divided into six chapters, comprising an introduction and theoretical framework, four core chapters and a conclusion. Of the central chapters, chapter II provides a historical context to the study, tracing developments in the relationship between Kyiv and the regions in the constitutional struggles of the early 1990s including pressures for and against greater sub-national autonomy. Chapter II also discusses what was happening inside Ukraine's public institutions during this period and the relative neglect of this issue by an international donor community more concerned with market reforms and reducing the size of the post-Soviet state.

Chapters III and IV are two case studies, on fiscal decentralisation and regional policy reform respectively, in the period 2000 to 2012. Evidence is presented on the progress of reform and the influence of external advice in both cases, based on the fieldwork carried out by the author in Ukraine between 2012 and 2014. Chapter V compares the findings from the case studies with the theoretical concepts drawn from the review of the literature in the introductory chapter, and proposes an explanatory framework for understanding the role of international technical assistance in supporting public administrative reform in Ukraine, in particular reform of the relationship between national and sub-national government.

The concluding chapter VI summarises the findings of the study with reference to the research questions of the first chapter and points to the wider implications of the case study evidence for the efforts of the international community to influence the course of reform in post-communist, post-Maidan Ukraine.

# Soviet and Post-Soviet Politics and Society (SPPS)
ISSN 1614-3515

Founded in 2004 and refereed since 2007, SPPS makes available affordable English-, German-, and Russian-language studies on the history of the countries of the former Soviet bloc from the late Tsarist period to today. It publishes between 5 and 20 volumes per year and focuses on issues in transitions to and from democracy such as economic crisis, identity formation, civil society development, and constitutional reform in CEE and the NIS. SPPS also aims to highlight so far understudied themes in East European studies such as right-wing radicalism, religious life, higher education, or human rights protection. The authors and titles of all previously published volumes are listed at the end of this book. For a full description of the series and reviews of its books, see www.ibidem-verlag.de/red/spps.

**Editorial correspondence & manuscripts** should be sent to: Dr. Andreas Umland, c/o DAAD, German Embassy, vul. Bohdana Khmelnitskoho 25, UA-01901 Kyiv, Ukraine. e-mail: umland@stanfordalumni.org

**Business correspondence & review copy requests** should be sent to: *ibidem* Press, Leuschnerstr. 40, 30457 Hannover, Germany; tel.: +49 511 2622200; fax: +49 511 2622201; spps@ibidem.eu.

**Authors, reviewers, referees, and editors** for (as well as all other persons sympathetic to) SPPS are invited to join its networks at
www.facebook.com/group.php?gid=52638198614
www.linkedin.com/groups?about=&gid=103012
www.xing.com/net/spps-ibidem-verlag/

## Recent Volumes

145 *Boris Popivanov*
Changing Images of the Left in Bulgaria
The Challenge of Post-Communism in the Early 21st Century
ISBN 978-3-8382-0667-7

146 *Lenka Krátká*
A History of the Czechoslovak Ocean Shipping Company 1948-1989
How a Small, Landlocked Country Ran Maritime Business During the Cold War
ISBN 978-3-8382-0666-0

147 *Alexander Sergunin*
Explaining Russian Foreign Policy Behavior
Theory and Practice
ISBN 978-3-8382-0752-0

148 *Darya Malyutina*
Migrant Friendships in a Super-Diverse City
Russian-Speakers and their Social Relationships in London in the 21st Century
With a foreword by Claire Dwyer
ISBN 978-3-8382-0652-3

149 *Alexander Sergunin, Valery Konyshev*
Russia in the Arctic
Hard or Soft Power?
ISBN 978-3-8382-0753-7

150 *John J. Maresca*
Helsinki Revisited
A Key U.S. Negotiator's Memoirs on the Development of the CSCE into the OSCE
With a foreword by Hafiz Pashayev
ISBN 978-3-8382-0852-7

151 *Jardar Østbø*
The New Third Rome
Readings of a Russian Nationalist Myth
With a foreword by Pål Kolstø
ISBN 978-3-8382-0870-1

152 *Simon Kordonsky*
Socio-Economic Foundations of the Russian Post-Soviet Regime
The Resource-Based Economy and Estate-Based Social Structure of Contemporary Russia
With a foreword by Svetlana Barsukova
ISBN 978-3-8382-0775-9

# Soviet and Post-Soviet Politics and Society (SPPS) Vol. 153
ISSN 1614-3515

General Editor: Andreas Umland,
*Institute for Euro-Atlantic Cooperation, Kyiv,* umland@stanfordalumni.org

Commissioning Editor: Max Jakob Horstmann,
London, mjh@ibidem.eu

### EDITORIAL COMMITTEE*

**DOMESTIC & COMPARATIVE POLITICS**
Prof. **Ellen Bos**, *Andrássy University of Budapest*
Dr. **Ingmar Bredies**, *FH Bund, Brühl*
Dr. **Andrey Kazantsev**, *MGIMO (U) MID RF, Moscow*
Prof. **Heiko Pleines**, *University of Bremen*
Prof. **Richard Sakwa**, *University of Kent at Canterbury*
Dr. **Sarah Whitmore**, *Oxford Brookes University*
Dr. **Harald Wydra**, *University of Cambridge*
**SOCIETY, CLASS & ETHNICITY**
Col. **David Glantz**, *"Journal of Slavic Military Studies"*
Dr. **Marlène Laruelle**, *George Washington University*
Dr. **Stephen Shulman**, *Southern Illinois University*
Prof. **Stefan Troebst**, *University of Leipzig*
**POLITICAL ECONOMY & PUBLIC POLICY**
Prof. em. **Marshall Goldman**, *Wellesley College, Mass.*
Dr. **Andreas Goldthau**, *Central European University*
Dr. **Robert Kravchuk**, *University of North Carolina*
Dr. **David Lane**, *University of Cambridge*
Dr. **Carol Leonard**, *Higher School of Economics, Moscow*
Dr. **Maria Popova**, *McGill University, Montreal*

**FOREIGN POLICY & INTERNATIONAL AFFAIRS**
Dr. **Peter Duncan**, *University College London*
Prof. **Andreas Heinemann-Grüder**, *University of Bonn*
Dr. **Taras Kuzio**, *Johns Hopkins University*
Prof. **Gerhard Mangott**, *University of Innsbruck*
Dr. **Diana Schmidt-Pfister**, *University of Konstanz*
Dr. **Lisbeth Tarlow**, *Harvard University, Cambridge*
Dr. **Christian Wipperfürth**, *N-Ost Network, Berlin*
Dr. **William Zimmerman**, *University of Michigan*
**HISTORY, CULTURE & THOUGHT**
Dr. **Catherine Andreyev**, *University of Oxford*
Prof. **Mark Bassin**, *Södertörn University*
Prof. **Karsten Brüggemann**, *Tallinn University*
Dr. **Alexander Etkind**, *University of Cambridge*
Dr. **Gasan Gusejnov**, *Moscow State University*
Prof. em. **Walter Laqueur**, *Georgetown University*
Prof. **Leonid Luks**, *Catholic University of Eichstaett*
Dr. **Olga Malinova**, *Russian Academy of Sciences*
Dr. **Andrei Rogatchevski**, *University of Tromso*
Dr. **Mark Tauger**, *West Virginia University*

### ADVISORY BOARD*

Prof. **Dominique Arel**, *University of Ottawa*
Prof. **Jörg Baberowski**, *Humboldt University of Berlin*
Prof. **Margarita Balmaceda**, *Seton Hall University*
Dr. **John Barber**, *University of Cambridge*
Prof. **Timm Beichelt**, *European University Viadrina*
Dr. **Katrin Boeckh**, *University of Munich*
Prof. em. **Archie Brown**, *University of Oxford*
Dr. **Vyacheslav Bryukhovetsky**, *Kyiv-Mohyla Academy*
Prof. **Timothy Colton**, *Harvard University, Cambridge*
Prof. **Paul D'Anieri**, *University of Florida*
Dr. **Heike Dörrenbächer**, *Friedrich Naumann Foundation*
Dr. **John Dunlop**, *Hoover Institution, Stanford, California*
Dr. **Sabine Fischer**, *SWP, Berlin*
Dr. **Geir Flikke**, *NUPI, Oslo*
Prof. **David Galbreath**, *University of Aberdeen*
Prof. **Alexander Galkin**, *Russian Academy of Sciences*
Prof. **Frank Golczewski**, *University of Hamburg*
Dr. **Nikolas Gvosdev**, *Naval War College, Newport, RI*
Prof. **Mark von Hagen**, *Arizona State University*
Dr. **Guido Hausmann**, *University of Munich*
Prof. **Dale Herspring**, *Kansas State University*
Dr. **Stefani Hoffman**, *Hebrew University of Jerusalem*
Prof. **Mikhail Ilyin**, *MGIMO (U) MID RF, Moscow*
Prof. **Vladimir Kantor**, *Higher School of Economics*
Dr. **Ivan Katchanovski**, *University of Ottawa*
Prof. em. **Andrzej Korbonski**, *University of California*
Dr. **Iris Kempe**, *"Caucasus Analytical Digest"*
Prof. **Herbert Küpper**, *Institut für Ostrecht Regensburg*
Dr. **Rainer Lindner**, *CEEER, Berlin*
Dr. **Vladimir Malakhov**, *Russian Academy of Sciences*

Dr. **Luke March**, *University of Edinburgh*
Prof. **Michael McFaul**, *Stanford University, Palo Alto*
Prof. **Birgit Menzel**, *University of Mainz-Germersheim*
Prof. **Valery Mikhailenko**, *The Urals State University*
Prof. **Emil Pain**, *Higher School of Economics, Moscow*
Dr. **Oleg Podvintsev**, *Russian Academy of Sciences*
Prof. **Olga Popova**, *St. Petersburg State University*
Dr. **Alex Pravda**, *University of Oxford*
Dr. **Erik van Ree**, *University of Amsterdam*
Dr. **Joachim Rogall**, *Robert Bosch Foundation Stuttgart*
Prof. **Peter Rutland**, *Wesleyan University, Middletown*
Prof. **Marat Salikov**, *The Urals State Law Academy*
Dr. **Gwendolyn Sasse**, *University of Oxford*
Prof. **Jutta Scherrer**, *EHESS, Paris*
Prof. **Robert Service**, *University of Oxford*
Mr. **James Sherr**, *RIIA Chatham House London*
Dr. **Oxana Shevel**, *Tufts University, Medford*
Prof. **Eberhard Schneider**, *University of Siegen*
Prof. **Olexander Shnyrkov**, *Shevchenko University, Kyiv*
Prof. **Hans-Henning Schröder**, *SWP, Berlin*
Prof. **Yuri Shapoval**, *Ukrainian Academy of Sciences*
Prof. **Viktor Shnirelman**, *Russian Academy of Sciences*
Dr. **Lisa Sundstrom**, *University of British Columbia*
Dr. **Philip Walters**, *"Religion, State and Society", Oxford*
Prof. **Zenon Wasyliw**, *Ithaca College, New York State*
Dr. **Lucan Way**, *University of Toronto*
Dr. **Markus Wehner**, *"Frankfurter Allgemeine Zeitung"*
Dr. **Andrew Wilson**, *University College London*
Prof. **Jan Zielonka**, *University of Oxford*
Prof. **Andrei Zorin**, *University of Oxford*

While the Editorial Committee and Advisory Board support the General Editor in the choice and improvement of manuscripts publication, responsibility for remaining errors and misinterpretations in the series' volumes lies with the books' authors.

# Part II: External Assistance and Domestic Reform – What the Literature Tells Us

Introduction

This chapter provides a brief overview of the literature on the role of external influence in promoting domestic reform. As there has been almost no academic research on the impact of international technical assistance on reform in post-communist states, the review involves a search of the wider literature on external influence in an attempt to place technical assistance to Ukraine in an appropriate theoretical framework.

The overview begins with an examination of the literature on the European Union's influence on reform in the accession states of Eastern Europe and in its post-enlargement 'neighbourhood' which includes Ukraine. Much of this is focused on the broad policy or macro-level. It then moves to two areas of research which address more directly the micro-level relationships of international technical assistance, although not necessarily in the context of post-communist countries. These are the bodies of literature on transnational policy transfer and on the management of international aid to developing countries.

The overview draws on literature from a number of areas, in particular Comparative Politics, EU Studies, Institutional Theory and Development Studies. It is one of the strengths of the Area Studies approach taken by the present study that it provides a useful platform for a cross-disciplinary analysis of a research problem of this scope and complexity.

Theorising External Influence (i): the EU and the Accession States

There is extensive literature on the influence of membership conditionality on the reform choices of the post-communist EU accession states of 2004 and 2008 (Checkel 2001, 2005; Jacoby 2004, 2006; Kelley 2004, Schimmelfennig & Sedelmeier 2005; Vachudova 2005; Wolczuk 2004, 2009). The central theme of the literature is a debate on the relative importance of domestic and external factors, in particular the incentive of EU membership, in persuading the political elites in these countries to follow a path of reform in accordance with the provisions of the *Acquis Communautaire*, the body of legislation which candidate countries must accept before joining the EU.

Since EU membership and its associated conditionality have not been on the agenda with regard to Ukraine, this literature will not be considered in any detail. However, there is a shared view amongst the majority of commentators that reform choices in the accession countries were shaped ultimately by a combination of domestic and external players working in tandem or coalition with one another, where the role of pockets of reform or 'minority traditions' within the state apparatus was particularly significant (Jacoby 2004: 238, 2006: 643, 645; Wolczuk 2009: 191). As chapters III and IV will show, these findings have a resonance in Ukraine also and there is ample evidence of pro-reform domestic constituencies in Ukraine working together with international actors in the context of programmes of technical assistance. The obvious difference is the absence of a clear external incentive to reform provided by the firm prospect of EU membership.

## Theorising External Influence (ii): the EU and its Eastern Neighbourhood

The European Neighbourhood Policy (ENP) was launched in 2004 with a 'new offer' to countries on the enlarged Union's eastern and southern border of 'deeper economic integration' and 'intensified political and cultural relations' with the EU. However, EU documents were at pains to make it clear that the prospect of membership was not open for discussion and neither was participation in EU institutions (EU Commission 2003: 5). The ENP was to be regarded as an alternative to further enlargement rather than a preparation for it (Landaburu 2006: 1), and the enlargement language of EU membership conditionality was replaced by the more ambiguous and opaque vocabulary of joint ownership and partnership. For Ukraine, with its long-held aspiration to EU membership, the new neighbourhood policy fell some way short of expectations.

The origins of the ENP lie in pressure from EU member states for progress towards a 'wider Europe' embracing Belarus, Moldova, Russia and Ukraine, a proposal which was agreed in principle by the European Council in Copenhagen in December 2002 (Smith 2005: 759). By the time of formal adoption in 2004 the numbers had increased to 16, including former Soviet republics in the Caucasus and Mediterranean states in the southern neighbourhood, but without Russia which preferred to maintain separate relations with the EU. The promise of the ENP was of step-by-step economic and political integration and a generous, if vague, offer of future inclusion in the single market (Wolczuk 2004: 20). Central to the ENP philosophy were the principles of shared values and common interests (Ganzle 2009: 1715). Tailor-made action plans for each partner country, based on its own choice of priorities, were to be the central operating instrument of the policy (Lanadbaru 2006: 1).

The ENP was thus conceived as a soft, participatory mechanism involving collaborative goal-setting (Sedelmeier 2007: 199-200) and its bilateral action plans as negotiated but non-binding documents (Dimitrova & Dragneva 2009: 856) aimed at approximation rather than precise harmonisation with the Acquis (Lavenex & Schimmelfenning 2009: 807; Boerzel 2010: 15). This arrangement has been characterised as one of 'network governance' where, in contrast to those with the accession states, the relationship between the EU and its neighbourhood partners was to be symmetrical in nature, with third countries invited to agree to areas of cooperation in a regime described as 'process-oriented…..voluntaristic and inclusionary' rather than one shaped by unilateral conditionality (Lavenex 2008: 943; Lavenex et al. 2009: 816) Ukraine under the ENP has been said to be 'enmeshed within a dense structure of European networks' (Youngs 2009: 904).

This somewhat sanguine assessment of the ENP accords rather too neatly with official pronouncements from the EU Commission which stress that 'there can be no question of asking partners to accept a pre-determined set of priorities. These will be defined by common consent' (EU Commission 2004: 8). When the 'constructive ambiguity' (Sedelemeier 2007: 199) of the ENP is taken into account it is an assessment which becomes difficult to sustain.

Constructive ambiguity stems from the Commission's own statements that the ENP relationship would not include a perspective on membership, at least *'in the medium term'* (EU Commission 2003: 5. Author's italics), and the implied encouragement this phrasing gives to those prepared to make most progress in adapting to EU rules (Leigh 2007: 2010). Arguably the ambiguity over the long-term membership prospects of the ENP's eastern partners cannot help but lead countries with strong membership aspirations, like Ukraine, to harbour hopes that accession will eventually become an option. In the meantime there is a clear incentive to conform to EU norms and practice and a corresponding increase in the capacity of the EU to require partner countries to meet its expectations. The ENP thus becomes an expression of the EU's desire to 'project its normative power' in its neighbourhood (Wolczuk 2008: 99).

On this interpretation the portrayal of the ENP as a symmetrical partnership of equals can be judged as 'entirely erroneous conceptually' since in practice it involves a 'one-way flow of EU directives......premised on a donor-recipient formula' (Korostoleva 2011: 6-8). The ENP becomes a 'neighbourhood context for the export of [EU] rules (Dragneva & Wolczuk 2012: 1), paying 'lip service.....to the principle of co-ownership' while in reality allowing the EU to monitor and patronise its partner countries and to oscillate between policies of inclusion and exclusion (Ganzle 2009: 1718, 1723).

Taking the argument further, the deliberate vagueness of the final aim of the ENP in relation to its eastern partners (Copsey & Mayhew 2006: 4) can be seen simply as a reflection of the Commission's wish to leave its future options open. Thanks to the ENP the EU has been able to secure the best of both worlds geopolitically, enabling it to relinquish the policy of enlargement but nevertheless retain its normative power. It is able to act as a 'normative hegemon' in the region by virtue of its strategy of building a set of highly asymmetric bilateral relationships to facilitate the active transfer of its norms and values to countries which are bound to the EU by the distant and elusive prospect of future membership (Haukkala 2008: 1611; 2009: 1762).

## Theorising External Influence (iii): Transnational Policy Transfer

Scholars employing policy transfer analysis or the related concept of lesson-drawing have generated a substantial body of literature (Bennett 1991; Rose 1991, 1993; Dolowitz & Marsh 1996, 2000; Evans & Davies 1998; Radaelli 2000; Stone 2000; Evans 2004a, 2004b). Policy transfer is defined as a 'process by which knowledge about policies, administrative arrangements, institutions and ideas in one political system….is used in the development of policies, administrative arrangements, institutions and ideas in another political system' (Dolowitz & Marsh 2000: 5) or as 'a theory of policy development that seeks to make sense of a process or set of processes in which knowledge about institutions, policies or delivery systems at one sector or level of governance is used in the development of institutions, policies or delivery systems at another sector or level of governance' (Evans 2004a:10).

As these definitions imply the policy transfer concept is employed to explain both a process taking place between two independent states and within the borders of one country, for example between government departments. However it is most commonly used in connection with the sharing of expertise and information between 'transnational groups of actors' (Stone 2000: 50), where 'through various channels of communication, policy makers learn of the programs of their counterparts in other countries, and this evidence influences the domestic policy process' (Bennett 1991: 32).

With regard to post-communist states the concept of policy transfer has been used by a number of scholars to conceptualise the promotion of EU institutional models in the enlargement and post-enlargement processes in Central and Eastern Europe. Thus the EU is described as a 'very active policy entrepreneur', with the *Acquis Communautaire* involving large scale policy transfer (Radaelli 2000: 26-27; Zabrowski 2005: 30). As a result policy transfer has become an isomorphic process, with candidates for membership required to adopt prescribed institutional forms and practices as a condition of future acceptance (Radaelli 2000: 27). A parallel argument can be made in relation to the exercise of the EU's normative power in exporting its norms and rules to states in the ENP neighbourhood with an aspiration to membership.

It has been argued that the post-communist states of Central and Eastern Europe have been particularly vulnerable to inappropriate forms of policy transfer not only as a result of the inherent asymmetry in relationships with international organisations like the EU but because of the enormous domestic pressure for change after the demise of the Soviet Union. This resulted in their being 'hungry, even starving', for policy transfer, with external advice invariably thought to be preferable in a situation where it there were few valid sources of relevant endogenous expertise (Ivanova & Evans 2004: 98, 109).

The multi-level approach to policy transfer (Evans & Davies 1999; Evans 2004a) takes the foregoing analysis closer to the dynamics of Wedel's 'relationships of aid' (1998: 9) and the practice of international technical assistance. It does so by conceptualising a set of vertical relationships linking intergovernmental or donor-recipient relationships at the macro-level with institutional and individual interactions at the micro-level where actual policy changes take place. The link is provided at a meso-level by transnational 'policy transfer networks' of domestic and external actors whose role it is to assist decision-makers to acquire knowledge and to mediate the process of policy change in individual institutions (Evans 2004a: 22-25). There are strong parallels here with the idea of coalitions of domestic and external actors working in tandem with each other (Jacoby 2006: 625; Wolczuk 2009: 191), with the policy transfer network offering a plausible framework for empirical investigation of how such alliances might function in practice.

## Theorising External Influence (iv): the Political Economy Analysis of International Aid

At first glance there is little in the literature of development theory which is of obvious relevance to post-communist states like Ukraine. Both academically and professionally the international aid community has consciously distanced itself from analysis of the external support to reconstruction in Russia and Eastern Europe following the dissolution of the Soviet Union in 1991. These after all were developed industrial societies even if, in the opinion of some commentators, they might more accurately be decribed as 'misdeveloped' (Sakwa 1999: 715). Nevertheless the study will argue that it is the literature of Development Studies which contains the most penetrating critique of the management of international expert advice and the role of external influence in building new institutions of public administration in developing countries, an objective which has become central to the strategy of international donors in Ukraine.

The political economy analysis argues that aid agencies in developing countries employ an overly technocratic approach to institutional development and are in denial about the political content of their activity (Fritz & Menocal 2007: 544). Donors prefer instead to maintain the 'sincere fiction of a disinterested exchange' with their partners without any clear analysis of how this will facilitate a process of reform (Bourdieu 1992; 113, cited by Brett 2009: 267). In the sphere of public administrative reform for example the technocratic approach assumes that the obstacles to better governance in developing countries are technical and managerial rather than political (Unsworth 2009: 886), a view indicative of a naively consensual view of power relationships (Hyden 2008: 262) and of the 'classic error' of isolating public administration from politics (Goldsmith 2010: 369). Political economy analysis argues that the key to increased aid effectiveness lies less with improving the efficiency of delivery mechanisms than with a better understanding of the social, institutional and political dynamics with which aid programmes are interacting, and a preparedness to become more politically engaged with the informal relationships underpinning the working of formal institutions. These are said to represent 'the grain' with which international agencies need to work (Hyden 2008: 267; Unsworth 2009: 891-892; Unsworth et al. 2010: 76).

The analysis is particularly critical of the tendency of international aid agencies to rely on the promotion of standardised and frequently inappropriate institutional models drawn from the experience of OECD[1] countries, and to make adherence to these a condition of continued financial support. Examples include the so-called 'good governance' agenda of the donor community which is criticised as dangerous and coercive institutional

---

[1] The Organisation for Economic Cooperation and Development

isomorphism lacking a sound basis in theory (Di Maggio & Powell 1991: 67-68; Andrews 2008: 379; Williams et al. 2011: S33; Duncan & Williams 2012: 134), and the New Public Management approach to public administration, with its questionable relevance to the circumstances of the developing countries to which it has been exported with great enthusiasm (Batley & Larbi 2004: 29; Fritz & Menocal, 2007: 545).[2]

The blame for this is said to lie primarily with expert policy networks which 'hammer out consensus and define world standards' and which have 'powers to filter norms and methods, designating some as "best practice" and excluding the rest' (Sogge 2002: 157-158). Donors resort to an overreliance on ideal-type, one-size-fits-all solutions regardless of context, rather than focusing on what can be accomplished in practice (Chang 2002: 130; Fritz & Menocal 2007: 579; Frodin 2011: S179). The institutional ethos of development agencies has thus become one of 'experts bringing solutions' (Unsworth 2009: 890), when the real question should be how to improve what already exists (Booth 2011b: 116) and work towards reform which represents 'best fit' rather than best practice (Williams et al. 2011: S53).

The argument that international donors in developing countries have a poor understanding of the institutional landscape in which they work is analogous to Wedel's argument that aid programmes to post-communist states lack basic institutional awareness (1998: 185-189). The political economy analysis of the importance of informal relationships and institutions also finds echoes in studies of neo-patrimonial networks in post-Soviet states, where the legal-bureaucratic and patrimonial spheres function in parallel with each other and have been able to flourish at the intersections of state, politics and business (Fisun 2003; Aslund & Paskhaver 2010; Malygina 2010; Whitmore 2010). Verena Fritz and others have also pointed to the growth of neo-patrimonialism in Ukraine and other post-Soviet states, arguing that it is a result of the

---

[2] New Public Management became popular in many OECD countries in the 1980s and 1990s and is associated with the marketisation of public services through, for example, increased competition in service provision by contracting out to the private sector and the introduction of public-private partnerships in capital project construction.

process of institutional erosion and fragmentation which followed the demise of the USSR (Fritz 2004, 2007; Roland 2002; Gel'man 2004). These observations are discussed in more detail in chapter V.

Conclusions

While the absence of scholarly literature on international advice on reform in Ukraine has necessitated an examination of the wider literature of Comparative Politics, EU Studies, Institutional Theory and Development Studies in order to suggest a theoretical framework for the analysis of the empirical findings of this study, the review has proved fruitful in offering a number of concepts which promise to be directly relevant to the two case studies in chapters III and IV.

*The Emergence of Pockets of Reform and Minority Traditions in the State Apparatus*

The evidence of the review is that domestic activism of this nature was a feature of pre-accession period in the enlargement states, with membership conditionality providing an incentive for pro-reform domestic actors to work in tandem with programmes of external advice and expertise (Jacoby 2004, 2006). Previous empirical studies in Ukraine have noted the emergence of comparable 'pro-reform constituencies' or 'enclaves' within the state apparatus, using the framework of the ENP action plan to promote convergence with EU rules and templates. This has been largely on the initiative of the officials concerned, more often than not acting without political support or oversight. (Solonenko 2008: 22; Wolczuk 2009: 202).

The case studies in chapters III and IV provide an opportunity for an in-depth examination of the evidence for such activism in the area of public adminstrative reform.

*The Concept of a Policy Transfer Network*

In relation to the accession processes of 2004 and 2008 the literature suggests that in order to have real purchase on the course of reform, external influence needs to establish alliances or 'informal coalitions' with domestic actors who seek reform (Jacoby 2006). The concept of a policy transfer network (Evans & Davies 1998; Evans 2004a) offers a framework for the empirical investigation of how informal coalitions or alliances of domestic and external actors are established and operate in practice, including exerting influence on the progress of reform.

The empirical evidence in chapters III and IV will compare two contrasting examples with regard to the establishment of pro-reform alliances. The case studies also present an opportunity to test the usefulness of the policy transfer network concept in explaining how such alliances function and are able to exert influence.

*Normative Institutional Isomorphism*

The findings of the review suggest that the normative power of an international organisation, in the case of Ukraine the EU, can be deployed to bring pressure to bear on recipients of external assistance to adopt prescribed institutional models (Radaelli 2000; Haukkala 2008; Ganzle 2009; Korostoleva 2011). The wider literature on international aid management in developing countries indicates that imported best practice institutional models are often recommended by external advisers with insufficient regard to their relevance in the domestic context (Andrews 2008; Unsworth 2009).

The case studies will examine whether external influence by the EU and other donors on the issues of fiscal decentralisation and regional policy can be characterised as isomorphic processes, and the extent to which they may have involved the transfer of institutional models inappropriate to the Ukrainian context.

*The Political Economy Analysis of International Aid*

Political economy analysis points to the institutional factors which have inhibited the efforts of external advisers to influence the course of institutional reform in developing countries (Unsworth 2009). Chapter II will discuss the process of 'institutional erosion' (Fritz 2007) which was a feature of post-independence Ukraine in the 1990s and the increasingly neo-patrimonial nature of its institutional relationships (Fisun 2003; Malygina 2010)

The empirical findings at chapters III and IV will suggest that the political economy analysis of international aid management in developing countries has resonance in Ukraine, and that donors' limited understanding of the neo-patrimonial nature of the Ukrainian state impacts negatively on their ability to influence reform outcomes.

# CHAPTER II: THE HISTORICAL CONTEXT - INTERGOVERNMENTAL RELATIONS IN THE NEWLY INDEPENDENT UKRAINE

Introduction

This chapter examines the decade following the dissolution of the Soviet Union and the establishment of Ukraine as an independent state. It was a period during which the country's longstanding regional tensions threatened to undermine the process of state building and when the distinction between regional policy and regional politics frequently became blurred and subject to political manipulation. It was also a time of profound uncertainty, even collapse, among post-Soviet institutions, including those at the local level of municipalities and districts. To advocate greater autonomy from Kyiv for regional and local governments in such a febrile atmosphere was to risk accusations of recklessness or, worse still, of separatist thinking.

The international community took little active interest in what were regarded as the internal affairs of Ukraine. After all, little harm could come from a reduction in the reach of state institutions in a country which had hitherto been the subject of too much government rather than too little. Donor interventions such as the European Union's TACIS programme and the United Kingdom's Know How Fund focused instead on questions which were seen as more central to Ukraine's anticipated transition to a market economy and liberal democracy. Foremost among these were enterprise restructuring and privatisation, reform of the banking system, electoral reform and, in the wake of the Chernobyl catastrophe of 1986, nuclear safety.

By the time international organisations turned their attention to the institutions of regional and local government at the beginning of the new millennium, the political arguments over the nature of the Ukrainian state and the acceptable degree of autonomy for sub-national units of administration had been largely settled, for the time being at least. A new Constitution had been agreed in June 1996, following the longest period of political wrangling and debate in any post-Soviet country, and new legislation governing the affairs of local and regional authorities had been enacted in 1997 and 1998. The result was a system of intergovernmental relations heavily skewed towards centralisation (Wolczuk 2002: 86), presided over by a political leadership which remained deeply suspicious of, even hostile to, arguments for any significant relinquishing of state authority.

The chapter is divided into two parts. Part I examines the institutional struggles of the first decade after independence which were to prove an important influence on the progress of reforming both regional policy and intergovernmental financial relations in the decade that followed. Part II of the chapter considers the response of the donor community to the challenge of post-communist transition, in particular the lack of attention to the weakening of state institutions which had occurred in the 1990s. When this was belatedly identified as a priority issue for international support at the end of the decade, there had been changes to the institutional landscape which were certain to compound the complexity of an already difficult environment for technical assistance.

# Part I: The Ukrainian State in the First Decade after Independence

The Challenge of State Building and the Threat of Disintegration

*Background: the Soviet Period*

A key factor distinguishing the task of economic and political reconstruction in the post-communist countries of the former Soviet Union, excluding the Baltic States, and those of Central and Eastern Europe was what Linz and Stepan describe as the severity of the 'stateness problem' (Linz & Stepan 1997: 449). In Ukraine's case the various regions which made up the newly independent country in 1991 had moved in and out of Ukraine's history at different times but had never interacted together as an ensemble (Wilson 1997: 25). Its territorial boundaries were largely a Soviet construct and in the aftermath of the break-up of the USSR there were serious doubts as to the feasibility of holding Ukraine together as an integrated political entity after centuries of statelessness (Wolczuk 2002: 66; Sasse 2001: 71).

While the regional cleavages which were to burden the process of state building during the first decade of independence were sharpened by political struggle and economic collapse, they were also a predictable outcome of tensions which had been apparent during the Soviet period and which forced their way to the surface in a less tightly controlled political environment. Indeed the USA's Central Intelligence Agency went so far as to forecast the disintegration of Ukraine under the pressure of latent ethnic conflict similar to that in post-communist Yugoslavia (D'Anieri 2007: 5). The analogy is not wholly satisfactory as the background to the inter-regional tensions in Ukraine was based not so much on ethnic grounds as on a complex mix of economic, political, historical and linguistic factors.

The faultlines threatening the integrity of the territory of Ukraine have historically been along its borderlands to the west, south and east. The western *oblasts* of the country were variously parts of Poland, Hungary, Romania and Czechoslovakia until the Second War when they were incorporated into the Soviet Union. At the time of their incorporation into the Ukrainian state they were economically backward in comparision with the more industrialised east and remained one of the least productive and poorest areas of the country (Birch 2000: 1026).

Politically however they had more recent experience of competitive elections than the rest of Ukraine and, having never been part of the Russian empire, their populations were inclined to regard themselves as Europeans as distinct from the 'Eastern Slavs' in the south and east (Birch 2000: 1017-18). Campbell comments on the longstanding tendency among Ukrainian nationalists in these western *oblasts* to refer somewhat dismissively to the eastern and southern parts of Ukraine as 'russified' and to assert that Ukraine would be in the European mainstream were it not for its links with Russia (1995: 123).

In contrast to the west the populations of Crimea in the south and Donbas in the east were historically over 90% Russian speaking (D'Anieri 2007: 7) and the question of their regional identity had been strongly politicised even in the pre-independence period (Birch 2000: 1028). Under Russian rule since the eighteenth century and part of the Russian Federation within the USSR until 1954 the special status of Crimea, including its strategic role as the base for the Soviet Union's Black Sea Fleet, led to pressure for a popular referendum in January 1991 and a subsequent upgrading of its political status from that of *oblast* to being an autonomous republic within the Ukrainian SSR (Birch 2000: 1029; Sasse 2001: 72).

For rather different reasons the Donbas region, which importantly straddles the territory of both Ukraine and Russia, also enjoyed privileged status prior to independence. The 'working class aristocracy' of its coalminers and steelworkers, who were better fed, clothed and housed than other working people, gave Donbas a unique place in Soviet culture (Birch 2007: 1027). The repeated miners' strikes of the late 1980s as its coal industry began to decline in competitiveness on world markets were an indication of the region's potential for political mobilisation. Even before the dissolution of the Soviet Union the Donbas miners had emerged has one of the USSR's most vociferous constituencies of political opposition (Sasse 2001: 84).

## Post-Independence: the Threat of State Disintegration

Following the declaration of Ukraine's independence in August 1991 the central struggle for political ascendancy to emerge was that between national and regional political elites, the latter including the leaderships at both *oblast* and major city level. As will be argued later the dynamics of this struggle continued to dominate the issue of public administrative reform well into the new millennium, in particular in the arguments over the reform of regional policy and intergovernmental finance.

It is important to see the political struggle of the 1990s in this wider context of a contest between national and regional elites rather than one which was driven solely by the need to contain the specific separatist threats on Ukraine's western, southern and eastern flanks, potentially serious as these undoubtedly were. The key question was the extent of decentralisation which an independent Ukraine's national ruling elite was prepared to concede or, to put it another way, how much power it was willing to share.

The settlement which was achieved in the adoption of a new constitution in June 1996, although formally presented as a compromise between centralist and decentralist pressures, was designed in practice to strengthen the vertical power of an executive president. However the political manoeuvring between national and regional elites, and at *oblast* level between President-appointed governors and the mayors of the bigger cities, remain to this day the site of Ukraine's sharpest political struggles.

With the exception of the western region of Zakarpats'ka, which took the opportunity to have its own referendum on becoming a self-governing territory within the new Ukrainian state to coincide with the national referendum on independence in December 1991,[1] the major precipitating factors behind the secessionist movements of 1992-94 were the economic

---

[1] 78% of those voting in Zakarpats'ka were in favour of greater independence from Kyiv, although the actual term 'autonomy' was not used in the referendum question after a personal intervention by President Kravchuk. The referendum was consultative in nature and did not lead to further claims for special autonomy arrangements (Sasse 2001: 83-84).

consequences for Ukraine of the dissolution of the USSR. The political and economic difficulties associated with the decline of the Soviet Union during the 1980s, and the view that Moscow had for a long time been drawing disproportionate revenue from Ukraine's rich agriculture and concentration of heavy industry, meant that expectations were high that the country would be better off on its own (Birch 2000: 1027; Fritz 2007: 112).

These hopes were confounded by the impact on living standards of the hyperinflation which followed independence and the collapse in Ukraine's overall GVA[2] by 65% between 1990 and 1995 (World Bank 2002b: 10). The popular reaction was strongest in the Russian-speaking regions of Crimea and Donbas whose populations felt they had been deceived by the promise of economic benefits flowing from separation from Russia (Wolczuk 2001: 140). If prior to independence the strongest centrifugal tendencies had come from the formerly Polish territories of western Ukraine, the centre of gravity of the secessionist movement now shifted to the south and east (Sasse 2001: 80).

The Crimean economy was strongly Sovietised and dependent on the now bankrupt military-industrial complex and on tourism from throughout the USSR (Sasse 2001: 86). The dislocation of trade links with Russia and the break-up of the highly integrated Soviet economy were also felt keenly in Donbas where the region's heavy industry was reliant on energy supplies from Russia and Turkmenistan (Birch 2000: 1028).

While the immediate causes of the separatist tendencies in Crimea and Donbas were broadly similar, the paths they followed in the period 1991-1994 reflected the differences in their historical and political backgrounds. In Crimea dissatisfaction with the new status quo was encouraged by Russia, with the unresolved issue of the Black Sea Fleet providing a convenient pretext, and pro-secession sentiments reached their climax with the election of a president for an 'independent' Crimean republic in 1994. Although this was to be quickly overturned by Kyiv in 1995 there was nevertheless a

---

[2] Gross Value Added (GVA) measures the contribution to the economy of each individual producer, industry or sector.

recognition that a special case would need to be agreed for Crimea, with extensive autonomy the price to be paid to placate long-running centrifugal tendencies and avert separation (Wolczuk 2002: 77). The 1996 Constitution thus accords Crimea the right to its own constitution and parliament and in effect the asymmetric status of a federal component within a unitary state (Sasse 2001: 70, Wolczuk 2002: 78).

In Donbas political demands for autonomy from Kyiv also appeared to reach breaking point in 1994, following repeated strikes by miners in 1993 against economic separation from Russia which ominously received wider regional support from the political leadership of Kharkivs'ka *oblast*, outside the Donbas (Campbell 1995: 121). A referendum called by the *oblast* councils of Donets'ka and Luhans'ka concurrently with the parliamentary elections of spring 1994 sought public support for a variety of proposals to strengthen links with Russia, including adoption of Russian as the official second state language and as the sole language of public administration in the Donbas region. Although the referendum proposals received public approval, the election of Leonid Kuchma as President in the summer of the same year, on a platform favouring stronger links with Russia and greater autonomy for the regions, was sufficient to forestall further moves towards secession. On the whole political mobilisation in Donbas over relations with Kyiv and the rest of Ukraine concentrated less on the prospect of outright secession and more on demands for greater control over regional resources, the protection of declining industries like coalmining and the role of the Russian language (Sasse 2001: 85), in contrast with the situation in Crimea where the threat of violent conflict, even civil war, was very real (D'Anieri 2007: 10).

*Strengthening the Presidential Vertical*

On a wider front the period 1991-1996 saw an independent Ukraine's first two Presidents, Leonid Kravchuck and Leonid Kuchma, both of whom were determinedly centralist, struggling to assert their executive authority over the regions. Between August 1991 and the adoption of the Constitution in June 1996 the *oblast* tier of government was by turns 'municipalised' and 'statified' (Matsuzato 2000: 45), depending on the changing balance of power between the President, the Parliament or *Verkhovna Rada*, and regional political elites.

Between March and April 1992 three laws[3] and one presidential decree[4] laid out the structure of intergovernmental relationships. Executive local self-government was to be granted to city, town and village councils only, with *oblast* and *raion* (district) administrations and their elected *radas* to be headed by the new executive post of President's Representative (Predstavnyk Prezydenta), an early statement of the intention to retain strong executive power from the centre. However, the ensuing economic collapse, with the sharpest fall in output occurring during 1993-94 (World Bank 2002b: 5), precipitated the passing of a new law by the *Verkhovna Rada* in February 1994 overturning the previous legislation and re-municipalising the *oblast* and *raion* councils. In the cities of Kyiv and Sevastopol the heads of their respective *radas* were to be directly elected and responsible for the executive as well as legislative function.

This was equivalent to the introduction of direct gubernatorial elections (Matsuzato 2000: 37) and presented the incumbents with virtually 'unconstrained executive power' over their mandate territories, able to decide for themselves to whom they owed allegiance at national level, the President, the *Verkhovna Rada*, or the Cabinet of Ministers (Wolczuk 2001: 139). It reflected the view among sections of the regional political elite, supported by the outwardly pro-decentralisation presidential candidate Leonid Kuchma, that Ukraine's economic performance would only be improved with a bottom-up approach to economic development and far less day-to-day interference from out of touch ministries in Kyiv (Wolczuk 2001: 151).

Paradoxically however, it was Kuchma who, on becoming President in July 1994, quickly reversed the earlier legislation in an August decree 're-statifying' the *oblast* and *raion* tiers of government by making their elected *rada* heads

---

[3] *Zakon Ukrainy vid 5 Bereznia 1992 Roku "Pro Predstavnyka Prezydenta Ukrainy"*;
*Zakon Ukrainy vid 26 Bereznia 1992 Roku "Pro Mistsevi Rady Narodnykh Deputativ ta Mistseve i Rehional'ne Samovriaduvannia"*;
*Zakon Ukrainy vid 27 Bereznia 1992 Roku "Pro Vnesennia Zmin do Zakonu URSR "Pro Mistsevi Rady Narodnykh Deputativ URSR ta Mistseve i Samovriaduvannia"*.

[4] *Polozhenia vid 14 Kvitnia 1992 Roku "Pro Mistsevi Derzhavni Administratsii"*.

directly accountable to him for the execution of state powers (Wolczuk 2002: 70). Kuchma's background as an industrial director in Dnipropetrovs'k and later as Prime Minister had convinced him that only a government with strong executive powers could be effective at a time of crisis (Wolczuk 2001: 148). The decree of August 1994 was later confirmed in the Constitutional Agreement of June 1995,[5] the precursor to the adoption of the Constitution by the *Verkhovna Rada* a year later (Matsuzato 2000: 38).

The Constitution of June 1996 maintained the strong presidential vertical to the executive branch at regional level, while remaining silent on the status of the *radas*. The right to full self-government, independent of the state, was confirmed for cities, towns and villages, in accordance with Ukraine's obligations under the Council of Europe's Charter of Local Self-Government.[6] Kuchma had long held the view that *radas* at *oblast* level should be indirectly elected so as to weaken regional councils' popular legitimacy (Wolczuk 2002: 80) and it was not until the passing of the Law on Local Self Government in Ukraine in 1997, vetoed three times by the President, that regional and district councils were accorded self-governing status although their executive branches continued to be responsible to Kyiv under the 1998 Law on Local State Administration.

This dysfunctional compromise remains in place to the present day. The structure of sub-national government in Ukraine is set out in Box I below.

---

[5] *Konstytutsional'nyiy Dohovir mizh Verkhovnoiu Radaiu Ukrainy ta Prezydentom Ukrainy - "Pro Osnovni Zasady Orhanizatsii ta Funktsinuvannia Derzhavnoi Vlady i Mistsevoho Samovriaduvannia v Ukraini na Period do Pryiniattia Novoi Konstytutsii Ukrainy"*.

[6] Ukraine was admitted to the Council of Europe in November 1995 and the Charter of Local Self-Government was ratified by the *Verkhovna Rada* in 1997. The Charter was less specific in its requirement for independence from the state at the regional tier than at city, municipality and village level (Wolczuk 2001: 160).

> **Box I: The Structure of Sub-National Government in Ukraine**
>
> *Ukraine is a unitary state with three levels of sub-national government. The top tier includes 24 oblasts, the Autonomous Republic of Crimea and two cities of oblast status, Kyiv and Sevastopol. The sub-regional level includes 488 raions or districts and 177 cities and towns of 'oblast significance', which include the capital cities of each region and other major population centres. The third tier of government is composed of almost 30,000 villages, settlements and smaller towns of 'raion significance', which are grouped together in approximately 12,000 administrative units.*
>
> *Oblasts and raions have similar administrative structures, consisting of an elected council with self-governing legislative powers and an executive body which is a deconcentrated form of state administration. The executive is nominally accountable to the council but its officials are appointed from Kyiv and have dual subordination to the oblast governor or raion head and to their line ministry. The regional governor is appointed by the President, not the oblast council.*
>
> *It is the hybrid nature of the oblast and raion levels of sub-national government, where elements of self-government in the form of elected councils exist alongside a strong state vertical unchanged from the pre-independence era, which has been at the centre of debates over the reform of Ukraine's system of territorial administration. In the 1990s it was these levels which were alternately 'statified' or 'municipalised' under policies of centralisation and decentralisation respectively (Matsuzato 2000: 45).*
>
> *By contrast the executive bodies of cities and towns of oblast significance, including the post of mayor, are directly elected and control their own executive branches. At the lowest tier the 12,000 smaller towns and villages are also self-governing and have their own elected councils. It is usual for these councils to delegate their executive functions upwards to the better resourced raion level.*
>
> *The cities of Kyiv and Sevastopol have a special status combining the features of self-governing cities and deconcentrated state oblast administrations. Thus the two cities have both a directly elected mayor and city council and an executive branch which is state-appointed.*
>
> *Sources: 'Positioning LGI/OSI Policy Dialogue to Support Decentralisation in Ukraine'. Local Government and Public Service Initiative (LGI) Budapest & FISCO Consulting Kyiv, 2008; OECD Territorial Review, Ukraine, 2013.*

A number of scholars (Birch 2000; Sasse 2001; Wolczuk 2001, 2002; Fritz 2007) focus on the conflict between presidential and parliamentary authority following independence, and the threat to Ukraine's territorial integrity posed by secessionist tendencies in its borderlands. The foregoing analysis suggests that an alternative lens through which to view the events of the 1990s is as a struggle between national and regional elites, including the leaderships of the largest cities.

This was at its sharpest, and most challenging to the nation building process in Ukraine, in the case of Crimea where a constitutional compromise had to be found in order to avert probable secession. In Donbas on the other hand, outright secession was not seriously mooted and it can be argued that this was primarily an example of regional elites using the demand for autonomy as a means of bargaining a better deal from the centre (Campbell 1995: 119). Sasse also suggests that political mobilisation in Donbas after independence was linked to Soviet institutional legacies and to the prominent role of administrative elites from Donets'ka and other regions of eastern Ukraine in the Soviet Communist Party *nomenklatura* (Sasse 2001: 86).

More broadly, Matsuzato argues that a distinguishing feature of the debate on centre-local relations in independent Ukraine has been the authority of *oblast* or regional government, and that the example of Ukraine in the 1990s is confirmation of the general proposition that a fundamental issue in post-communist state building is the status of what he terms the 'meso-elites' and 'meso-governments' at regional level (2000: 45). For the purposes of this study this provides a useful context for the closer examination of two aspects of centre-local relations, regional policy and intergovernmental finance, following independence and in the first decade of the new millennium, and for an analysis of the impact of the international community in advising on reform.

## Regional Policy and Intergovernmental Finance in the Decade after Independence

*Regional Policy*

Attitudes to regional policy in the first years after independence mirrored the prevailing hostility of political elites in Kyiv towards any suggestion of more autonomy for the regions. To advocate regionalism was to legitimise regions as independent political actors and to threaten Ukraine's territorial integrity (Sasse 2001: 76), and while lively and open discussion about the right to local self-government in the towns and villages might be acceptable, to argue the case for a specifically regional dimension to government policy was to risk being labelled as a separatist.[7] Nevertheless, elements of a differential economic policy towards the regions were beginning to emerge in the mid-1990s and by the end of the decade the sharp variation in the ability of regions to come to terms with the move towards a market-based economy had forced the issue of regional policy closer to the top of the government agenda (World Bank 2002b: v).

In the Soviet system of central planning regional policy as such did not exist. Rather than treating regions as distinct economic entities which play an important developmental role in their interaction with other economic agents, planning for a given territory was the sum of centrally organised sectoral and branch activity and the region was simply a recipient of a range of national policies in its domain (World Bank 2002b: 16).

The early years of independence saw a continuation of this top-down ministry-driven approach, albeit accompanied by elements of a changing understanding of the economic significance of regions. A proposal was made to introduce five economic super-regions (Karpats'ky, Polis'kyi, Podils'kyi, Ukrains'kyi Prychornomors'kyi and Predniprovs'kyi),[8] and the Cabinet of Ministers prepared comprehensive progranmmes for their economic and

---

[7] Interview with Serhiy Maksymenko, regional policy expert, Kyiv, 22 March 2013.

[8] These have been described as 'economic management complexes' (*teritorial'no-gospodars'ki kompleksy'*, Romaniuk, 2013: 211) and did not coincide with either existing *oblasti* or Ukraine's historical regions (Transcarpathia, Galicia, Bukovina, Volynia, Podila, Cherhihiv, Sloboda Ukraine, Nova Rossiya and Donbas: Wolczuk 2001: 160/161).

social development in the period 1996-2000, at an estimated cost of 60 billion UAH (World Bank 2002b: 21; Romaniuk 2013: 211). This followed the economic collapse of 1992-1994 and pressure from regional elites for a more region-focused economic policy as a strategy for recovery, but the measure was later abandoned. In addition to the significant cost, there was doubtless fear of the creation of politically powerful mega-regions, since the proposal involved the introduction of a new tier of territorial administration (Romaniuk 2013: 211). In 1997 a draft law passed by the *Verkhovna Rada* which included provision for a reduction in the number of *oblasts* from twenty-five to eight was vetoed by President Kuchma for similar reasons (Swianiewicz 2006: 602).

If the period from 1995 saw the steep decline in economic activity beginning to flatten out and modest annual growth returning to stronger regions, nationwide the picture was very uneven. Only four regions (Crimea, the City of Kyiv, Mykolaivs'ka, Zaporiz'ka) experienced real growth in excess of 0.5%, while six (Chernihivs'ka, Chernivets'ka, Khersons'ka, Sums'ka, Ternopil's'ka, Zhytomyrs'ka) contracted by over 4.5% a year (World Bank 2002b: 7). Furthermore while it might have been expected that the benefits of returning economic growth, however limited, would be felt across the country, the difficult adjustment of all but a few regions to market conditions and the collapse of inter-regional economic relationships (Romaniuk 2002: 182) meant the reality was quite different. By the end of the decade only eight regions had per capita GVA above the national average, with the great majority up to 20% below. The GVA figure in three *oblasts* (Chernihivs'ka, Ternopil's'ka and Zakarpats'ka) was less than 60% of the average and the indications were that these disparities were increasing over time (World Bank 2002b: 10).

National government meanwhile appeared unable to respond with compensatory measures. State capital investment in the regions, which in 1995 had varied from a maximum of 51.4% of all capital expenditure in Kyiv *oblast* to a minimum of 10.6% in Poltavs'ka, fell away sharply so that by 2000 only five regions were in receipt of more than 10% of their annual capital investment from the state budget (Romaniuk 2013: 212). The reduction was particularly marked following the economic crisis of 1998 and by the end of the decade state capital investment had ceased to play any significant role in infrastructure development at regional level, and was targeted primarily at dealing with civil emergencies and other short-term problems (Romaniuk 2013: 212).

Prompted by a reform to the legal framework,[9] the mid- to late 1990s was also a period during which regional and city authorities increasingly began to prepare their own programmes for medium to long term social and economic development (Romaniuk 2002: 183), an indication of a growing understanding of the region as a significant economic actor. The impact of this change is discussed in detail in chapter IV.

*Intergovernmental Finance*

Approaches to the conduct of intergovernmental finance, the mechanism of national government support to the recurrent spending of local and regional government on the delegated state functions of education, health and social protection, remained under similarly tight direction from the centre following independence. This was in part because of the perceived chaos at town and district level with the loss of the controlling influence of local Party committees. As with broader regional policy however, by the end of decade the impact of Ukraine's economic collapse and the resulting contraction in budget support going to sub-national tiers of government began to force a change in thinking about intergovernmental finance. But this was not before the intervening period had brought about a profound and corrosive change in institutional behaviour.

The Soviet *Matryoshka* pyramid of 'nested' budgets followed logically from the notion of a hierarchy of organs of government, each layer of which was part of an integrated structure of state power. In such a system there is no conceptual distinction between local, regional and national authorities, which are all aspects of a single state apparatus (Wolczuk 2002: 69). Thus while the

---

[9] Under article 142 of the 1996 Constitution territorial communities were entitled to prepare their own programmes for socio-economic and cultural development, to be financed from state and/or local budget sources.

budget for each *oblast* was determined by the Ministry of Finance in its preparation of the consolidated annual budget for the country as a whole, the individual budgets for districts, cities, towns, villages and settlements were settled through the state vertical of *oblast* and *raion* administrations.

Each level in the hierarchy was thus responsible for determining the budget allocation to the level below: regions to districts and cities of *oblast* subordination, districts to municipalities of *raion* subordination, villages and settlements. Budget decisions were based on expenditure needs stemming from the input norms laid down by line ministries and the costs of maintaining the existing network of institutions in each territory (Martinez-Vasquez & Thirsk 2010: 34).

Following independence, from the point of view of national government, there was little incentive to change this supply-driven model of budget preparation which, for all its inherent inefficiencies, seemingly had the advantage of affording Kyiv a high degree of financial control over the regions and localities. Now that the close day-to-day supervision by the Communist Party of municipal and district soviets and their executive committees no longer applied (Ross 2009: 29), there was recurring concern over a 'perceived crisis of governability' in the localities (Wolczuk 2002: 69) and a sense that state authority should be reasserted in order to overcome what was seen as the 'prevailing anarchy' (Wolczuk 2001: 161). Subordination of all budgets to *oblast* state administrations would help to achieve this aim.

It is conceivable that the *Matryoshka* model of intergovernmental relations might have survived had it not been for the impact of Ukraine's flagging economy and the shrinking revenue base for local government. In reality the model became untenable as the state budget was increasingly unable to support the existing level of public services and its associated network of institutions as prescribed by ministry norms. Eventually only one-third of expenditure needs for delegated state functions in education, health and social protection were being met by transfers from the state budget (Martinez-Vasquez & Thirsk 2010: 12, 35). This was in conflict with the 1996 Constitution of Ukraine which stipulated in article 142 that expenditures of local self-government arising from the decisions of state bodies should be reimbursed in full by the state.

The allocation of annual budget transfers between regions, and onwards from regions to towns and districts, now became a matter of hard bargaining in which there were few if any rules of engagement (Martinez-Vasquez & Thirsk 2010: 14). Heated bureaucratic negotiations ensued (World Bank 2004: 6), involving a steady stream of *oblast* officials travelling to Kyiv to secure a better deal, and one regional Director of Finance recalls that he would work until the early hours to reach an agreement with ministry officials over the financial settlement for the following year, only to be telephoned the next morning to be told that the figure had been reduced by 50 million UAH as a result of a decision taken elsewhere.[10] The tortuous process was repeated at *oblast* level downwards with the result that, as the final links in the *Matryoshka* chain, the budgets of small towns and villages were often not agreed until well into the financial year (Martinez-Vasquez & Thirsk 2010: 15).

Striking anomalies resulted from this largely subjective and opaque process. According to the budget figures for 1997 per capita spending on health in the city of Kyiv was 61% higher than in the relatively poor *oblast* of Zakarpats'ka, expenditure on education per school student 65% higher in Dnipropetrovs'ka than in neighbouring Luhans'ka, and on social protection a massive 268% higher per capita in Dnipropetrovs'ka than in Volyns'ka (Fiscal Analysis Office 1998: 17).

As 'fiscal turbulence' swept across sub-national budgets all over the country during the financial crisis of 1998 (Martinez-Vasquez & Thirsk 2010: 53), pressure for reform increased and the USAID-financed Fiscal Analysis Office, established with a brief to advise the Budget Committee of the *Verkhovna Rada*, recommended immediate adoption of an objective and formula-based system for calculating intergovernmental transfers as a mechanism for achieving greater per capita equalisation between regions (Fiscal Analysis Office 1998: 19).

---

[10] Interview with Yuriy Balkoviy, Director of Finance Department, Luhans'ka *Oblast* State Administration, Luhans'k, 27 June 2013.

The issue was taken up by the powerful Association of Ukrainian Cities, whose membership included the elected mayors of the major cities. A campaign was started to do away with the *Matryoshka* system and replace it with one which would establish the budgets for local government without *oblast* interference and in accordance with the provision for financial independence of local governments set out in article 143 of the 1996 Constitution. The alliance of the Budget Committee of the *Verkhovna Rada*, chaired by Yulia Tymoshenko, and the Association of Ukrainian Cities was to prove instrumental in the reforms that followed in the new millennium, as is discussed in chapter III.

In the meantime however the continuing operation of the Soviet-era *Matryoshka* in the post-independence context of sharply declining budgetary resources had already left its mark on institutional behaviour. Not only did it encourage arbitrary and unpredictable decision-making (Wolczuk 2002: 85) but, in bestowing what was in effect absolute power of each tier of the pyramid over the tier below, it led to the paradoxical situation where the Ministry of Finance had little or no influence on budget formation beyond the *oblast*. In so doing it created the ideal conditions for unconstrained rent-seeking by officials and politicians at every level (Maynzyuk & Dzhygyr 2008-9: ?).

## Institutions under Pressure

### Institutional Erosion

What was happening in intergovernmental budget relations is an example of what Verena Fritz describes as 'institutional erosion' (2007: 4). Fritz argues that in the period from independence to 1995 Ukraine experienced a steady weakening of its institutions as the *ancien regime* of Soviet politics, bureaucracy and a planned economy crumbled without a new order immediately taking its place. The use of the term 'erosion' is intended to convey a qualitative change and not simply a downsizing of state institutions and the numbers they employed, though this also occurred (2004: 3). The change entails a weakening of the constraints on the behaviour of state actors as the boundaries between the formal and informal 'rules of the game' which define institutions (North 1990: 3) become blurred, and informality begins to conflict with and ultimately undermine the purpose and values of the institution.

As Shlapentokh (1989) has argued, well before the break-up of the USSR the degree of institutional erosion was already high, with the credibility of state and Party organisations in long-term decline and alternative informal behaviour involving expropriation of state property for private gain increasingly widespread. Independence in Ukraine, far from arresting the process of erosion, spawned a growth in informal practices and rising dysfunctionality among state institutions as political elites at national and regional levels contested the balance of power between the executive and legislature, and between Kyiv and the regions (Fritz 2007: 109).

Gel'man (2004: 1024) and Wedel (2003: 429) note similar processes at work in Russia and other newly independent states of the former Soviet Union. Overall the problems associated with institutional erosion were said to have been far less severe in post-communist Central and Eastern Europe than in most post-Soviet states (Fritz 2007: 62). The latter were faced with the additional questions of identity and 'stateness' following the USSR's disintegration (Linz & Stepan 1997: 449) and were quickly consumed by political struggles over the task of nation building in the midst of economic collapse.

Growing informality and increasing dysfunction within Ukraine's state institutions in the early 1990s opened the door to networks of 'opaque groups', intertwining business, political and bureaucratic interests which straddled the boundaries between the private and public realms and were able to exploit their access to state institutions to extract economic rents (Fritz 2007: 110). The emergence of neo-patrimonial relationships and their penetration into state institutions at every level in post-independence Ukraine has also been noted by Fisun (2003) and Malygina (2010), and as a wider phenomenon in contemporary post-Soviet societies by Mendras (1999), Franke et al. (2009), Whitmore (2010), and Stewart et al. (2012). Malygina defines a neo-patrimonial state as one in which informal (patrimonial) and formal (bureaucratic) logics of action co-exist. Public and private spheres are separated *de jure,* but *de facto* such differentiation does not exist (2010: 10).

Here again there is continuity with the late Soviet period where informal networks between state enterprises and local authorities were frequently employed to advance their mutual interests (Smith & Swain 1998: 37-38). However opinions differ over the extent to which historical legacy is the key to an understanding of institutional behaviour in the 1990s (Nielson et al. 1995; Smith & Pickles 1998), or whether the tensions of the first decade after the break-up of the USSR were equally influential (Wedel 2003; Fritz 2007). In any event by the turn of the century as state capacity was gradually restored, a changed institutional order had evolved in both Ukraine and Russia, as a result of which all 'meaningful actors were forced to accept new rules of the game' (Gel'man 2004: 1028; Fritz 2007: 57).

*Strains in the Localities*

In 1990s Ukraine the responsibilities of sub-national government, particularly at municipal and district levels, were expanding rapidly, and this in a system of local public administration described as 'skeletal....lacking the wherewithal for major initiatives'. At the time of independence local government in Ukraine had employed fewer than 100,000 staff for a population of 52 million, compared with Russia where the figure was 900,000 for population only three times larger (Campbell 1995: 116).[11] However, with the demise of the Soviet system the range of tasks for which local governments were to be responsible was dramatically increased.

In the superficially monolithic Soviet structure of municipal administration local governments frequently had to rely on the goodwill of factory directors to provide their citizens with social and cultural amenities. In practice it was powerful local enterprises, responsible to central ministries, which provided the majority of communal services including housing, polyclinics, children's

---

[11] Hague et al. put the Ukraine figure at 425,000 but still regard this as small compared with western European countries with similar populations. In their view the state apparatus inherited by the newly independent Ukraine was 'drastically inadequate in personnel and material resources' (1995: 422).

nurseries, recreation facilities and other essential elements of urban infrastructure. In the 1970s, in the USSR as a whole, state controlled enterprises were responsible for the construction and annual running costs of 70% of housing, 65% of kindergartens and day care centres and 30% of hospitals and polyclinics (Ross 2009: 33-34). In mono-industrial cities public transport was often provided by the town's dominant employer (Healey et al. 1999: 263). In Kyiv during the same period, the city controlled only 30% of the housing stock, and in the country generally about half of all municipal utilities such as water, gas and waste water management were in the hands of local factories (Ross 1987: 156). Similarly in rural areas it was the collective and state farms which organised school transport and deliveries of coal and wood in winter to older people confined to their homes.

Research findings from Russia provide an indication of what happened in Ukraine after 1991 following the programme of rapid privatisation of state-owned industry. The heavy costs of supporting communal services compelled newly-privatised enterprises to divest themselves of their social assets,[12] which were in most cases transferred to the ownership of local municipalities with predictable consequences. Between 1993 and 1997 in Russia, 80% of housing, 75% of children's nurseries and 82% of hospitals and polyclinics previously in the ownership of enterprises were transferred to municipalities, many of whom were either unwilling or unable to shoulder the burden of taking over their running costs. By 1999 there was an estimated shortfall of 70% in the financing of housing and other divested social assets (Healey et al. 1999: 272-273).

In mid-1990s Ukraine one research study described local government as having little or no authority or control over its revenues but with a range of new and important responsibilities for communal and municipal services (Hague et al. 1995: 419). What was happening in post-communist local government during the 1990s was almost equivalent to establishing municipal and rural administration *ab initio*, and comparable in many ways to similar

---

[12] This was often an explicit condition of privatisation (Healey et al. 1999: 263).

processes in developing countries (Campbell & Coulson 2006: 545),[13] Even so the international donor community was to show little interest in assisting Ukraine during such a critical period in the evolution of its local government.

Conclusions to Part I

A number of the factors described here were to have significant bearing on the attempted reforms to local government finance and regional policy that followed after 2000 and are the subject of the case studies in chapters III and IV. The consolidation of the strong presidential vertical extending through the state-appointed posts of *oblast* and *raion* heads of administration was confirmation of a continuing hostility in Kyiv to the devolution of authority to sub-national government. At the same time however, the 1996 Constitution and the State Law on Local Self-Government which followed it in 1997 led to the emergence of a powerful lobby of political leaders from Ukraine's biggest cities, ambitious for greater autonomy and with a democratic legitimacy which regional governors could not claim.

A weakening of the constraints on the behaviour of state actors in the post-independence period, together with a near collapse of communal services at the level of municipal and district government, opened the door to new forms of political and bureaucratic patronage. Meanwhile international advice to Ukraine, as in other newly independent states of the former Soviet Union, was directed primarily towards the rapid dismantling or downsizing of the machinery of state. Academic theorists of post-communist transition were also more interested in the impact of transition on political regimes and political institutions than in what was happening more widely to the functioning of the state (Popov 2004: 108; Fritz 2007: 2)

---

[13] Campbell & Coulson (2006) refer particularly to the experience of local government in Central and Eastern Europe but their observation is no less true of Ukraine and other states of the former Soviet Union.

# Part II: Post-Soviet Transition and the Sharing of International Know How

Introduction

From the outset of international assistance to reform in the newly independent states of the former Soviet Union there were tensions between the political and developmental purposes of programmes of donor intervention. In the case of the UK for example the combining of the two objectives was implicit in the structure established to deliver the British government's assistance programme, the UK Know How Fund. The Fund was to be jointly managed by the Foreign and Commonwealth Office and the Overseas Development Agency, the body responsible for Britain's aid programme in developing countries and the precursor to the Department for International Development.

The involvement of the Foreign Office in the so-called Joint Assistance Unit signalled the British Government's wider political and diplomatic motivation for supporting transition in post-Soviet countries, which in the case of Ukraine centred on consolidating its political and economic independence from Russia (Hamilton 2013: 122). Tensions between the political and developmental objectives of international intervention would lead eventually to a distancing and disengagement of international aid scholars and practitioners from the provision of technical assistance to post-Soviet states including Ukraine.

As the international community began to appreciate the full extent of the challenge it had taken on, so thinking shifted from simplistic transition-based assumptions to a strategy which recognised the need for longer term institutional re-building. This was common to all major donors to Ukraine. However the changes that had occurred in Ukraine's institutional landscape in the first years of independence meant that this was now a considerably more complex task than it may have been a decade earlier.

## The Challenge of State Building and the Response of International Donors

*The Influence of the Transition Paradigm*

It has been observed that the collapse of the socialist regimes of Eastern Europe coincided with the dominance of two inter-related paradigms, neoliberalism and globalisation (Sakwa 1999: 713). To this might be added a third, that of the 'transition paradigm' (Carothers 2002), which gained strong currency among academics and political leaders alike in the aftermath of the events in Central and Eastern Europe in 1989 and the eventual dissolution of the Soviet Union in 1991, and which was to have a profound impact on the nature of the international advice provided to Ukraine in the early years of independence.

'Transitology' argued that the transition from communism was conceptually and theoretically analogous to the breaks with authoritarian rule that had occurred in Southern Europe and Latin America during the 1970s and 1980s (Schmitter & Lynn Karl 1994: 184) and that comparison with these earlier efforts to liberalise and democratise authoritarian regimes might ultimately contribute to the development of a generalised theory of post-communist transition (Bova 1991: 137). The debate over transitology in the academic community was at its sharpest between scholars from an Area Studies background and those from the field of Comparative Politics, and at root was a disagreement about the uniqueness of Russia and the former Soviet Union as an object of scholarly research (Sakwa 1996: 181).

Nevertheless in the early 1990s at least, even those who argued forcibly that the state socialism of post-communist countries was a distinct phenomenon along virtually every dimension that economists, sociologists and political scientists recognised as important, were not against the concept of transition as such, only asserting that in the case of post-communism it should not be regarded as a mere variation on a larger theme but as a process meriting separate study (Bunce 1995: 111, 119).

The language employed by both the European Union and the UK

Government in explaining their strategies for supporting reform in Central and Eastern Europe and the former Soviet Union speaks to their endorsement of the concept of transition. An interim evaluation of the EU's TACIS programme in July 1997 describes its purpose as to 'bring about the transition to the market economy and the reinforcement of democracy' through the transfer of knowledge and skills (EU Commission 1997a: 4), and a review of its programme in Ukraine one year later defines as the goal of its technical assistance 'to support the reforms to establish a market economy and a democratic society' (EU Commission 1998: 2). The European Bank for Reconstruction and Development (EBRD), in the 1995 edition of its annual report on economic transition in post-communist states, listed nine 'transition indicators' against which the performance of individual countries could be benchmarked (1995: 11). Similarly the newly elected UK Government of 1997, justifying its continued use of the international aid budget for programmes in the relatively developed countries of the former Soviet bloc, stated that 'countries in transition to full democratic societies and market economies face particular difficulties. Help for them is a finite commitment, reflecting our interest in their stability and development' (UK DFID 1997: 40).

The rapid expansion of government sponsored donor assistance from the EU, Britain, the USA and others gave birth to what was described as a 'transition industry' (see chapter I), comprising the three interlocking networks of international financial institutions, academic advisers, and consultants employed by international development agencies (Swain 2006: 208). It was also viewed with scepticism by Development Studies scholars and the mainstream international development community, who protested that aid budgets were being raided by western governments for diplomatic and foreign policy purposes, and that the peoples of some of the poorest countries in the world were being 'forsaken' as the demands from countries of the former Soviet Union increased (White 1998: 156).

These tensions led on the one hand to a distancing of the Development Studies discipline from research into the impact of international advice to the so-called transition states, and on the other to increasing doubts within governments, particularly in the UK and the EU, over the efficacy of technical assistance programmes designed to bring about 'fast transition'.[14]

*Building Market Economies and Democratic Societies*

The European Community launched its TACIS programme immediately upon the dissolution of the Soviet Union in December 1991, while the UK Know How Fund had been established as early as the summer of 1989 in response to political developments in Poland (Hamilton 2013: 2). The first intimations of an extension of the Fund to what was then still the Soviet Union were given by Foreign Secretary Douglas Hurd in an announcement in November 1990, motivated by a wish to show support for Gorbachev's attempts at reform and a mounting concern that a looming economic crisis would undermine these (Hamilton 2013: 53).

A year later, before the final decision to dissolve the USSR, 5m GBP had already been committed to Russia for specific projects in the financial, small business and food processing and distribution sectors. By 1992 the UK Know How Fund had a budget of 17m GBP available for disbursement to nations of the former Soviet Union,[15] compared with an EU TACIS figure of 450m ECU for the same year. In both cases Russia was the recipient of the largest share of expenditure, at 12m GBP and 111m EUR[16] respectively, with Ukraine in second place at 4m GBP and 48.3m EUR. By 1996 the outlay of the Know How Fund in Ukraine had increased to 9m GBP and that of EU TACIS to 76m EUR Between 1991 and 1996 the Know How Fund financed over 150 separate projects in Ukraine (Figures from EU Commission 2007a: 2; Hamilton 2013: 82, 83, 88, 122).

The transition goals of building a market-based economy and a pluralist political system were underscored by the sectoral focus of both the Know How Fund and EU TACIS in Ukraine during the 1990s. Priority sectors for

---

[14] The phrase 'fast transition' appeared in an internal review of the UK Know How Fund's activities in Hungary and Ukraine carried out in 1999 (Hamilton 2013: 145).

[15] Plus Mongolia.

[16] All figures for 1992 and 1996 are shown in EUROs rather than ECUs in the 2007 EU TACIS report.

the UK were banking and finance, privatisation, employment and small business, management training and limited activities in the areas of parliamentary links, media development and support to the police and legal reform (Faint 2004: 9).

Public administrative reform, including support to reforms in regional and local government, was not identified as a priority, although in 1995-96 some 15% of Know How Fund expenditure in Ukraine was used on 'good government' activities, principally study visits to Britain for political figures (over a third of *Verkhovna Rada* deputies either visited the UK or took part in related seminars) and expert consultancy to selected ministries. Overall, however, there were doubts about the effectiveness of such assistance and a feeling that other donors might be better placed to provide it (Hamilton 2013: 122). This was in marked contrast to the activities of the Know How Fund in the Czech Republic, Hungary, Poland and Slovakia, where assistance to the reform of local government had been identified as a priority sector at an early stage.[17]

EU TACIS had a similar focus on transition-related interventions, with 30% of its 1991-1998 expenditure in Ukraine going to projects supporting enterprise restructuring and development and 23% to non-nuclear energy and the environment. The Human Resource Development sector, which included advice and training to government institutions, received 16% of total expenditure over the period, sufficient to finance 16 individual projects valued at ECU 62.3m. Of these, two relatively small programmes, together costing ECU 4.3m, were targeted to public administrative reform and both were principally concerned with the creation of a national system of training for state servants under the aegis of the President's Academy of Public Administration. Only two programmes, on the social impact of privatisation and assistance to the housing sector, jointly costing ECU 4.8m, addressed issues of direct relevance to the institutions of regional and local government (EU Commission 1998: 20, 21, 104).

---

[17] Interview with Professor Kenneth Davey, lead adviser to the UK Know How Fund programme in the Czech Republic, Hungary and Slovakia, Cheltenham, 27 August 2013.

Like the UK Know How Fund TACIS allocated a small share of its resources specifically to the issues of democratisation and improved transparency in government, although in this case it was through a dedicated 'Democracy Programme' established in 1992 with an expenditure of ECU 31.2m ECU between 1993 and 1996. Ukraine received around 20% of the programme's larger grants over this period, and Russia close to 50%. Only 3.5% of the overall programme, including its Central and Eastern Europe component, was spent on projects promoting greater openness in public administration and these were delivered mainly by in-country non-governmental organisations. Indeed the Democracy Programme as a whole was on a bottom-up rather than government-to-government basis, and was not subject to formal approval by recipient countries (EU Commission 1997b: 33, 39, 95).

*A Reactive or a Proactive Policy?*

It was somewhat ironic but perhaps inevitable that politically driven initiatives hastily packaged in response to the dramatic dissolution of the Soviet Union in December 1991 would themselves have a less than smooth transition to the implementation stage. So it was with the EU TACIS programme and the newly extended UK Know How Fund. Both had initially made a virtue of being demand-led, minimally bureaucratic and flexible enough to respond quickly to the needs of their new partners (Faint 2004: 12; Frenz 2007: 1), a policy which was increasingly called into question as the programmes became better established.

The interim evaluation of TACIS in July 1997 concluded that the programme was too thinly spread, with starts made on some 2000 projects across the former USSR between 1991 and 1996. While the demand-driven approach may have been justified in the early years it had led ultimately to a lack of strategic thinking and a consequent weakening of impact. The evaluation also found that annual action programmes for the implementation of projects bore little relation to the ongoing policy dialogues and Partnership and Cooperation Agreements (PCAs) with individual states. It was strongly recommended that in future the PCA machinery be used to give political guidance and strategic direction to the sectors in which TACIS was operating (EU Commission 1997a: 5, 60, 62).

The shift from a demand-led approach was now underway. A follow-up to the interim evaluation, this time addressing TACIS activities in Ukraine specifically, found that programme content was increasingly a 'dialogue driven exercise' with up to 50% of projects scheduled for implementation in 1998 originating in proposals from the EU side. This was regarded as a welcome contrast to the collection of 'unrelated small actions' which had been a feature of earlier action programmes (EU Commission 1998: 2).

Doubts over the virtues of a demand-led philosophy followed a similar trajectory in the evolution of the UK's Know How Fund. While at 17m GBP in 1992 the British intervention in post-Soviet states had been minor compared with the 450m ECU available to TACIS in the same year[18], its relatively small size was seen as an advantage. Comparisons were made between an under-resourced but speedy and responsive Know How Fund and the slow and cumbersome procedures of the EU, which were regarded as delivering very little to recipient countries while providing a great deal of well-paid employment for Western European consultants (Hamilton 2013: 100).

Nevertheless, when management of the Know How Fund was eventually absorbed into the incoming Labour Government's new Department for International Development (DFID) in 1997, questions were asked about the reactive and opportunistic approach of the Fund's early years and its overreliance on personal contacts and the opinions of local activist groups which, in the initial period of transition, were said to be necessarily flawed (Hamilton 2013: 146). DFID, with its world-wide remit for international aid and poverty relief, was determined to be both more proactive and more prescriptive in its procedures for selecting projects in (Faint 2004: 12).

This was not universally welcomed by British diplomats who regarded the new ministry's approach as unnecessarily bureaucratic and far less responsive. Many were more concerned with the foreign policy benefits of Know How Fund interventions, which in the case of Ukraine centred on

---

[18] As a member of the EU the UK Government made a contribution to the annual budget for TACIS which was in excess of the figure set aside for the Know How Fund (Hamilton 2013: 83).

consolidating its political and economic independence from Russia (Hamilton 2013: 122, 146). As noted earlier it was this ambiguity of purpose that also led Development Studies scholars to distance themselves from researching the impact of international advice to post-communist states.

*Questioning the Institutional Impact*

One of the more important conclusions of a 1997 evaluation of the TACIS programme overall was the acknowledgement that while initially the former USSR was regarded as a developed economic giant in need of short-term transition-oriented assistance, there was now an appreciation that the complexity of the institutional changes needed had been grossly underestimated (EU Commission 1997a: 13).

A parallel review of TACIS activities in Ukraine found that while there had been tangible benefits to individual partners from study programmes and training, these had not been translated into changes in decision-making mechanisms in government institutions or acceleration in the process of reform. In short the impact on public administration and the effectiveness of government had been minimal (EU Commission 1998: 2, 7). The view within DFID was much the same, with critics of the Know How Fund approach arguing that insufficient attention had been given to the need to redevelop state institutions (Hamilton 2013: 155). The World Bank was also critical of international aid in general, with donor responses agencies too often cocooning their programmes in free-standing technical assistance projects and making little attempt to understand or improve the institutional environment (1998: 22).

These assessments tallied with views in the academic literature. It was argued that the 'minor technocratic efforts' of programmes designed to support post-Soviet transition had neglected altogether the issue of state building and instead recommended a weakening of executive power and a diffusion of state authority (Carothers 2002: 17). The lack of engagement with the working of state institutions could be traced back to the early 1990s and an international focus on the dismantling of the institutional legacy of the USSR.

Donor governments had failed to anticipate that the downsizing of the state which followed would be accompanied by increasing dysfunctionality and a process of 'de-institutionalisation' which was far more marked than any comparable processes in Central and Eastern Europe (Roland 2002: 30; Fritz 2004: 3; 2007: 2, 4, 46:).

The stage was set for a fundamental re-think and change in approach which was to coincide with the start of the new millennium.

Conclusions

The 1990s were a period of pivotal change in Ukraine, the full complexity of which was not well understood by the international community. As the case studies which follow in chapters III and IV will show, the continuing ramifications of these changes would have a considerable impact on the efforts of international donor programmes to influence the course of reform.

The struggle for power between national and regional or meso-level (Matsuzato 2000) political elites was central to the challenge of state building in the newly independent Ukraine. At issue was the degree of regional autonomy which could be secured from the centre. At its most extreme, in the largely russophone regions of Crimea and Donbas, the struggle came close to threatening fragmentation of the state through secession. These tensions were at their highest in the period 1992-1994 when Ukraine's economic collapse was felt most keenly in those areas with traditionally strong economic and political ties with Russia and the former Soviet Union.

Alternating policies of 'statification' and 'municipalisation' of regional and local government throughout the first half of the decade were a reflection of the shifting balance between forces in favour of centralisation or decentralisation. Ultimately the constitution adopted by the Ukrainian parliament in June 1996, together with subsequent enabling legislation on regional and local government in 1997 and 1998, signalled that the argument had been won by the centralists. The result was a system of intergovernmental relations heavily skewed towards strong executive power from Kyiv, exercised through a presidential vertical extending through deconcentrated state administrations at *oblast* and *raion* levels.

A form of decentralised local self-government was granted only to the major cities, towns and villages. Towards the end of the decade, however, imbalances in the capacity of regions to deal with economic collapse and adapt successfully to a market-based economy led to pressure on national government to adopt a more differentiated approach to the regions, and this was reflected in perceptible changes in thinking about both regional policy and intergovernmental finance.

Meanwhile the struggle for political power, sharpened by a severe economic collapse, had virtually sabotaged the task of state building. In the face of increasingly dysfunctional public administration at all levels, a process of institutional erosion led to a weakening of the constraints on state actors and a blurring of the boundaries of acceptability between formal, rule-based behaviour and informal actions for private gain. While this was to a degree a continuation of a phenomenon already apparent in the late soviet era as the Communist Party itself fell into disrepute, the early years of independence saw a variety of new actors moving into the previously confined space of the ruling *nomenklatura*.

At the same time the institutions of local government at municipal and district level were experiencing traumatic change as a result of the obligation to take responsibility for a network of utilities and social sphere facilities which had previously been provided by state-owned enterprises, and to do so at a time of massive decline in budgetary resources. What was happening to Ukraine's local government in the 1990s was almost equivalent to establishing municipal and district administration from scratch.

Advice to Ukraine from the EU and the UK during this transformative period paid virtually no attention to the challenges facing both local government and state public administration in general. The priorities of programmes of technical assistance were driven largely by the political imperative to support Ukraine's transition to a successful market economy with pluralist democratic politics, and the focal sectors for donor advice were therefore concentrated on private sector and capital market development, and on opportunities for national and local politicians to learn from the experience of their Western European counterparts.

Only towards the end of the decade, in the context of increasing international disillusion with the progress of reform, did attention shift towards the role of public administration in facilitating or obstructing transition, and the capacity of Ukraine's public institutions to carry through a programme of change. By this time however those institutions had themselves moved on, moreover without the help of donor intervention, and were operating under new rules often based on opaque, neo-patrimonial relationships between political, bureaucratic and business interests. This was the far from promising ground on which the international community, having previously distanced itself almost entirely from questions of public administration, began to regard institutional development as the overriding priority for the new millennium.

# CHAPTER III: CASE STUDY I
# THE BUDGET CODE REFORM OF 2000/1

Introduction

The first case study examines the role of international advice in the reform of financial relations between national, regional and local government as a result of the adoption of a new Budget Code for Ukraine in the autumn of 2000, in time for phased implementation starting in 2001. As discussed in chapter II the financing of local government expenditure was one of the most problematic areas of the post-independence period. The stand-off between successive national governments determined to keep a tight rein on the actions of sub-national administrations, and local political elites emboldened by the promise in the new constitution of greater financial autonomy for Ukraine's towns and cities, created formidable domestic pressure in support of reform.

Even so, when it came the reform was surprisingly bold in its ambition, described by one Ukrainian source as 'the most striking attempt to fight against the pervasive feudalism in centre-local relations' (Maynzyuk & Dzhygyr 2008/9: 4). In dismantling the *Matryoshka*[1] pyramid of nested budgets, each layer of which was part of an integrated structure of hierarchical state authority (see chapter II), the reform was a decisive break with the Soviet past and in keeping with the decentralising logic of the 1996 Constitution, the 1997 Law on Local Self-Government, and Ukraine's adoption of the European Charter of Local Self-Government. It was also a deliberate strategy to bring local government finance under more predictable and rule-based control and to overcome the increasingly informal and corrosive practices in settling the level of financial settlements with individual local authorities which had been a growing feature of the 1990s.

As a case study of the influence of international technical assistance, the

---

[1] The correct transliteration from the Russian is *Matreshka*, but the more common usage is employed here.

Budget Code reform of 2000/1 is of particular interest because it is an example of external advice contributing directly both to the adoption of new legislation and to its implementation in practice. While it has not been uncommon for international experience and expertise to be used in the preparation of legislation in Ukraine, the step from 'rule selection' to 'rule application' has usually been far more challenging (Langbein & Wolczuk 2012: 14-15). It has been argued that the distinctive feature of the donor-recipient relationship in this case was the trust and confidence placed in the advice of international experts by the Government of Ukraine, which enabled it to have a decisive influence on both the content of the reform and its execution (Martinez-Vazquez & Thirsk 2010: 165).

More generally it has been suggested that the Budget Code reform represented a significant strengthening of Ukraine's formal institutions and was a genuine first step in triggering improvements in de facto practice (Fritz 2007: 197). Given that it was so fundamental in nature, and therefore likely to lead to strong opposition from influential vested interests, this was no small achievement. Opposition to the reform was indeed strong and from powerful quarters, in particular from state-appointed regional governors who were the principal actors in the network of patronage which the *Matryoshka* had spawned. The eventual adoption of the new Budget Code by the *Verkhovna Rada* and its signing off by President Kuchma were achieved in the context of a political environment which remained highly hostile to any notion of de-centralisation, regardless of the constitutional and legislative commitments in that direction in the 1990s (Maynzyuk & Dzhygyr 2008: 6).

On the international donor side the Budget Code reform was a rare example of three donors working collaboratively, with each taking responsibility for a defined area of policy advice and interaction with the Government of Ukraine. The three were the World Bank, the USA's Agency for International Development (USAID), and the UK's Department for International Development (DFID). The institutional assemblage in favour of the reform on the Ukrainian side was no less impressive. It included the powerful Budget Sub-Committee of the *Verkhovna Rada* chaired by the recently elected and ambitious Yulia Tymoshenko, and the influential Association of Ukrainian Cities, whose membership comprised the elected mayors and other leading figures from Ukraine's largest urban and industrial centres.

In addition the reform was driven on the technical side by a small team of young and equally ambitious officials in the Ministry of Finance, all experts in the financing of local government, recruited from senior posts in the regions and intent on reforming the system of intergovernmental finance. The period 2000-2001 thus witnessed an unprecedented conjunction of political, civil society and governmental forces, each exhibiting a strong will and enthusiasm for fundamental change (Maynzyuk & Dzhygyr 2008: 6).

The case study is divided into two parts: Part I explains the background to the reform, the respective roles of domestic and external actors in preparing reform proposals, and the main points of the draft Budget Code as they affected intergovernmental financial relations; Part II examines the process of securing adoption of the code in the face of powerful opposition, subsequent problems at the implementation stage and the response of international donors. This is followed by a brief conclusion summarising the principal findings of the case study.

Throughout the chapter, the terms 'fiscal decentralisation', 'reform of intergovernmental financial relations' and 'Budget Code reform' are used interchangeably.

# Part I: Preparing the Reform

Fatal Flaws Appear in the *Matryoshka*

The Soviet-era *Matryoshka* system for distributing the state budget between Ukraine's regions and cities, designed for a centrally planned economy, became increasingly dysfunctional in the context of the transition to a market economy and sharply declining revenues from taxation during the 1990s. Budgetary arrears at sub-national level reached a crisis point in 1998 when they accounted for three-quarters of the total overspend incurred by government institutions for the year. Pressures to restrain expenditure and the pyramid nature of the *Matryoshka* had resulted in increasingly arbitrary decision-making and a rapid growth in patronage and rent-seeking behaviour by politicians and officials at every level. In the period 1998-1999 a number of discrete domestic and international interests converged with a common purpose to use the crisis in sub-national budgets as a lever to introduce a new model of intergovernmental financial relations.

*The Matryoshka Pyramid*

Post-independence Ukraine inherited the Soviet system of financing the running costs of local and regional governments. This was generally known as the '*Matryoshka*', since the annual budget for each level of administration, ranging from the 27 *oblasts*[2] to the 12,000 or so villages and settlements, was nested within the budget for the tier immediately above in a manner reminiscent of the traditional Russian doll.

Under the 1991 Law on the Budgetary System of Ukraine, which perpetuated the *Matryoshka* model and regulated intergovernmental financial relations in Ukraine throughout the 1990s, the Ministry of Finance prepared an annual consolidated budget for the whole country which divided the available financial resources for the year between ministries in Kyiv and the 27 *oblasts*. The process of calculating each *oblast*'s budgetary requirements for the

---

[2] 24 regions plus the Autonomous Republic of Crimea and the Cities of Kyiv and Sevastopol which have *oblast* status.

coming year compared its expected revenue from a variety of taxes levied in the region, both national and local, with its expenditure needs arising from detailed national norms for each area of its spending authority.

These norms, also largely inherited from the Soviet era, stipulated a prescribed level of staffing and set of budget institutions per head of the population, an input-led approach to financial planning which followed 'volumetric and network indicators – numbers of beds, clubs, metres of premises, length of roads, etc.' (Maksiuta et al. 2004: 13). The difference between a region's expected revenue and its norm-based expenditure needs was bridged by annual subsidies or transfers from the national exchequer, which were intended to equalise the spending capacity of wealthier and less well-off regions.

While this budget model may have worked reasonably well in the conditions of a centrally planned economy 'where cash played a secondary role' (Maksiuta et al. 2004: 13), in the context of a changed economic model and the conditions of a sagging economy and shrinking revenue base, Ukraine could no longer afford the level of public services it had previously enjoyed. A growing discrepancy emerged between the norm-based expenditure requirements of sub-national governments and the revenue capacity of regions to satisfy them (USAID 2004: 4).

By 1997 only seven *oblasts* were net contributors to the national budget under this arrangement, while in eight of the poorest regions equalisation payments from national government represented 50% or more of total revenues. The city of Kyiv, with the largest tax base of any region, contributed over half its annual income to the exchequer (Fiscal Analysis Office 1998: 16-17). 'Own revenues' to sub-national government, the proceeds from purely local taxes and charges rather than a share of nationally levied personal or enterprise taxation, accounted for only 3.5% of all regional and local government income (Maksiuta et al. 2004: p.7).

With each level of sub-national government responsible for determining the budget of the tier below in a context of sharply declining revenue for public expenditure, there began a 'protracted sequential process' of argument and negotiation over disputed estimates of income and expenditure (Martinez-Vazquez & Thirsk 2010: 12), a process which cascaded down from *oblasts* to the larger cities and districts, and then on to smaller municipalities and villages or settlements. At each level the gap between an input-led expenditure calculation and a control figure for the budget resources available was contested by leaders of the subordinate authority, an argument which often continued well into the financial year and which, according to the former deputy mayor of one large city, invariably led to ill-feeling on both sides extending over two or three months every year.[3]

In the newly independent Ukraine, where the conditions of the Soviet planned economy no longer applied, the final allocation of resources for the coming year was determined less by any objective assessment of need, or by the content of any policy programmes there might be, than by the availability of hard cash and a 'pervasive climate of budget bargaining.'[4]

The opaque nature of these negotiations provided ample opportunity to reward one's friends and punish ones enemies by bestowing or withholding patronage.[5] In extreme cases responsibility for important national infrastructure such as a major defence installation, together with the associated budget provision, would find its way onto the balance sheet of a small village in return for a past favour,[6] a practice made possible by the continuation of the Soviet practice of a single establishment being under the subordination of several different levels of government authority (Maksiuta et al. 2004: 13).

At a more general level the absence of transparency encouraged the increasing use of 'soft' budget constraints, where gap-filling transfers from national or

---

[3] Interview with Pavlo Kachur, Deputy Director of the Association of Ukrainian Cities and formerly Deputy Mayor of the city of L'viv, Kyiv, 20 March 2013.

[4] Interviews with Wayne Thirsk, formerly financial adviser with the Verkhovna Rada Fiscal Analysis Office, Kyiv, 27 November 2012, 29 November 2012, 28 March 2013.

[5] Interviews with Wayne Thirsk, Kyiv, 27 November 2012, 29 November 2012, 28 March 2013.

[6] Interview with Yuriy Dzhygyr, intergovernmental finance expert, FISCO Consulting, Kyiv, 29 November 2012.

regional government offered the opportunity for lower level authorities to be bailed out before the end of the fiscal year as a result of lobbying or subjective judgements and deals made at the negotiating table (World Bank 2002a: 22-23; Martinez-Vazquez & Thirsk 2010: 14).

The existence of soft budget constraints and the ever-present opportunity for special pleading behind closed doors also introduced a perverse incentive for local governments to overstate their expenditure needs and underestimate their revenue so as to receive a more favourable settlement from the state budget at the beginning of the financial year. Conversely any initiative to economise on expenditure voluntarily was likely to result in a clawing back of government grants, as evidenced by the case of Luhans'ka *oblast* which in 1996-1998 made swingeing reductions in its education spending in an effort to balance the regional budget, only to find that its transfers from Kyiv were reduced by the corresponding sum.[7] Examples like this sent a clear message to others and became the principal reason for the subsequent arrears in budgets at all levels and a growing problem of indebtedness. In practice there was no effective limit to sub-national government expenditure and no serious attempt to bring spending into line with the available resources (Maksiuta et al. 2004: 13). The outcome was a growing crisis in local and regional government finance.

Between 1993 and 1996 per capita real spending by sub-national governments fell by 63% (Fiscal Analysis Office 1998: 15), reflecting the sharp decline in revenues from personal income, enterprise and local taxes during this period. Despite this fall in spending, budget execution was consistently in excess of the figure approved by the Ministry of Finance and over the course of the decade the arrears of sub-national government grew steadily.

City and district authorities continued to be responsible for the bulk of national spending in key public services such as education (76% of all budget expenditure in 1998), health (90%), housing and communal services (99%), and by 1998 in the Education and Health sectors regional and local

---

[7] Interviews with Wayne Thirsk, Kyiv, 27 November 2012, 29 November 2012, 28 March 2013.

governments were overspending their budgets by 68% and 24% respectively (World Bank 2002a: 29-30). Between January 1996 and August 1998, when they reached their peak, overall sub-national government arrears grew from 1.09 billion UAH to 4.7 billion UAH, or almost three-quarters of the total overspend by government institutions in that year (Martinez-Vazquez & Thirsk 2010: 43).

This clearly unsustainable situation was in part also the result of a deliberate policy of national government. From 1994 onwards, faced with an increasing budget deficit, the Cabinet of Minsters embarked on a policy of decentralising responsibility for social protection payments to regional and local governments. This included the social welfare allowances or concessions payable to groups such as war and labour veterans and the subsidies available to individuals on lower incomes for housing and communal service charges. The right to these concessions was enshrined in legislation and the rates of benefit determined at a national level, but the burden of financing programmes of social assistance was progressively shifted to the local level without any accompanying transfer of budgetary provision.

This gave rise to the phenomenon of the 'unfunded mandate', where the responsibilities of regional and local governments fail to match their decision-making authority or their resources to finance them (World Bank 2002a: 30-31). The growth in the sub-national share of public spending from 31% in 1994 to 47% in 1998 reflected this radical off-loading of responsibility by national government, and by February 2000 social protection payments accounted for 56% of all arrears in the regions (Martinez-Vazquez & Thirsk 2010: 32-33, 43). The politically unacceptable outcome was that the level of benefits paid to members of the community in the greatest need was dependent largely on the tax base of the city or district in which they happened to live.

*First Stirrings of Budget Reform*

The years 1998-99 were critical in providing the momentum for the reform of intergovernmental financial relations which was to follow from 2000 onwards.

The period saw the convergence of a number of discrete influences and pressures. These ranged from growing political support for a vision of a self-determining form of local governance as expressed in the 1996 Constitution, the European Charter of Local Self-Government signed in 1997 and the adoption of the State Law on Local Self-Government in the same year, and finally the reform ambitions of key individuals and institutions.

Each of these factors, for different reasons, provided an opportunity to use the crisis in sub-national government finance in order to drive through a new model of intergovernmental relations. International donors were drawn into this emerging network, often as a result of the perceived dynamism of individual pro-reform politicians or state officials, and here again the apparent opportunity to make a meaningful breakthrough in the reform of public administration in Ukraine acted as the catalyst for a rare example of collaboration between members of the donor community.

On the Ukrainian side the principal institutional interests advocating radical reform of intergovernmental financial relations reflected the views of political, civil society and intra-governmental lobbies, and were as follows:

- **The Budget Committee of the** *Verkhovna Rada* - the influential Budget Committee was responsible for formulating parliamentary policy on the financing of regional and local government, in addition to wider issues concerning the state budget. Following the Rada elections in the summer of 1998 the committee was chaired by a young and ambitious new deputy from Dnipropetrovs'k, Yulia Tymoshenko;

- **The Association of Ukrainian Cities** - the Association was founded in 1994 as a non-governmental organisation aiming to promote and strengthen urban self-government and to represent municipal interests to national and regional levels of administration. Its membership comprised the leaderships of city and municipal governments, including the elected mayors of Ukraine's largest cities;

- **The Territorial Budget Department of the Ministry of Finance** - the Department was responsible for dealing with a growing problem of local government arrears over which it had little effective control, thanks to the *Matryoshka* system. It was headed by a young economist, Anatoliy Maksiuta, recruited in the mid-1990s from Zhytomyrs'ka *oblast* where he had held senior positions in financial management at regional and district levels.

In the international donor community, three major donor programmes associated themselves in different ways with the growing reform pressures among their Ukrainian counterparts:

- **The World Bank** – fiscal management issues figured largely in the Bank's discussion of reform with the Government of Ukraine all the way through the 1990s, and overhauling local government finance was central to these. An unpublished review by Bank experts, prepared between 1997 and 1999, recommended *inter alia* the replacement of the *Matryoshka* system;[8]

- **The United States Agency for International Development (USAID)** - as part of a broader programme of support to fiscal reform in Ukraine, the USAID sponsored Fiscal Analysis Office of the *Verkhovna Rada* was established in 1998 to provide advice on budget reform to members of the *Rada* Budget Committee. USAID had also provided financial and expert assistance to the Association of Ukrainian Cities since its foundation in the mid- 1990s;

- **The United Kingdom Department for International Development (DFID)** - as the UK Know How Fund the British international assistance programme to post-Soviet Ukraine had supported the setting up of a National Academy of Public Administration, a civil service training institution which was to play an important role in the professional development of a number of individuals who would later be central to the

---

[8] E-mail correspondence from Deborah Wetzel, formerly the World Bank's chief adviser on budget reform to the Government of Ukraine and author of the unpublished report, received 18 May 2014.

budget reform of 2000. Following its establishment as a free-standing ministry, in 1999 DFID sent an expert team to Ukraine to assess the scope for more comprehensive technical assistance to the development of local and regional self-government, including in the area of intergovernmental finance.

As discussed in chapter II, while the adoption of the 1996 Constitution, the signing of the European Charter of Local Self-Government, and the passing of the 1997 State Law on Local Self-Government together indicated a step-change in the political climate with regard to the powers of sub-national government in Ukraine, they were not matched by any accompanying changes to the financing of local authorities to enable them to make use of their new powers.

The Constitution (arts. 140, 142, 143) had confirmed the right to full self-government, independent of the state, for cities, towns and villages, in accordance with Ukraine's obligations under the Council of Europe's Charter of Local Self-Government, and empowered local governments to approve spending programmes for socio-economic development within their territory. Similarly, the 1997 Law on Self-Government attempted to delineate more clearly the 'own' and 'delegated' spending authority of cities and municipalities, with delegated spending limited to the state functions of education, health and social protection.

However this championing of the idea of budgetary independence for the lower tiers of government was in reality more a statement of intent than an explicit legislative commitment, and under the 1997 Law the procedures for determining sub-national budgets were to remain unchanged from those set out in the 1991 Law on the Budgetary System of Ukraine until such time as new budget legislation was introduced (Fiscal Analysis Office 1998: 20). This impasse was to have a galvanising effect on pro-reform activists

The Emergence of Personal and Institutional Networks

Beginning in 1999 political interests at national and big city level combined to press for greater autonomy in the determination of sub-national budgets and, paradoxically, found common cause with a small group of pro-reform officials in the Ministry of Finance whose main concern was to bring the local budget process under better control and to eradicate as far as possible the corrosive practices of patronage and rent-seeking between different levels of government. A similar convergence of interests was evident in the international donor community where the World Bank, USAID and more recently UK DFID had each identified the reform of intergovernmental finance as a priority for their intervention. A network of overlapping personal and professional relationships within and between both Ukrainian and international institutions was already becoming apparent at this stage. This was a factor which was later to prove central to the effort to push through the Budget Code reform.

*A 'Unique Concurrence' of Interests*

There are contrasting narratives on the question of who was to take the leading role in pressing for new legislation on intergovernmental finance. On one account it was the new intake of parliamentary deputies on the *Rada* Budget Committee, led by their 'hyperactive' chair Yulia Tymoshenko, which 'roused a sleepy Ministry of Finance' into action and prodded city governments to set up their own associations and lobby for change (Oberemchuk 1999).

On another view the Ministry of Finance, which itself had recently had an injection of new blood in the shape of Territorial Budget Department Head Anatoliy Maksiuta, felt overburdened by the interminable wrangling over budget settlements with sub-national government and the escalating level of arrears. Furthermore a radical overhaul of intergovernmental financial relations formed part of a reform programme already agreed between the Government of Ukraine, the International Monetary Fund (IMF) and the World Bank (Maksiuta et al. 2004: 17-18).

Yet another analysis emphasises the role of the USAID-funded Fiscal Analysis Office which was said to have played a pivotal role in forging close working relationships with both the Budget Committee and the Ministry, and as a result being 'instrumental in building consensus around the most appropriate direction for reform' (USAID, 2004: 8). What is in no doubt is that there was a 'unique concurrence' in the interests of several bodies frustrated, albeit for different reasons, with the financing arrangements for regional and local government (Maksiuta et al. 2004: 16), and a window of opportunity for reform brought about by a rare alignment of interests between the legislative, executive and local spheres of state authority.[9]

## The Budget Committee of the *Verkhovna Rada*

For politicians in this period being a so-called 'regionalist' among *Rada* deputies, in other words taking the side of regional and local governments in budget and other disputes with the centre, brought a degree of prestige and was considered beneficial to future political careers (Oberemchuk 1999). In the parliamentary intake of June 1998 there were a number of deputies like Yulia Tymoshenko who had prior connections with regional or local government and who, following their election to the *Rada*, set about exploiting their image as defenders of regional interests. Part of their platform was to build public and political support for the idea of a second chamber in Parliament to represent the interests of the regions.

In the Budget Committee this group allied itself with a number of longer-standing deputies who had devoted their energies to the field of intergovernmental finance for a number of years.[10] In her role as chair of the Budget Committee from 1998 Yulia Tymoshenko became the 'unstoppable political champion' of budget reform,[11] attracting to the cause the support of the leaderships of many of Ukraine's largest cities and municipalities. Before long the Budget Committee was able to 'set a mousetrap' for the Ministry of Finance by preparing a draft Budget Code for the reform of intergovernmental financial relations and a draft state budget for 1999 based on the methodology contained in its proposed Code.[12]

---

[9] E-mail correspondence from Deborah Wetzel, received 18 May 2014.

[10] Valeri Asadchev, Yuri Kliuchkovs'kyi, Boris Andresiuk, Leonid Kosakovs'kyi, Vladymyr Rybak. *'Lyubit Mestnyi Biudzhety Stalo Modno'*, *Ukrains'ka Pravda*, 24 November 1999

[11] Interview with Ihor Shpak, formerly Director of the Verkhovna Rada Fiscal Analysis Office, Kyiv, 20 March 2013..

[12] *'Lyubit Mestnyi Biudzhety Stalo Modno'*, *Ukrains'ka Pravda*, 24 November 1999.

Meanwhile a model of what shape that reform might take was being developed in the rooms of the *Verkhovna Rada*'s USAID-funded Fiscal Analysis Office (Fiscal Analysis Office 1998). The purpose of the model was to define more clearly the spending responsibilities of national and sub-national tiers of government, to rid the system of behind-closed-doors bargaining between successive levels of administration, and to introduce greater stability and predictability into the revenue flows to local governments. It would also bring to an end the unacceptable practice of 'unfunded mandates' for expenditure on social benefits, which had resulted from deliberate government policy.

The centrepiece of the reform was to be a formula-based system of intergovernmental transfers, under which the spending requirements of local authorities were to be calculated mathematically on a uniform needs-led basis determined by demographic factors, replacing the current input-led approach which started from the network of existing institutions. On the income side the formula would take into account the revenue-raising capacity of individual authorities, but would do so in a way which no longer punished local governments for taking initiatives to increase their income. On the contrary it would guarantee them the right to retain the benefits of efficiency gains, the 'long-standing dream of city mayors and local finance officials.'[13]

Most radically, because the reformed transfer system was to be objective and formula-based, there was no longer a need for it to be overseen by *oblast*-level authorities. Instead, the Ministry of Finance would make an annual calculation for each sub-national unit of government and make the transfer directly to them.

Over the course of the 1998 financial year Fiscal Analysis Office experts were actively discussing the expected benefits of the bold new approach, separately and jointly with the Budget Committee of the *Verkhovna Rada* and with officials in Territorial Budget Department of the Ministry of Finance. Already in March 1998 Yevhen Zhovtiak, vice-chair of the Budget Committee, was confidently predicting that the reformed transfer system would be adopted

---

[13] '...*davnia mriia meriv ta mistsevykh finansystiv*', from Yevhen Zhovtiak, '*Za Mistsevi Biudzhety Zamovyty b Slovo,*' Polityka, 2 March 1998.

by parliament in time for inclusion in the 1999 state budget.[14]

## The Association of Ukrainian Cities

The Association of Ukrainian Cities was established in 1994 with the help of funding from USAID's Municipal Financing and Management Project (USAID 1996), and as early as 1996 had identified the lack of discretionary powers of city governments over budgetary issues as a priority concern. Contrary to the view that the larger cities were spurred into action primarily by the inspirational leadership of Yulia Tymoshenko, figures who were active in the Association at the time argue that it was a powerful lobby in its own right, with the mayors of Ukraine's major cities taking a leading role. In the context of the increased authority bestowed on local self-government by the 1996 Constitution and the 1997 State Law on Local Self-Government, directly elected city mayors had become an influential political force. 'If the Association asked for a meeting with the President or with the Cabinet of Ministers, its wish would be granted.'[15]

Regular conflicts over the annual budget settlement between democratically mandated city councils and state appointed *oblast* administrations were a feature of the increasingly anomalous *Matryoshka* system of intergovernmental finance, and reflected the contradiction between the rights of self-government as established by recent legislation and the *de facto* omnipotence of the *oblast* authorities (Maksiuta et al. 2004: 18). Long-running disputes had occurred in Odesa, Vinnytsya, Kirovohrad, Luhans'k and other cities, with the most celebrated example being the regional capital of Khmelnytsky. Here the municipal government had deliberately and substantially increased its 'own revenues' from local taxes and charges, to a level of 10% of annual income rather then the more typical 4%, only to find it was penalised by the *oblast* administration which correspondingly reduced the share of nationally levied taxes the city was allowed to retain (World Bank 2002a: 29).

---

[14] Yevhen Zhovtiak, 'Za Mistsevi Biudzhety Zamovyty b Slovo,' *Polityka*, 2 March 1998.

[15] Interview with Pavlo Kachur, Deputy Director of the Association of Ukrainian Cities in the 1990s and formerly Deputy Mayor of the city of L'viv, Kyiv, 20 March 2013.

From 1997 onwards city mayors, understanding that their future electoral success would be dependent on serious investment in municipal development and that this would only be achieved if there were less interference in their financial affairs, embarked on a well-organised campaign for reform through their association.[16]

## The Ministry of Finance

Within the hierarchy of the Ministry of Finance, both nationally and regionally, there were pockets of pro-reform activity involving individual officials who were responsive to the idea of formula-based transfers as a means of bringing to an end the apparently ceaseless round of negotiation and deal-making which characterised the present system, and which had contributed to the crisis of arrears in sub-national spending. These were middle-ranking state servants operating on their own and frequently without the support of their top management.

Anatoliy Maksiuta, described by a senior World Bank official as 'always a champion' of intergovernmental finance reform,[17] made a first attempt to introduce a formula approach in the first draft of the 1999 state budget. However, his initiative was 'labelled as premature' by more senior ministry officials (USAID 2004: 5) and 'scuttled at the last minute' by the Deputy Minister.[18]

There were similar initiatives at regional level. Yuriy Balkoviy, Director of Finance for the Luhans'ka *oblast* administration, was the first regional finance head to experiment with a formula approach to transfers to municipalities and districts, also in the 1999 budget, for which he had the support of the chair of the *oblast* council budget committee. His initiative was warmly welcomed by Yulia Tymoshenko who, 'in her rather informal western style of disregarding protocol and hierarchy', approached Balkoviy directly,

---

[16] Interview with Pavlo Kachur, Kyiv, 20 March 2013.

[17] E-mail correspondence from Deborah Wetzel, received 18 May 2014.

[18] Interviews with Wayne Thirsk, Kyiv, 27 November 2012, 29 November 2012, 28 March 2013.

without reference to the ministry, to take part in a *Verkhovna Rada* working group preparing proposals to put to parliament.

The group was to include finance officials from a small number of other regions who shared Balkoviy's thinking.[19] But when he presented his formula approach to a ministry *Kollegia* in Kyiv, Balkoviy's ideas were roundly condemned by Deputy Minister Bukovinsky as unconstitutional. Seemingly the ministry as an institution was opposed to any move towards a more objective method of calculating transfers, wishing to maintain as much manual (*ruchnoe*) control as possible.[20]

As to the motivation of these reform-minded national and regional officials, from their point of view the rationale may have been less about decentralisation and granting greater authority to the localities, and more about bringing better order and control to a chaotic local budget process which had become increasingly subject to patronage and rent-seeking by politicians and officials at every level (Maynzyuk & Dzygyr 2008-9: 2). After all, under the *Matryoshka* regime the ministry had little real influence on the formation of budgets below *oblast* level and it is perhaps revealing that Maksiuta himself describes the major weakness of the pre-2000 process for the annual determination of local expenditure as being that it was non transparent and 'unenforceable' (Maksiuta et al. 2004: 13).

Professor Kenneth Davey, DFID's senior adviser to Maksiuta on reforming intergovernmental finance, argues in a similar vein that the ministry was under extreme pressure to bring local budgets under firmer control. The introduction of a transfer formula would 'allow the Ministry of Finance to off-load the responsibility for prioritising expenditure onto local governments and bring to an end the annual wrangling that took up so much time and left

---

[19] One name mentioned in this regard is Serhiy Mel'nik from Khmel'nyts'ka region, where there had been a running conflict between oblast authorities and the leadership of the regional capital.

[20] Interview with Yuriy Balkoviy, Director of Finance Department, Luhans'ka Oblast State Administration, Luhans'k, 27 June 2013.

the ministry with all the hard decisions and all the blame. The transfer formula enabled them to say 'OK, that's it, that's all you're getting – you decide from here on.'[21]

*The International Donor Community*

**The IMF and the World Bank**

The convergence of interests among key Ukrainian institutions and a few well-placed individuals within them was paralleled by analogous developments in the international donor community. The IMF, which was providing 2.6 billion USD in budget support to the Government of Ukraine to shore up the mounting state budget deficit, made overhaul of the entire budget process a condition of its continued assistance.[22] Similarly, the World Bank regarded overhaul of intergovernmental finance as the focal point of budget reform, in particular the transition to a formula-based system.

The Bank was proposing a Municipal Development Loan facility, enabling the newly self-governing cities to access credit for much needed investment in communal infrastructure. While the loan was not explicitly conditional on budget reform,[23] in all likelihood it would only proceed if the financing of municipal budgets were placed on a more stable and predictable footing. In response, in November 1999 the Ministry of Finance invited the Bank to take part in the Ministry's own working group tasked to develop a new model of intergovernmental finance (Martinez-Vazquez & Thirsk 2010: 56).

The World Bank also developed close working relationships with Yulia Tymoshenko in her capacity as chair of the *Verkhovna Rada* Budget Committee. Deborah Wetzel, the Bank's chief adviser to Ukraine on budget reform, had discussed the need for reform at length with Ms Tymoshenko and was thought to have gently dissuaded her from pushing ahead with an early but

---

[21] Interview with Professor Kenneth Davey, Senior Adviser with DFID's LARGIS project, Cheltenham, 27 August 2013.

[22] Interview with Anatoliy Maksiuta, First Deputy Minister of Economic Development and Trade, formerly Director of the Territorial Budget Department of the Ministry of Finance, Kyiv, 25 May 2013.

[23] E-mail correspondence from Deborah Wetzel, received 18 May 2014.

rather ill-conceived version of a formula-based transfer system which retained too much of the old *Matryoshka* approach.[24]

## The United States Agency for International Development (USAID)

In March 1998, as part of a wider programme of advice on macroeconomic and taxation reform,[25] USAID launched the Fiscal Analysis Office (FAO). Originally conceived as an embryonic budget office for the *Verkhovna Rada*, the FAO quickly honed in on the issue of fiscal decentralisation and the reform of intergovernmental finance.

Its close working relationships with both the Budget Committee of the *Rada* and the Territorial Budget Department of the Ministry of Finance, between whom it acted as an informal broker, stemmed from its expert staff being in the main Ukrainian specialists in sub-national budget finance and the office thus being widely perceived as a local institution rather than as a donor project. It became a focal point for reform discussion and debate between Budget Committee members, officials from the Territorial Budget Department, and FAO experts. Importantly these discussions would take place informally, 'within the confines of the FAO' and away from the day-to-day pressures of government (USAID 2004: 8).

USAID also played a significant role through its decision to finance the establishment of the Association of Ukrainian Cities in 1994, and to provide expert advice and training from both international and Ukrainian consultants on strengthening the Association's role as a lobby for city and municipal governments. This became increasingly important as legislative changes in the status of local self-government enhanced the political power of elected leaders at this level. In the view of Pavlo Kachur, formerly deputy mayor of the city of L'viv and in the late 1990s the Association's deputy director, it was the advice and training of USAID experts[26] which helped to transform the

---

[24] Interviews with Wayne Thirsk, Kyiv, 27 November 2012, 29 November 2012, 28 March 2013.

[25] USAID 'Fiscal Reform in Support of Trade Liberalization', contract no. PCE-1-03-00-00015-00 (USAID 2004).

[26] Experts were employed by the American Research Triangle Institute which was contracted by USAID to support the Association.

role of the Association and turn it into a successful campaigning organisation.[27]

## The United Kingdom International Development Agency (DFID)

DFID's principal contribution to the Budget Code reform was to come from 2000 onwards but two of its interventions in the 1990s were to have significant implications for what happened later. In one of its few incursions into the field of public administration reform the United Kingdom Know How Fund supported the work of a new Institute of Public Administration in Ukraine.

The Institute was the brainchild of Bohdan Kravchenko, a Canadian of Ukrainian descent, who had come to Kyiv in 1991 having previously worked as Director of the Canadian Institute of Ukrainian Studies in the University of Alberta. The aim of the Institute was to provide training for existing and new civil servants, to a standard comparable with the best international standards of contemporary public administration, an objective requiring 'a very substantial attitude change….a change in patterns and value systems that had become deeply entrenched' (Glentworth 1995: 9). Kravchenko was influential and well-connected and the Institute had successfully attracted funding from the Cabinet of Ministers and from international sources including the George Soros Foundation.

Support from the Know How Fund consisted mainly of a partnership arrangement with the University of North London, whose task was to assist the Institute to develop a Masters of Public Administration programme capable of receiving international validation in Western Europe. Kravchenko and his colleagues were in many ways the ideal technical assistance partners, themselves deciding when and what support was needed from UK experts and whether in the process of implementation any changes were required to the original agreement with the donor. This proactive approach from a partner was regarded by the Know How Fund as desirable in all aid projects but in practice all too rarely the reality.[28] The Institute was later to become the

---

[27] Interview with Pavlo Kachur, Kyiv, 20 March 2013.

[28] Interview with Dr Garth Glentworth, formerly UK DFID Governance Adviser, London, 18 February 2014.

Ukrainian National Academy of Public Administration, which remains to the present day the country's leading in-service training institution for civil servants.

For the purposes of the present study what is significant about the Institute is its role in the formation of a network of figures who were later to be key actors in the reform of the Budget Code. Among the small group of 15 or so graduates of the 1993-1994 Masters programme were: Anatoliy Maksiuta, later Director of the Territorial Budget Department; Pavlo Kachur, later Deputy Director of the Association of Ukrainian Cities and Adviser to Prime Minister at the time of the reform; and Yuriy Hanushchak, later expert for the Research Triangle Institute which advised the Association of Ukrainian Cities.[29]

The period at the Institute of Public Administration under Kravchenko's intellectual leadership and the long-term relationship between these individuals are mentioned by all three as decisive influences on future attitudes and career patterns. Anatoliy Maksiuta in particular recalls a month-long internship in the Finance Department of the London Borough of Islington, arranged through the University of North London, where he first learned about the UK practice of formula-based intergovernmental transfers and even chose it as the topic for his Masters dissertation.[30]

DFID's second significant intervention in the 1990s was to send two experts to Ukraine, one British and one Polish, to do a 'scoping' study on the need for a British project to support the reform of local and regional government. Jim Amos was the former Chief Executive Officer of Birmingham City Council and employed as a DFID adviser on public administration reform in Eastern Europe. Pawel Swianiewicz was Project Manager for the UK's Local Government Assistance Programme (LGAP) in Poland and was also an expert

---

[29] Another participant in the 1993-1994 programme, although not directly involved in budget reform, was Vasyl Kuiybida, later Mayor of L'viv City and subsequently Minister of Regional Development and Construction.

[30] Interviews with Anatoliy Maksiuta, Kyiv, 25 May 2013; Pavlo Kachur, Kyiv, 20 March, 2013; Yuriy Hanushchak, Kyiv, 21 March, 2013.

on local government, having cooperated with British finance advisers on the reform of Poland's arrangements for intergovernmental finance.

LGAP was seen by DFID as a highly successful programme which, it was thought, might be capable of replication in Ukraine. Over a period of six months in 1998 Amos and Swianiewicz visited Kyiv and several regions, and their recommendations were to provide the basis for DFID's Local and Regional Government Institutional Strengthening project (LARGIS) which was launched in December 1999.[31]

International Technical Assistance in the Preparation of Budget Reform

The launch of DFID's LARGIS project towards the end of 1999 marked a major change in objectives for programmes of technical assistance to Ukraine, with the emphasis moving from the know-how and skills sharing approach of the early 1990s to the more process-oriented task of institution building. In the area of intergovernmental finance the focus of this task was to be on constructing a new relationship between national and sub-national governments which would simultaneously accommodate pro-reform politicians' drive for greater autonomy for local government and reform-minded state officials' wish to establish a less politicised and more technocratic method for settling local budgets.

Despite initial tensions on the Ukrainian side, in the early months of 2000 DFID and USAID experts worked collaboratively with both political leaders and ministry specialists to prepare a policy instrument which would meet both requirements. The formula-based transfer model which emerged from this process replaced the *Matryoshka* system and allocated finance from the state budget direct to local government without the controlling intervention of *oblast* administrations. Similarly the mathematical nature of the annual transfer calculation introduced greater predictability into the setting of local

---

[31] Interview with Pawel Swianiewicz, formerly Project Manager of the UK Know How Fund Local Government Assistance Programme in Poland, later expert for the DFID LARGIS project in Ukraine, Warsaw, 12 October 2013.

budgets, eliminating the need for bargaining and negotiation and with them much of the scope for patronage.

*The LARGIS Project: UK DFID Prioritises Institutional Development in Ukraine*

DFID's LARGIS project, which ran from late 1999 to the end of 2002 with a budget of GBP 1.5m, was the new ministry's most ambitious planned intervention to date in the field of institutional development in Ukraine, reflecting a widely held view in the donor community at the end of the 1990s that more attention should be given to the perceived weakness of Ukraine's state institutions and to systemic rather than partial reform (EU Commission 1998: 2, 7; Hamilton 2013: 155).

The broad objective of LARGIS was to assist the Government of Ukraine to establish a new framework for relations between national, regional and local government, and this was to include developing a 'stable and transparent system of intergovernmental finance.'[32] The project's senior expert on funding arrangements for local government was Professor Kenneth Davey from the University of Birmingham, who had wide experience of consultancy on public administrative reform in Asia, Latin America and Eastern Europe, and who had been lead adviser to the UK Government's programme of assistance to local government reorganisation in the Czech Republic, Hungary and Slovakia in the 1990s.[33]

In November 1999, at a briefing meeting in DFID's London offices between senior ministry officials and the LARGIS project management team from the University of Birmingham, the importance of achieving rapid results on budget reform was underscored and it was remarked that the presence of both Professor Davey and Pawel Swianiewicz (from the successful Polish

---

[32] From a report of the International Development Department, University of Birmingham, UK National Archives, www.webarchive.nationalarchives.gov.uk/20090316045905/http: //www.liveweb29.bham.ac.uk/consult/LARGIS.shtml (Accessed 8 May 2014).

[33] Professor Davey was well known to Deborah Wetzel, the World Bank's chief adviser to Ukraine on budget reform, with whom he had worked on the question of intergovernmental finance in Hungary and other post-communist countries. This professional relationship was important in shaping the approach of the LARGIS intervention on the ground.

Local Government Assistance Programme) in Birmingham's project proposal had been important factors in the decision to award the contract to the University's International Development Department.

The World Bank was particularly anxious to press ahead with reform while there appeared to be strong political momentum in favour of doing so. It proposed that LARGIS experts should service the working group structure established in late 1999 by Anatoliy Maksiuta and representatives of the leading interests arguing for reform, the Budget Committee of the *Verkhovna Rada*, the Association of Ukrainian Cities, and the Territorial Budget Department of the Ministry of Finance. The working group's task was to elaborate and build consensus behind a formula-based transfer system with a view to its incorporation in the 2001 state budget. Exceptionally, because of the urgency to move forward while there was political will to do so, the World Bank was also requesting that DFID allow the payment of nominal honoraria to working group participants as an additional incentive to undertake the detailed technical work as quickly as possible. This was outside the normal practice of technical assistance programmes and potentially in contravention of Ukrainian legislation on the payment of state officials.[34]

By mid-January 2000 the LARGIS team was on the ground in Kyiv and was greeted initially with some suspicion by USAID's project on Fiscal Reform in Support of Trade Liberalization, which had been operating since 1997. USAID experts were sceptical that the UK Government had anything useful to contribute in a situation where, as noted above, top officials in the Ministry of Finance had already rejected the advice of their own specialists in relation to the 1999 state budget, and successfully resisted the combined pressure of the *Verkhovna Rada* Budget Committee and the Association of Ukrainian Cities. USAID was also critical of the policy of providing honoraria payments to officials, which were seen to be creating a dangerous precedent and

---

[34] The World Bank argued, and DFID accepted, that the device had been used successfully by projects in Indonesia where Professor Davey had been involved, and that small honoraria could legitimately be made as a per diem expense to state officials taking part in research and training.

undermining the approach of other donors.[35]

Relations between Ukrainian partners were also less than straightforward. The initial impression of the LARGIS team, gained through a series of separate meetings with the principal actors on the Ukrainian side, was that Budget Committee politicians and Ministry of Finance officials were working quite separately on the question of intergovernmental finance reform.

Reform was a key priority for members of the *Verkhovna Rada* Budget Committee bent on a radical decentralisation of authority and less interference from Kyiv. Yet for the Ministry of Finance it was only an element of a broader drive to overhaul the chaotic process of preparing and executing the annual state budget. The Ministry was fully aware that the financing of local government, because it would attract political interest, was a useful locomotive for wider reform, capable of dragging the rest with it.[36] However its principal concern in relation to local budgets was almost certainly one of introducing more order and control.

This tension between politicians and officials was evident in the LARGIS project's inaugural round-table to discuss the setting up of small task groups to prepare the formula-based transfer scheme. The meeting was hosted by Yevhen Zhovtiak, Deputy Chair of the Budget Committee, and was held in the Committee Rooms the *Verkhovna Rada* in February 2000, indicating the clear intention of politicians to take the leading role. Ministry of Finance officials, among them Maksiuta's deputy Anatoliy Miarkovskyi,[37] were initially excluded from the round-table and kept waiting for an appreciable time at the entrance to the committee rooms because their names did not appear on a list of invited participants provided by the Budget Committee. When they did finally gain entry, the officials were subjected to a barrage of

---

[35] Interviews with Wayne Thirsk, Kyiv, 27 November 2012, 29 November 2012, 28 March 2013.

[36] Interview with Ihor Shpak, Kyiv, 20 March 2013.

[37] Maksiuta had by this time been appointed Head of the Ministry of Finance's overall Budget Department and had appointed Miarkovskyi as his deputy. Like Maksiuta, Miarkovskyi had a background in local finance, in his case from the Dnipropetrovs'ka region.

criticism from both *Verkhovna Rada* members and Association of Ukrainian Cities representatives for placing bureaucratic obstacles in the path of reform of local government finance.[38]

If relations between the key institutional protagonists on both the Ukrainian and donor sides were at times strained, by contrast intergovernmental finance experts from DFID's LARGIS and USAID's Fiscal Analysis Office were quick in establishing a rapport. In discussion with Yevhen Zhovtiak it was agreed that LARGIS experts Kenneth Davey and Pawel Swianiewicz would assist the proposed task groups to elaborate the expenditure side of the transfer formula, while Fiscal Analysis Office experts Ihor Shpak and Wayne Thirsk would focus on local government revenues and a methodology for ensuring that authorities were not penalised through claw-back if they were successful in increasing the share of overall income coming from local sources.

This agreement played to the respective experience and strengths of the two expert teams and worked well. In Professor Davey's words 'the division was agreed from the beginning, at the very first meeting. Wayne and Ihor were very co-operative about it all, where they could have felt that we were moving in on the Fiscal Analysis Office's territory. They did not attend the expenditure side task groups but we kept them up to date with what we were doing. Relations were remarkably smooth and we met regularly, in meetings or less formally'.[39] The strength of these relationships is testimony both to the experience and mutual respect of the individuals involved and also to an unusual willingness to cooperate at donor level, itself largely the outcome of past professional contacts.

*Technical Assistance in Action: Advice to the Task Groups Preparing Budget Reform*

The challenge for LARGIS experts Kenneth Davey and Pawel Swianiewicz was considerable. It was one thing for Yulia Tymoshenko and Anatoliy Maksiuta to be convinced of the necessary direction of reform, but

---

[38] Interview with Professor Kenneth Davey, Cheltenham, 27 August 2013.

[39] Interview with Professor Kenneth Davey, Cheltenham, 27 August 2013.

introducing the formula-based transfer system into Ukraine's complex intergovernmental budgetary arrangements could only be successfully achieved if the ministry specialists who would eventually be responsible for implementing the new system were also persuaded that it would work.

In the late winter and spring of 2000 LARGIS experts met regularly with task groups of Ministry of Finance officials organised on a sector basis reflecting the three main areas of expenditure delegated from national to sub-national government: education, health care and social protection.[40] The role of each task group was to prepare a mathematical formula to allow for the transfer of funds from the state budget to local authorities in such a way as to equalise the capacity of local governments, regardless of their population size or individual tax base, to provide a given level of service in the three delegated areas. The membership of the task groups comprised the team of senior Ministry of Finance officials responsible for each sector, augmented from time to time by finance officials from the line ministries concerned.

It was also important to maintain the involvement of the key domestic actors who had been pressing for the reform, and to ensure that these potentially divergent interests were pulling in the same direction. At the hub of the task group structure was a Steering Committee composed of *Verkhovna Rada* Budget Committee members, representatives of the Association of Ukrainian Cities, and Anatoliy Maksiuta and Anatoliy Miarkovskyi from the Budget Department of the Ministry of Finance. The Association representatives on the Committee included two of Maksiuta's former contemporaries at the Institute of Public Administration, Yuriy Hanushchak and Pavlo Kachur, the latter now also working as an adviser to the Prime Minister of the time, Viktor Yushchenko. The Steering Committee was jointly advised by both LARGIS and Fiscal Analysis Office experts and its brief was to prepare the final draft of the Budget Code for submission to the Cabinet of Ministers and the *Verkhovna Rada*.

---

[40] Sport and culture are a fourth but much smaller area of delegated expenditure.

This sophisticated and inclusive approach to public policy analysis, drawing simultaneously on the views and expertise of political lobbies and technical specialists and developing a shared approach to problem-solving between them, was fostered by Anatoliy Maksiuta. Maksiuta in turn was much influenced by the teaching of Vira Nanivska at Kyiv's International Centre for Policy Studies. The Nanivska Centre was at the forefront of encouraging what was seen as a European-style, consensus-building approach to the development of public policy.[41]

Given the initial difference in assumptions and approach between Ministry specialists on the sector task groups and their LARGIS advisers, the speed with which proposals for the expenditure element of the transfer formula were completed was impressive. As previously discussed, the still-surviving Soviet practice of input-based budgeting meant that the starting point for the process was the finance required to sustain the network of existing institutions and their associated staffing. If, as was increasingly the case, there were insufficient funds to meet these costs, the extent of the shortfall would be settled in a process of hard political bargaining. Nevertheless, the staffing or service-level 'norm' remained the guideline figure and the baseline assumption regarding the required level of provision.

The model proposed by LARGIS experts, following closely the practice of both the UK government and the post-communist governments of much of Central and Eastern Europe, made no attempt to link the allocation of central government grants to the existing pattern of institutions in the localities and was sceptical of the concept of staffing and service norms, which it regarded as unrealistic and a relic of the Soviet past. Instead the model claimed simply to provide a means of delivering an equitable and transparent division of available state budget resources which were inevitably finite. It deliberately left little or no room for negotiation since it was based on the application of

---

[41] E-mail correspondence from Deborah Wetzel, received 18 May 2014. Post-Soviet Ukraine's first independent think tank, the International Centre for Policy Studies (ICPS) was established in 1994 with finance from the George Soros Open Society Institute. Vira Nanivska joined ICPS as Director in 1997, having previously been employed by the World Bank in Ukraine.

the same mathematical formula to all sub-national units of government, employing what Yevhen Zhovtiak from the Budget Committee had earlier described as 'uncompromisingly objective indicators.'[42]

LARGIS experts would meet with each of the three sector task groups over a full day, deliberately away from the day-to-day pressures of the Ministry in a quiet and neutral location. In the morning experts would explain a particular aspect of the expenditure calculation to be included in the transfer formula, followed by work in the afternoon when group members would start applying the methodology to their own sector. Homework would be given to each task group in order to complete a given piece of work before the next visit of experts. Group members were said initially to be 'horrified' by the scale and complexity of the formula approach, and its lack of regard for the spending norms of each service. They would frequently spend the morning of a day-long meeting questioning the detail with great scepticism. After a break for lunch however, they would come back and say 'ok, so where do we start?' According to LARGIS expert Kenneth Davey, motivation was never a problem and the groups got on with their work in and between meetings very diligently. 'They knew the work had to be done, that their managers wanted it done, and so they just got on with it. All of them were tough and hardworking specialists in their field, used to pushing things along and doing what they had been asked to do by their superiors.'[43]

The style of the LARGIS experts was arguably no less important. Speaking of Professor Davey's interaction with Ukrainian counterparts, Anatoliy Maksiuta commented on his comprehensive knowledge of the intergovernmental finance system in a variety of countries and how to build it in new environment. Also 'his personal, quiet style, offering an opinion when needed in order to overcome a blockage in the process of policy formulation…..just the type of partnership approach the Ukrainian side appreciated.'[44] Similarly Yuriy Hanushchak, a Ukrainian expert working for the Association of

---

[42] '…bezkompromisni ob'ekiyvni pokaznyky', Yevhen Zhovtiak, 'Za Mistsevi Biudzhety Zamovyty b Slovo…,' Polityka, 2 March 1998.

[43] Interview with Professor Kenneth Davey, Cheltenham, 27 August 2013.

[44] Interview with Anatoliy Maksiuta, Kyiv, 25 May 2013.

Ukrainian Cities, remarked that 'expert advice to the Ministry of Finance could be taken wrongly if it made officials feel inadequate in some way, but the style of experts like Ken Davey and Pawel Swianiewicz was gentle, reasonable and low-key, making it all sound possible and not overly complicated.' Ironically it also gave more credibility to Ukrainian experts like Yuriy Hanushchak himself, who had previously offered similar advice to the Ministry and received short shrift.[45]

Professor Davey puts it as follows: 'the standard method of addressing each practical reform issue was to convene a meeting of the task group of Ukrainian specialists representing the different interested parties, outline a range of optional solutions based on international practice, then provide intermittent but not constant dialogue and comment at the stage of draft recommendations. LARGIS did not supply blueprints and effectively left the groups to make up their own minds within an agreed timetable and with financial and administrative support. The result was a greater commitment on the Ukrainian side to the reform solutions proposed.' The international nature of the advice was also important. Professor Davey recalls that because of the background of the LARGIS team they were 'able to call on experience of a range of Central and Eastern European countries which had to reform systems of intergovernmental finance based previously on the same model as Ukraine's.'[46]

*The Draft Budget Code Proposals*

By June of 2000 the Steering Committee already had a draft of the proposed new Budget Code, including a major section on the reform of intergovernmental finance. Kenneth Davey and Pawel Swianiewicz from the LARGIS project, and Ihor Shpak and Wayne Thirsk from the Fiscal Analysis Office, had completed their work on the expenditure and revenue sides of the transfer formula respectively, and the recommendations of the various sector

---

[45] Interview with Yuriy Hanushchak, expert with the Association of Ukrainian Cities, Kyiv, 21 March 2013.
[46] Interview with Professor Kenneth Davey, Cheltenham, 27 August 2013.

task groups were incorporated in the draft after discussion in the Steering Group. The draft Code offered a radically changed vision of the relationship between the national, regional and local tiers of government in Ukraine.[47]

First, building on the principles set out in the 1997 Law on Local Self-Government, the draft Code attempted a further clarification of the responsibility of each level of government for the financing and delivery of public services. National government was assigned responsibility for defence, state security, foreign policy, assistance to regional development and crucially, in view of the growing problem of 'unfunded mandates', the financing of social benefit payments. Sub-national government at *oblast*, city[48] and district levels were to share responsibility for the financing of education and health care, but with the large part of day-to-day service delivery to the public delegated to regional and local governments with an accompanying transfer from the state budget to meet a proportion of the cost. Regional and local governments were also to be responsible for the payment of social benefits, but these were to be fully compensated by subventions from the state budget. City and district governments were to be wholly responsible for the provision and financing of the so-called housekeeping elements of local community infrastructure – roads, housing maintenance, waste management and transport.[49]

Secondly, transfers from the state budget for the financing and execution of the delegated functions of education and health care were no longer to be channelled through the *oblast* level. Where previously cities and districts were subordinated for budget purposes to the *oblast* administration, each of these 688 units of local government was now to have a separate and direct relationship with the Ministry of Finance in Kyiv. It would no longer be

---

[47] The Budget Code reform of 2000/1 addresses the state budget system overall, including the procedure and timetable for preparation and adoption of the annual budget, rules for accounting and execution of the state budget, regulations for national and sub-national borrowing, and so on. The discussion here is limited to reforms in the area of intergovernmental financial relations.

[48] Cities are here defined as the larger cities and towns of 'oblast significance' in each region, as distinct from the smaller municipalities which are subordinate to district authorities.

[49] Interview with Wayne Thirsk, Kyiv, 27 November 2012.

possible for regional governors to manipulate the budgets of city and district authorities as they might wish. The Steering Committee held back from recommending a further decentralisation to the 12,000 or so smaller municipalities and villages, many of which lacked the financial and administrative resources to maintain an independent relationship with the ministry. This tier of local government was to remain financially subordinate to the district level of administration.[50]

Lastly a mathematical formula, uniform across all units of regional and local government and known in advance to all recipients, was to replace individual bargaining and negotiation as the method of calculating transfers from the state budget. And the basis of the formula, rather than being the cost of maintaining the existing network of institutions and their associated staffing, was to be a per capita of population expenditure norm for education and health care services based on a division of the sum available in the state budget. Adjustments were built into the formula to allow for the additional per capita cost of providing services in certain conditions, for example the higher cost of education in less densely populated rural areas or of health care for populations with a high proportion of older people.[51]

On the income side of the transfer formula, the Steering Committee had adopted two recommendations from Fiscal Analysis Office experts designed to encourage local governments to maximise their own revenues. Income was to be divided into two revenue 'baskets', own and delegated, the former composed of various local taxes and charges and available for the housekeeping services for which authorities were wholly accountable, the latter the product of national taxes levied in the locality. Authorities' own revenues were to be outside the transfer formula calculation and therefore not subject to offsetting against the government grant. In addition, the Fiscal Analysis Office had devised a 'fiscal capacity index' which measured local authorities' relative capacity to generate income for its two revenue baskets. This index was incorporated in the transfer formula, which in theory meant

---

[50] Interview with Anatoliy Maksiuta, Kyiv, 25 May 2013.
[51] Interview with Professor Kenneth Davey, Cheltenham, 27 August 2013.

that greater fiscal capacity would result in a higher payment back into the state budget in order to equalise capacity between revenue-rich and poorer and authorities. However, on the advice of the Fiscal Analysis Office, the index was to be subject to review on a three-yearly basis only, thus avoiding disincentives to local government to increase their income.[52]

Conclusions to Part I

Part I of the case study has described the growing economic and political pressures to reform Ukraine's system of local government finance which had continued to follow a Soviet model for the first decade after independence. By the late 1990s, from the point of view of national government, there was a problem of persistent overspending at sub-national level. For the larger cities, which had grown more powerful with the adoption of a new constitution, the problem was of a continuing lack of autonomy in the control of local budgets. Underlying both was the deeper malaise of the opportunities for political manipulation and patronage which the perpetuation of *Matryoshka* system encouraged.

A 'unique concurrence' of interests, involving domestic and external actors, provided a window of opportunity for addressing these problems in a comprehensive manner. The centrepiece of the proposed reform was to be a formula approach to determining state budget transfers to local governments, based on a methodology used in the European Union and much of post-communist Central and Eastern Europe. The reform promised simultaneously an increase in local autonomy over spending decisions and, paradoxically, tighter control by the Ministry of Finance over the level of sub-national budgets. The circle was to be squared by the exclusion of the powerful *oblast* governors from the budget process and directly threatening their scope for political manipulation. Perhaps not surprisingly it was the *oblast* level which proved to be the principal site of the ensuing struggle to gain acceptance for the reform.

---

[52] Interview with Wayne Thirsk, Kyiv, 27 November 2012.

# Part II: Reform Adoption and Implementation

Introduction

While there was little problem in gaining parliamentary support for the draft Budget Code, given that the *Verkhovna Rada*'s Budget Sub-Committee was one of its leading proponents, the process of ensuring the code finally passed into law was to result in determined resistance from the opponents of decentralisation and the principal losers from the dismantling of the *Matryoshka*. Foremost among these were the President-appointed *oblast* governors who stood to lose their influence over the budgets of big cities and the considerable powers of patronage this bestowed. It could be confidently predicted that governors would be supported in their opposition by the President himself, as indeed turned out to be the case.

This was also a situation in which the professional risks taken by the small group of reformist state officials in the Ministry of Finance might be exposed and the chances of future career progression threatened as a result. The final adoption of the code in early 2001 was due largely to the strength of the coalition formed between the broad alliance of interest on the Ukrainian side and the well-coordinated support of the three international donors.

Despite this apparent success and its declared commitment to longer term institution building, UK DFID adhered to its usual three year project cycle for technical assistance and by the end of the budget reform's first full year of operation the British government had switched its priorities in Ukraine away from fiscal decentralisation to work with two *oblast* administrations on the issue of regional development. USAID followed much the same strategy but with a focus on municipalities. By the end of 2002 neither donor was engaged in any significant activity at national level, and no further interventions were planned in the area of intergovernmental finance.

The net result was that no international expertise was available when the Budget Code ran into problems of implementation. These stemmed largely from the incomplete nature of the original reform and its incompatibility with other unamended areas of legislation which undermined its effectiveness. The system of formula-based transfers which had been designed to bring greater predictability and transparency to the financing of local government degenerated rapidly into what the World Bank described as an opaque and incomprehensible 'black box' (2008: 36), allowing the former practices of manual interference and patronage to reassert themselves as strongly as ever.

### The Passing of the Law on the State Budget for 2001
*Overcoming Fierce Opposition from Powerful Veto-Players*

The new Budget Code was incorporated into a draft Law on the State Budget for 2001, which was sent quickly by the Cabinet of Ministers to the *Verkhovna Rada* in July 2000 where it was given its first formal reading approval with little opposition. Preparations began in the Ministry of Finance for a second reading by Parliament planned for September, which would virtually assure the Code's adoption into law subject only to a formal third reading and the signature of the President.

For reformist forces in the Ministry of Finance this was an anxious time. On a professional level there was concern whether such a complicated process for intergovernmental transfers would succeed, as the Ministry, instead of negotiating with 27 *oblast*-level authorities, would now have to calculate the budgets of almost 700 individual units of local government. The chances of the whole thing going badly wrong seemed high.[53] There was real risk that questions would be raised about the position of individual state officials who had pioneered work on the Budget Code, to the probable detriment of their future careers.

A Ukrainian expert close to the machinations inside government describes the Budget Code reform process within the Ministry of Finance as having been driven by the '3 Ms' - Maksiuta and his deputy Anatoliy Miarkovskyi, together with Minister of Finance, Ihor Mitiukov. However Minister Mitiukov had 'allowed' the work to proceed rather than actively encouraging it, fully aware perhaps that there would be strong opposition from powerful

---
[53] Interview with Anatoliy Maksiuta, Kyiv, 25 May 2013.

directions.⁵⁴ For while the reform seemed clearly to be in the interests of city and district government leaderships, who would now be able to settle their annual budgets without the intervention of the *oblast* administration, it correspondingly ran directly counter to the interests of the politically powerful *oblast* governors whose powers of patronage were seriously threatened. And since *oblast* governors were appointees of the President and important guarantors of his authority in the regions, it was safe to assume that they would be able to rely on his support against the Ministry.

That this was indeed the case became clear at the beginning of September, when a more detailed version of the draft Law on the State Budget for 2001 was published, prior to being sent to the *Rada* for second reading. The draft had been completed over the summer by Maksiuta and Miarkovskyi, with assistance from Ihor Shpak in the Fiscal Analysis Office, and included the two radical proposals of using a formula-based approach to intergovernmental transfers and the by-passing of *oblast* administrations in the setting of budgets for cities and districts. According to the newspaper *Fakty i Kommentarii* a meeting was convened in the offices of the President's Administration, to hear a presentation from the Ministry of Finance on proposals for the 2001 state budget.

The meeting was attended by President Kuchma himself, the Prime Minister and other members of the Cabinet of Ministers, the Speaker and several *Rada* members, as well as by *oblast* governors and the chairs of *oblast* councils. Unsurprisingly, governors were quoted as being 'less than delighted' (*ne v vostorge*) at the Ministry's proposals for a new scheme of intergovernmental financial relations which sought to limit their participation in the process of agreeing local budgets. In their view this was in direct contravention of existing legislation on local self-government since it prevented *oblast* councils from fulfilling their co-ordinating and supervisory responsibilities in the regions.⁵⁵ On the following day, 4 September, described by Wayne Thirsk as 'Black Monday', it was made clear that the President was strongly opposed

---

⁵⁴ Interview with Ihor Shpak, Kyiv, 20 March 2013.

⁵⁵ '*Zachem Poslam USA i Kanady Ponadobilos' Vmeshivat'sia vo Vnutrennie Dela Ukrainy?* Irina Kotsina, *Fakty i Kommentarii*, 29 September 2000.

to the legislation proceeding in its present form, which the meeting had concluded would 'ruin the country', and that the Ministry of Finance had been instructed to prepare a new draft retaining the *Matryoshka* model. It looked very much as if the attempt to reform intergovernmental finance was dead in the water (Martinez-Vazquez & Thirsk 2010: 59).

The precise timing of some of the events that followed is unclear, since they involved an intensive round of behind-the-scenes negotiations between the Administration of the President, the *Rada* and the Cabinet of Ministers (Martinez-Vazquez & Thirsk 2010: 59). However, the outcome was that President Kuchma appeared to back down and reverse his decision to oppose the reform. It is evident that the institutional and personal networks involved in the preparation of the new Budget Code continued to play an important role in ensuring its survival through this decisive period.

According to Pavlo Kachur's account Minister of Finance Ihor Mitiukov concluded that, in the light of mounting opposition, including from the President himself, the draft law could not now be sent to the *Rada* without fundamental revision. His intention was to withdraw it at the scheduled meeting of the Cabinet of Ministers in the week following the President's intervention. Knowing his minister's position, Anatoliy Maksiuta telephoned Pavlo Kachur at 7.30 in the morning of the Cabinet meeting to brief him on Mitiukov's decision. Kachur, who was not only a member of the Steering Committee which had prepared the reform but also an adviser to the Prime Minister on matters including intergovernmental finance, was thus able to forewarn Viktor Yushchenko. In the meeting of the Cabinet later that day Yushchenko - himself a strong supporter of the reform - overruled his minister and instructed Mitiukov to proceed with referring the draft to the *Verkhovna Rada* for its second reading, in apparent defiance of the President's instructions.[56]

At about the same time a controversial letter was sent to President Kuchma bearing the signatures of the American and British Ambassadors to Ukraine

---

[56] Interview with Pavlo Kachur, Kyiv, 20 March 2013.

and the Directors of the World Bank and European Bank for Reconstruction and Development in Kyiv.[57] The letter, actually drafted in the Fiscal Analysis Office, expressed regret on behalf of the international donor community at the President's decision to discontinue on the path to reform despite support for the new Budget Code from the Cabinet of Ministers and the *Verkhovna Rada*. It was donors' belief that the reform marked an important step towards increased accountability and transparency at all levels of government, on the basis of which the international community was already planning future assistance in the form of investment projects.

The letter was roundly condemned as 'international blackmail' (*mezhdunarodnyi shantazh*) and 'tactless interference in Ukraine's internal affairs' (*bestaktnoye vmeshatel'stvo vo vnutrennie dela Ukrainy*) by an article in *Fakty i Kommentarii*. At the same time however, the article's author seemed to leave the door open for a change in Presidential thinking by asserting that the draft Law had yet to be formally received by the President's Administration, let alone reviewed by the President himself, and that accusations of 'anti-reformist' decisions were therefore premature and unwarranted. The author went on to hint strongly that Prime Minister was at fault for stirring up a fuss about nothing, and concluded that 'it's hard to find a black cat in a darkened room, especially if it isn't there' (*'trudno naiti chornuyu koshku v tyomnoi komnate, osobenno, esli ee tam net'*).[58]

There followed an apparently dramatic shift in President Kuchma's position. The Ambassadors' letter had served to raise the political stakes of opposing reform and it is probable that the President was wary of alienating the *Verkhovna Rada*, the Cabinet of Ministers, powerful big city mayors and the international community 'all in one swipe' (Martinez-Vazquez & Thirsk 2010: 59). It is also possible that Kuchma himself was not wholly averse to seeing some weakening in the authority of regional governors who, in Ihor Shpak's

---

[57] Interview informants were not able to recall the exact date of the letter.
[58] *'Zachem Poslam USA i Kanady Ponadobilos' Vmeshivat'sia vo Vnutrennie Dela Ukrainy?'* Irina Kotsina, *Fakty i Kommentarii*, 29 September 2000. The newspaper *Fakty i Kommentarii* was owned by President Kuchma's son-in-law, the oligarch Viktor Pinchuk, and may be assumed to have had some insight into the President's thinking.

words, had come to regard themselves as 'omnipotent landlords of their *oblasts*'.[59] However when faced with a virtual 'mutiny' against the threat the Budget Code posed to the governors' 'limitless powers',[60] the President may have decided that the more expedient course was to offer them his backing rather than oppose them en bloc. When his position changed he was able to soften the blow by ensuring that full implementation would not take place until 2002 and that *oblast* adminstrations would continue to have a role in the execution of the state budget for 2001.

Regardless of President Kuchma's motives, it is clear that the strong alliance of interests on the Ukrainian side, including personal and professional links which dated back to the early 1990s (see chapter II), was a decisive factor in maintaining the momentum of reform. Equally important however was the role of donors in 'bringing the leading actors together in the Steering Group [and helping to develop] a cohesion which overcame divergent approaches to key issues in drafting the Budget Code, and stood firm in the face of the opposition which it inevitably encountered.'[61] The Law on the State Budget for 2001 received its third reading in February 2001 with an overwhelming majority and was signed off by the President in April.

*The Short-Term Impact of Budget Code Reform*

The temporary hiatus resulting from conflicting views as to whether the Budget Code reform should be allowed to proceed in its present form inevitably led to its having to be implemented in stages. As noted above, in the execution of the 2001 budget settlement for local authorities below regional level state transfers were still mediated by *oblast* administrations although, following a decision of the Cabinet of Ministers, the size of these transfers was to be based on a formula calculation set out by the Ministry of Finance. A final de-linking of *oblast*, city and district budgets did not take place until the 2002 financial year.

---

[59] Interview with Ihor Shpak, Kyiv, 20 March 2013.
[60] Interview with Ihor Shpak, Kyiv, 20 March 2013.
[61] Interview with Professor Kenneth Davey, Cheltenham, 27 August 2013.

The major gainers from the disaggregation of sub-national budgets were the mayors of the larger cities, whose representative association had campaigned so effectively for the reform. Not only were they freed from financial dependence on *oblast* administrations, they were also able to retain a larger proportion of their independently raised revenue for use on development priorities of their own choosing (Maksiuta et al. 2004: 39). Viewed overall, there were both winners and losers from the move away from a facility-based calculation of local budgetary requirements, the losers tending to be those cities or districts with a relatively better endowed network of well financed and well maintained institutions (World Bank 2002a: 34). However the Ministry of Finance was able to mitigate these losses, partly through conscious policy and partly by good fortune.

The inclusion of a five-year 'transition fund' in the legislation allowed for variation of the formula calculation to avoid sudden falls in the transfer finance available to individual cities and districts. This, together with a period of robust economic growth of 6% during 2000/1, meant that in terms of per capita spending hardly any sub-national budgets were reduced from their 2000 level (Martinez-Vazquez & Thirsk 2010: 82). And disparities between individual units of local government were significantly reduced by a transfer formula which appeared to provide for more effective equalisation between richer and poorer authorities. Where in 2000 the 'coefficient of variation' between city budgets had been 46%, in 2001 it was reduced to 21%. In the districts the figures also narrowed, from 25% to 18% (World Bank 2002a: 33).

For the Ministry of Finance and the World Bank, both anxious to make progress in introducing the Municipal Development Loan facility, the greatest achievement of the reform was that local budgets ceased to be the major source of fiscal instability which they had become in the late 1990s. The growing crisis of 'unfunded mandates' in social protection seemed to have been resolved as a result of national government's acceptance of financial responsibility for social benefit and other payments, and the indebtedness of local budgets in the social protection sphere had been more or less eliminated.

More widely, the Code had introduced new rules of the game and intergovernmental financial relations had assumed an economic rather than political character (Maksiuta et al. 2004: 31, 33). The increased predictability of local financial resources was said to have successfully revived budget discipline and allowed more space for strategic thinking and the necessary restructuring of education and health provision. The World Bank was particularly impressed by the efforts of the city of Berdyansk, a port in the south-eastern *oblast* of Zaporiz'ka, which had gone to great lengths to rationalise its services to children and older people and was said to have successfully combined a net reduction in the network of establishments with an increase in the quality of the provision (World Bank 2002a: 36).

However it is important to note that while the Budget Code reform appeared to grant all local governments real authority over the use of their financial resources, including those transferred from national government, the differences of interpretation on this central issue were wide enough to suggest that there might be problems later. Martinez-Vazquez and Thirsk in their account of the reform argue that under the Code transfers from the state budget were to be unconditional rather than earmarked for spending on delegated functions only, and that this adhered deliberately to the provisions of the European Charter of Local Self-Government (2010: 105). This view is supported by a report from the World Bank in 2002 which confirms that under the Code 'local councils are free to determine how the equalisation grant received from the state budget will be used' (World Bank 2002a: 34). Kenneth Davey also concurs with this interpretation, saying that 'local governments were free to use their expenditure transfers as they chose and not necessarily on delegated functions. This was one of the questions that officials on the task groups found difficult to grasp, though they did finally go along with it. In this sense [the reform] was a truly decentralising step.'[62]

In contrast Anatoliy Maksiuta writes that in his view 'the transfer of the greater part of budgetary resources to the local budgets requires the development of a system which would guarantee that these resources are

---

[62] Interview with Professor Kenneth Davey, Cheltenham, 27 August 2013.

used in the manner envisaged by the central authority', and that the it was the responsibility of national government to ensure that local authorities had received not only the delegated function but also the funds for its execution (Maksiuta et al. 2004: 38). This significant difference in perception between donor experts and their ministry counterparts, over the extent of local autonomy the Budget Code reform should ultimately allow, seems not to have been much discussed while the Code was in preparation but was to prove crucial at the implementation stage.

## Budget Code Reform and the Challenge of Implementation

### *The Changing Agenda of International Donors*

The period following President's Kuchma's final signing of the Budget Code reform in April 2001 through to its full implementation in the course of the 2002 financial year saw a gradual phasing out of assistance to the Ministry of Finance by both USAID and DFID. By the time the reform had completed its first year of operation in December 2002 neither donor had an active programme of cooperation with the ministry.

The usual three year project cycle for technical assistance projects meant that USAID's contract for the running of the Fiscal Analysis Office came up for renewal at the end of 2000, with the result that the Barents Group consulting company which had managed the project since its inception in early 1998 were replaced as lead contractors by Development Alternatives Incorporated. Ihor Shpak, who had worked as Director of the Fiscal Analysis Office, was in the losing tender for the contract and left the project.

Under its new management the focus of Fiscal Analysis Office activity in 2001 was on monitoring the immediate impact of the reform in the regions and localities and the implementation of a 'training for trainers' programme to prepare a cadre of Ukrainian specialists whose task would be to build the capacity of finance officials in the regions to operate the new system. DFID's LARGIS project also moved much of its attention to the regions and, following fieldwork studies in Donets'ka, Kharkivs'ka, L'vivs'ka and Odes'ka *oblasts*, recommended refinements to the coefficients used in the education and health transfer formulae to take better account of variations in demography and population density between authorities.

Olga Sandakova, who was working as project manager for DFID's Kyiv office in early 2002, recalls that the transfer to other duties of Garth Glentworth, the UK ministry's Governance Adviser, heralded a change in approach from DFID's senior management in London.[63] Increased emphasis was to be placed on project logical frameworks and other results-based management tools to which the rather gradualist approach of public administration reform – an area described by one senior DFID official as a 'morass' – was not well suited. In spite of apparent success in the area of intergovernmental finance, there was scepticism that DFID's interventions were resulting in significant systemic change. An internal DFID memorandum at the time states that the LARGIS project had 'laid solid foundations for continued mainstreaming of good governance agenda….including budgetary reform' but at the same time 'demonstrated that systemic change [was] still to happen in public administration.'[64]

There was a need for 'good stories' of DFID achievements in strengthening governance in Ukraine and it was felt in London that these would be more likely to come from work in the regions rather than from continued cooperation with ministries.[65] In common with USAID, DFID operated a three year project cycle, and when the LARGIS contract came up for renewal or extension a draft proposal from DFID's Kyiv office to extend assistance at national level for a further three years, pointing to the 'proven value of an engagement both at a national policy level and the local implementation/pilot level'[66] was rejected by DFID's senior management in London.

---

[63] Interview with Olga Sandakova, formerly Project Manager for DFID Ukraine, Kyiv, 17 October 2013.

[64] Zayarna, A. European Standards in Ukrainian Public Administration: DFID/World Bank Partnership. 15 December, 2003. [Internal Memorandum]

[65] Interview with Olga Sandakova, Kyiv, 17 October 2013.

[66] From unpublished draft terms of reference for the project 'Towards European Standards of Public Administration in Ukraine' (TESPA), August 2002.

It was agreed instead to shift the focus of public administration support to two major regional programmes in Donbas and L'vivs'ka *oblast*, neither of which was to include a national component.[67] From the start of 2003 onwards DFID's cooperation with the Government of Ukraine was to be largely confined to 'exploratory and diagnosis' work, with a particular focus on capacity for policy analysis and management of the civil service.[68]

It was widely rumoured among foreign experts at the time, though never officially confirmed, that a further contributory factor to DFID's decision to focus its interventions on the regions was a request from USAID to follow its example and cease work with government ministries in the aftermath of the 'Kolchuga' scandal. In September 2002 the news broke that the US Government had obtained secret recordings of President Kuchma authorising the illicit sale of the Kolchuga early warning system, manufactured in Donestk, to Saddam Hussein's Iraq.[69] NATO took action by pointedly excluding Kuchma from its summit in Prague in November 2002, in spite of ongoing discussions about Ukraine's possible future membership, while the US imposed sanctions which involved restrictions on technical assistance to the Government of Ukraine.

Among these restrictions was an instruction to staff of the Fiscal Analysis Office to keep their contact with Kyiv ministries, including the Ministry of Finance, to an absolute minimum[70] and while continued cooperation with the Budget Committee of the *Verkhovna Rada* was permitted, politicians had by this time moved on to other concerns and this was effectively the end of the

---

[67] Economic Regeneration & Social Mitigation of the Donbas Region (Action Donbas), 2002-2008; Lviv Development Project, 2003-2007.

[68] Internal memorandum from Alexandra Zayarna, DFID Governance Adviser, dated 15 December 2003. Before the closure of its programme in Ukraine in February 2008 DFID made two small national-level interventions in the area of public administration reform: LARGIS II, 2005-2006; SuFTAR (Sustainable Financing of Territorial Administrative Reform), 2005-2006.

[69] 'Analysis: From West's Favourite to Pariah', Stephen Mulvey, 26 September 2002. Available at: http://news.bbc.co.uk/1/hi/world/europe/2282229.stm . [Accessed 21 May 2014]

[70] Interview with Wayne Thirsk, Kyiv, 27 November 2012.

USAID contribution to the implementation of the Budget Code reform.

The focus of USAID's interventions overall, like those of DFID, was soon to switch to the regions. The Agency's Country Strategy 2003-2007 identifies the strengthening of government institutions as a strategic priority, but at national level this was directed towards increasing the capacity of parliament and the judiciary to act as effective counterweights to the power of the executive (USAID 2002). Its flagship intervention, launched in 2004, was to be an ambitious Local Economic Development project working in partnership with over 70 municipalities across all *oblasts* in Ukraine (USAID 2009).

*The Failings of an Incomplete Reform*

In its overview of progress in Ukraine's intergovernmental budget relations written in 2008, the World Bank pointed to the continuing lack of transparency and predictability in the preparation of sub-national budgets in spite of the Budget Code reform. Employing language almost identical to that it had used a decade before in its critique of the *Matryoshka*, the Bank described the transfer formula as an opaque and impenetrable 'black box' (2008: 36, 37).

The problem was one of a partial and incomplete reform. The previous supply-driven approach to local budgeting had been replaced with the demand-led transfer formula, but the reform was not supported by corresponding changes in the rights of local governments to make their own decisions on staffing levels and service priorities in the cities and districts for which they were responsible. The World Bank had anticipated this problem as early as 2002 although it seems to have had no influence on USAID and DFID's decisions to move on to other issues (2002: 38).

By seeking to address the problems of a hierarchical, overly-centralised system of responsibility for local budgets without at the same time confronting the broader question of the division of accountability for the delivery of public services between different levels of national, regional and local government, the widely praised Budget Code reform of 2000/1 had in practice led to a deepening of 'institutional uncertainty' ('*instytutsiyna nevyz-*

*nachenist'*) as two incompatible systems of public administration operated alongside one another (Maynzyuk 2008: 3).

The outcome was not simply a question of institutional or bureaucratic muddle, but rather one which was to have far-reaching consequences for the fate of the whole reform. A kind of quasi-delegated authority began to co-exist as an element of 'courageous decentralised decision-making', alongside the basic characteristics of a planned hierarchical system (Maynzyuk & Dzhygyr: 2008/9: 5).

In reality, even after the introduction of the Budget Code, city and district authority decision-making on spending continued to be subject to a rigid vertical structure of input norms dictated by central line ministries. These norms were laid out in detailed guidelines stipulating staffing ratios and other requirements based on a prescribed set of local institutions, in practice determining how the formula-based transfers for the delegated functions of education and health must be allocated. For local governments these two sectors on average accounted for some 85% of current expenditure and since ministry norms were mandatory with potentially harsh penalties for non-compliance, the spending autonomy supposedly granted by the new Budget Code was quickly understood to be purely notional. (Maynzyuk & Dzhygyr 2011: 15; World Bank 2008: iv; Maynzyuk 2008: 5).

The position was made even worse when, in 2006, the Ministry of Finance reversed its policy on the 'index of fiscal capacity' which had assumed no growth in a local authority's income from personal and other taxation over a three year period, and instead began to offset any increased revenue in the annual transfer calculation. Maksiuta, who had been replaced in the Ministry in 2003, describes this decision as a 'tragedy' in its implications for the consequences of the reform.[71]

The resulting impact on perceptions of the Budget Code reform in the regions was predictably negative. Since the new transfer formula was designed simply to divide existing resources on a more transparent and equitable basis

---

[71] Interview with Anatoliy Maksiuta, Kyiv, 25 May 2013. Maksiuta was replaced in the Ministry of Finance in 2003, following the appointment of a new Minister in a re-shuffle of the Cabinet of Ministers.

rather than to increase the funds available in the state budget overall, the continued prevalence of input-based ministry norms and the disincentive to increase local revenues meant that the perennial problem of unfunded mandates imposed on local governments went unresolved, even in the social protection sphere where it had been most burdensome (World Bank 2008: 21). Inevitably, hardest hit were the poorer municipal and district authorities where staffing and other recurrent costs accounted for a high percentage of annual budgets and the ability to retain increases in local income, however small, had been most crucial.

In the words of one broadly sympathetic Ukrainian critique of the Budget Code reform, 'the new hybrid delegated/deconcentrated model [of intergovernmental finance] became a notoriously inadequate instrument for the allocation of notoriously insufficient resources among a notoriously ineffective system of existing institutions'. In the resulting institutional vacuum it was all too easy for the familiar practices of 'steering by hand' (*'ruchnoe upravlenie'*) and 'rent-seeking behaviour' (*'rento-orientirovannoe povedenie'*) to re-emerge in the settling of local budgets between one level of government and another (Maynzyuk & Dzhygyr: 2008/9: 2, 7).

*The Return to Feudalism*[72]

Ukrainian and foreign observers alike have commented on the distortions to the purpose and content of the transfer formula in the years that followed its introduction in 2001. Intended as a transparent and relatively simple instrument understandable to both financial specialists and regional or city leaderships, the formula rapidly degenerated into one of 'astronomical complications' (Maynzyuk & Dzhygyr: 2008/9: 6), encompassing around 70 sub-formulae and literally hundreds of factors and adjustment coefficients for estimating expenditure needs and revenue capacity (World Bank 2008: 36). One of the original Fiscal Analysis Office advisers on the reform later wrote of the 'thick fog' that had come to obscure the transparency and simplicity of the transfer calculations (Martinez-Vazquez & Thirsk 2010: 122).

---

[72] The 'feudalism' of intergovernmental financial relations pre-the Budget Code reform (Maynzyuk & Dzhygyr 2008/9: 4).

Responsibility for this is usually laid at the door of local government leaderships for attempting to extract an advantage for their city, municipality or district by special pleading to the Ministry of Finance for their supposedly exceptional needs which required the addition of a new coefficient, or by such devices as re-naming institutions or even moving clients from one institution to another which attracted more finance (World Bank 2008: vii; Maynzyuk & Dzhygyr: 2008: 8; Maynzyuk & Dzhygyr: 2008/9: 7).

A rather more generous but arguably more plausible interpretation of the actions of local governments in manipulating the formula to protect their existing network of institutions and current staff establishment is as a survival or coping strategy to mitigate the mismatch between their budgetary resources and their delegated responsibilities (Maynzyuk & Dzhygyr: 2008/9: 7; Maynzyuk & Dzhygyr: 2008: 8). Politically there was clearly little to be gained from allowing a local facility to close or teaching and healthcare staff to lose their jobs, but the pressure not to do so came also from the continuing hegemony of ministry norms and the potentially severe consequences of ignoring them.

A senior finance official from Luhans'ka *oblast* asked rhetorically 'who takes the blame if we don't have the money to pay teachers' salaries in the last quarter of the year because we didn't secure a sufficient transfer allocation from Kyiv – I do of course!'[73] It was hardly an exaggeration to claim that local executors of delegated functions 'remain total hostages' (*'polnost'yu ostayutsya zalozhhikami'*) to centralised decision-making, aimed not at meeting a particular quality standard but rather at a rigid model of service delivery which must be uniform across the whole country (Maynzyuk & Dzhygyr: 2008/9: 5).

Thus, in spite of the high ambitions of the alliance of Ukrainian interests who fought so hard for it and the unique collaboration of international organisations which supported them, the reality of the Budget Code reform of 2000/1 began to look not very different from the *Matryoshka* system it was

---

[73] Interview with Yuriy Balkoviy, Director of Finance, Luhans'ka *Oblast* Administration, Luhans'k, 27 June 2013.

intended to replace. In the 'institutional confusion' ('*institutsional'naya smes'*) (Maynzyuk & Dzhygyr 2008/9: 6) which followed the reform there was reversion to the familiar absence of any clear rules of the game as players from national and sub-national governments once again expended their energies in hard bargaining behind closed doors, this time over the inclusion or not of new formula coefficients proposed by city and district leaderships.

This return to 'steering by hand' ('*ruchnoe upravlenie*') was also evidenced in a new 'cult of targeted subventions' ('*kul't teseleviykh subventsiiy*') (Maynzyuk & Dzhygyr 2008/9: 7). These were national government grants outside the Budget Code transfer mechanism, usually in the gift of the Cabinet of Ministers or *Verkhovna Rada* deputies and very hard to identify clearly in the state budget where they appeared as a one line general description.[74]

In Maksiuta's words '…groups in the government and in Parliament are gradually returning to the unsystematic administration of the process, solving concrete issues in the interest of concrete regions…..the critical number of "manual interferences" can lead to global changes in the regulation of inter-governmental fiscal relations' (Maksiuta et al. 2004: 43). From 2005 to 2007 the proportion of financial allocations to sub-national government in the form of targeted subventions increased from 21% to 43%, as 'feudal relationships – the total privatisation and fragmentation of state authority' were once again able to impose themselves on Ukraine's system of financing local government (Maynzyuk & Dzhygyr 2008/9: 7, 3).

The short attention span of international donors was itself a significant contributory factor to this disappointing outcome. In one account of the Budget Code reform a former expert with the Fiscal Analysis Office begins by describing the reform as 'spectacularly successful' and the role of international donors as 'remarkably positive', but adds somewhat ruefully in his conclusion that 'it is not enough for donor agencies and others to rest on their laurels and take comfort from knowing that the reform legislation has passed and is being implemented. Without steady attention to how the reforms are working and to what is required to ward off legislative and ad-

---

[74] Interview with Ihor Shpak, Kyiv, 20 March 2013.

ministrative threats to the reform, the reform benefits may turn out to be smaller than anticipated' (Martinez-Vazquez & Thirsk 2010: preface, 163, 165/166). In interview the same expert was more blunt in saying 'donors missed the boat......misjudged the time they were needed and should have stayed around to monitor the medium term outcomes of the reform.'[75]

There had also been early indications of a difference in perception between donor advisers and their Ukrainian counterparts with regard to the degree of local autonomy the transfer formula implied. As noted above, Ministry of Finance officials had always found the idea of unconditional transfers for the execution of delegated state functions hard to grasp and counter to their understanding of role of ministry norms. For their part international advisers were consistently opposed to supply-led stipulations for institution and staffing levels. Pawel Swianiewicz, expert with the DFID LARGIS project, felt that errors of judgement were made in relation to the broader policy context of the reform: '.....on norms we didn't give this as much attention as we should have.....the inconsistency and contradiction between nationally determined service norms and the decentralisation logic inherent in the transfer formula approach.'[76]

Anatoliy Maksiuta, writing in 2004 after his replacement at the Ministry of Finance and aware that the international donor community had moved on to other agendas, makes his frustration clear in commenting that in spite of the serious problems arising in the implementation of the reform there is a widespread view that donors had already achieved what they wanted from the reforms and 'have not stated new intentions' or 'clarified what else is needed' (Maksiuta et al. 2004: 49). The international donor community was already busy on other matters and was no longer on hand to proffer advice if and when things started to go wrong.

As of 2014 international technical assistance has yet to return to the question of fiscal decentralisation and the reform of intergovernmental financial relations.

---

[75] Interview with Wayne Thirsk, Kyiv, 28 March 2013.
[76] Interview with Pawel Swianiewicz, Warsaw, 12 October 2013.

## Conclusions

This account of a failed attempt to introduce radical reform into Ukraine's system of financing regional and local government is on one level a contest between the opposing forces of centralisation and increased local autonomy, in which the centralisers were the clear victors. Paradoxically however it was at the same time an attempt to impose stricter administrative control from the centre over a wholly unregulated system in which networks of patronage were able to flourish at every level. Ultimately, in spite of the broad political alliance formed in support of the reform, the introduction of formula-based transfers was a narrow technocratic solution to a much wider problem and one which the old networks had little difficulty in circumventing.

Leading pro-reform figures acknowledge today that reform of Ukraine's territorial administrative structure, and above all a clear delineation of authority and accountability between tiers of government, should in principle have preceded or at least accompanied budget reform. But given the powerful opposition to the reform itself and the absence of any political consensus on wider decentralisation, the chief protagonists in the campaign to secure adoption of the Budget Code were forced to accept that the terms on which it was agreed would necessarily be limited (Maynzyuk 2008: 4). In interview both Anatoliy Maksiuta and Pavlo Kachur took the view that 'you have to take reform opportunities as they arise.....if we had waited, we would still be waiting now.'[77]

Despite the major problems with implementation the reform of intergovernmental finance of 2000-2001 has continued to be viewed positively in many quarters, not only for its radical break with past practice but also as a rare political compromise in an environment more accustomed to the zero-sum-game (Maynzyuk & Dzhygyr 2008: 6). Many of those who were closest to the process of securing agreement to the reform are reluctant to criticise the longer-term outcome, variously describing it as a 'spectacular success' (Martinez-Vazquez & Thirsk 2010: preface), and 'easy to find problems with

---

[77] Interviews with Anatoliy Maksiuta, Kyiv, 25 May 2013; Pavlo Kachur, Kyiv, 20 March, 2013.

in hindsight' but 'its basis, the transfer formula, is still intact after twelve years.'[78]

One of the leading figures on the Ukrainian side, who became a regional governor under the presidency of Viktor Yushchenko, insists that 'despite some failings the system today is much preferable to what happened before 2000. If you are a governor or city mayor today you know for sure what your transfers will be and you know that your social benefits will be covered 100%. All the interminable wranglings and bad feelings between the *oblast* administration and municipalities over the annual budget settlement have gone.'[79]

The account has also provided positive evidence of the key role of pro-reform groupings of officials at middle levels of the state apparatus (Wolczuk 2008: 103) and how alliances or 'informal coalitions' (Jacoby 2006: 625) with other domestic actors and external advisers can enable these officials to achieve what Fritz describes as significant 'improvements in formal institutions' and in '*de facto* practices' (2007: 197).

Lastly, it is clear that international donors played an influential role in the reform, both in providing the model on which the transfer formula was based and in helping to bind the alliance of initially divergent interests on the Ukrainian side which led to the defeat of the reform's opponents and the adoption of the Budget Code. However the substantial achievements on the donor side were compromised by an inadequate appreciation of the wider context of intergovernmental financial relations and, more seriously, by the institutional short-termism of programmes of technical assistance which meant that expert advice was no longer available at the time when it might have been most useful. Successful institutional reform of this complexity 'requires sustained technical attention over many years' (SIGMA 2006: para. 4.8), which is exactly what the international donor community was not prepared to offer.

---

[78] Interview with Ihor Shpak, Kyiv, 20 March 2013
[79] Interview with Pavlo Kachur, Kyiv, 20 March 2013.

# CHAPTER IV: CASE STUDY II - REGIONAL POLICY REFORM IN UKRAINE 2000-2012

Introduction

Regional policy has been one of the most complex and troubled areas of government in post-independence Ukraine. As discussed in chapter II in the early 1990s any leading political figure arguing in favour of greater autonomy for the regions risked being accused of being an advocate for separatism, and the case study on fiscal decentralisation has shown how the hostility of political elites in Kyiv towards any serious moves in the direction of decentralisation has continued well into the new millennium. Nevertheless two related factors have combined to force the issue of regional policy closer to the top of the agenda for successive administrations. First, the sharp variation in the capacity of regions to deal with the economic and social impact of the dismantling of the centrally planned economy which has resulted in growth and income differentials which are politically unacceptable and socially divisive. Secondly, Ukraine's continuing aspiration to EU membership and the priority attached by the European Community to regional policy as the principal instrument for reducing social and economic disparities.

International donors have been very active in advising on the reform of Ukraine's regional policy with at least a dozen major projects operating in the area of assistance to regional or municipal development between 2000 and 2012.[1] Over half of these were from the EU or from EU member states acting

---

[1] **EU TACIS/ENPI:** Assistance to Regional Development in Ukraine 2004-2006, Support to Sustainable Local Development 2007-2011, Support to Sustainable Regional Development 2008-2011; **USAID:** Local Economic Development 2004-2009, Local Investment and National Competitiveness 2009-2012; **UK DFID:** Local and Regional Government Institutional Strengthening (LARGIS) 2000-2002, Economic Regeneration & Social Mitigation of the Donbas Region (Action Donbas) 2002-2007, Lviv Development Project 2003-2007; **CIDA:** Regional Governance and Development 2005-2010, Municipal and Local Economic Development 2010-2015; **Swiss Agency for Development & Cooperation:** Support to Decentralisation in Ukraine (DESPRO) 2006-2017; **United Nations Development Programme/European Union:** Community-Based Approach to Local Development 2007-2015.

bilaterally and were aimed at assisting the Government of Ukraine to approximate its approach to regional policy to that of European Union countries. Projects from USAID and CIDA, while not explicitly aimed at EU harmonisation, have had broadly comparable terms of reference.

Despite this substantial input of international expertise, in 2012 Ukraine still had no settled legislation or government programme for the implementation of regional policy, and its approach to regional development was being described by the EU as remaining 'fragmented and ineffective' (EU ENPI SURDP 2011: 2). The case study documents the apparent failure of the donor community to make a greater impact.

As with the attempted reform of intergovernmental relations in the previous chapter, the leading figures on the Ukrainian side are middle-ranking state servants setting out largely on their own initiative to bring elements of the country's public administration closer to accepted practice in the international community, in particular that of the European Union. The themes of increased self-determination for sub-national governments and a reduction in the scope for political patronage are again central to the reformers' purpose. However, in contrast with the introduction of formula-based budget transfers to local government, the pro-reform officials in Ministry of Economy who attempted to 'Europeanise' Ukraine's regional policy found themselves with few domestic allies, and the ill-coordinated and at times misdirected interventions of programmes of international technical assistance could do little to help them.

The case study is organised in two parts, as follows. Part I examines the progress of attempted reform from the Ukrainian perspective, drawing on interviews with some of the leading actors involved. It begins with an analysis of the domestic pressures to reform regional policy and how these were counter-balanced by continuing resistance at national level to the notion of granting more autonomy to sub-national government. After ten years of independence the topic remained as politically contentious and open to manipulation as it had been in the struggles of the mid-1990s.

The narrative then traces the struggle to introduce settled legislation on regional development and the emergence of key pro-reform figures in the Ministry of Economy who argued in particular for the introduction of Contracts for Regional Development, an instrument drawn directly from EU practice and intended to bring greater transparency to state investment in the regions. This is followed by a description of the failure to implement reforming legislation, including the provision for regional contracts, and the increasing marginalisation of the officials from the Ministry of Economy who had argued for their introduction.

Part II presents an analysis of international donor activity in support of regional policy reform through the same period and examines the influence that programmes of external assistance had on the course of reform, including on the reasons for its eventual failure. It begins with the change in donor strategy noted in chapter II, from the relatively straightforward skills and know-how sharing of the early post-independence period, to the more complex task of longer-term institutional development. The objectives of all five donor projects examined in the case study were expressed in the terms of this far more ambitious goal, entailing assistance to the Government of Ukraine in establishing a stable legislative base for regional policy reform and building institutional capacity to support its implementation.

Detailed accounts follow, based on interviews with both donor and Ukrainian informants, of the attempts of British, European Union and Canadian programmes to meet these objectives and of the circumstances of their failure to make the intended impact.

The responsibility for Ukraine's erratic progress towards reform and by extension the disappointing outcomes of the programmes of external advice, has usually been attributed to domestic causes (for example Solonenko 2008: 32). Perceived problems include the lack of a political consensus among key interest groups on the appropriate path of reform, poor levels of competence in the management of regional and local development, and even the low 'absorption capacities' of regions for the knowledge and skills transfer of technical assistance (EU ENPI SURDP 2011: 2, 4).

The case study provides an opportunity to examine the evidence for these assertions in the area of regional policy, but also to document the institutional behaviour of donors and to question whether the interventions of international technical assistance projects have themselves contributed to the continuing impasse in making progress with reform.

# Part I: the Struggle for Settled Legislation

Regional Policy Reform in Ukraine in a National and International Context

Economic pressures in the post-independence period led to increasing demands for more effective state policies to promote balanced regional development. As these emerged early in the new millennium they showed clear signs of being influenced both by changes in international thinking about regional policy and by Ukraine's aspiration to membership of the European Union.

*Domestic Reform Pressures*

As the events of 2013/14 have amply demonstrated, in Ukraine the question of national government's relations with the regions continues to be a matter which provokes deep political division. Reluctant to relinquish control from the centre, successive post-independence governments in Kyiv may have paid lip-service to the principle of devolving authority but, in spite of many proposals for administrative reorganisation and an abundance of advice from Council of Europe experts on how this might be achieved, Ukraine's strong state vertical extending through *oblast* and raion levels has remained firmly in place.[2]

Meanwhile regional elites have been able deliberately to blur the distinction between decentralisation and political regionalisation (Maynzyuk & Dzhygyr 2008: 17) and have freely adapted the vocabulary of regional policy for their own purposes, re-packaging it as regionalism or federalism (Mrinska 2006: 1) and breathing new life into the constitution-building struggles of the 1990s.

Making progress with regional policy reform has therefore been one of the most problematic areas of public administrative reform generally, even if there has been broad agreement that decisive action of some kind is needed

---

[2] Council of Europe expert Gerard Marcou has commented on 12 separate drafts of legislation on reforming local self-government in Ukraine since 2001, none of which has ever reached the stage of being put before Parliament. Interview, Paris, 22 November 2013.

to address the growing disparities in development between Ukraine's regions. The legacy of the two-thirds reduction in the country's productive capacity following independence has continued into the new millennium, with striking contrasts between the relative wealth of a limited number of relatively prosperous cities and the majority of smaller towns and rural districts. In 2004-5 five of Ukraine's twenty-seven regions together accounted for almost 50% of the country's GVA,[3] and Kyiv City and the Dnipropetrovs'ka region were the beneficiaries of a third of total foreign direct investment in the country (GoU SSRD 2006: 7, 16). In 2007 overall investment per capita, foreign and domestic, was 78 times greater in Kyiv city than in the Ternopil's'ka region (Kuiybida et al. 2010: 40). The 2006 State Strategy for Regional Development summarised the position as follows:

> The key problem which has emerged in Ukraine in recent years and which needs a step-by-step solution is the increase in disparity in the socio-economic development of regions. The deepening inequalities…
> ..severely complicate implementation of socio-economic reform, expose the regions to crisis and can lead to disintegration of the national economy.
>
> (GoU SSRD 2006: 21)

*Changing International Paradigms in Regional Policy*

Internationally regional policy has been described as 'one of the most complex areas of government policy-making' capable of meaning 'different things to different disciplines, jurisdictions and countries' (EPRC 2001: 1). Debates in international thinking about regional policy have centred particularly on the question of whether regional policy is primarily a national government responsibility exercised through programmes of state intervention from the centre, or whether a region-led approach leads to more sustainable outcomes.

Post-war policies to address the growing regional disparity in many industrialised countries were traditionally concentrated on a 'top-down, interventionist approach….in the productive sphere', with the declining traditional sectors of coal, steel and shipbuilding identified as the priority sectors (World

---

[3] Gross Value Added is the Ukrainian measure which broadly approximates to GDP.

Bank 2002b: 2). State subsidies, tax incentives and grants were deployed in an attempt to shelter local economies from the impact of international competition and to promote to growth of new industry by investment in hard physical infrastructure or encouraging the relocation of enterprises in more promising sectors to areas of high unemployment (Hildreth 2009: 322; OECD 2014: 110).

Growing scepticism regarding the effectiveness of these top-down interventions, together with wider political pressure for increased devolution of state authority, led to the emergence of a 'new paradigm' of regional policy in the early 1990s (Hildreth 2009: 324). This changed thinking on regional policy emphasised opportunity rather than disadvantage, applying to all regions and not just those which were seen to be lagging behind (OECD 2014: 110-111), and was no longer solely concerned with the equalisation of outcomes. More fundamentally, regions ceased being the passive objects of policy or recipients of state aid and were seen instead as able to act as 'subjects that influence, make and implement policy' themselves (Hudson 2007: 1151).

National governments were exhorted to take on a proactive role, first in providing a regulatory and policy framework within which the 'endogenous assets' of regions, particularly the soft infrastructures of institutional capacity and human capital, could be utilised to the maximum advantage (World Bank 2002b: 19; OECD 2014: 111). Secondly government regional policy became a 'synergy policy' focused on integrating the sectoral and territorial impact of national and sub-national government interventions, and achieving a much stronger effect than the sum of individual sectoral policies (Mrinska et al. 2013: 3).

*New Thinking in Ukraine's Regional Policy*

A reflection of this change in international thinking can be found in the evolution of Ukraine's approach to regional policy, although as the case study will show this has remained very much what Jacoby (2006: 629) terms a 'minority tradition'. The approach has remained largely top-down and sector-based, a legacy of the Soviet policy of centrally determined annual programmes managed by line ministries. Even today these can be very numerous, with well over 100 individual programmes operating in parallel to each other in a given region or city and frequently contradictory in their impact on the ground.

Nevertheless, the beginnings of a fundamental change in thinking have been evident since 2001 with the drafting of Ukraine's first Concept of State Regional Policy. The Concept document was much influenced by the Council of Europe's Charter of Local Self-Government, to which Ukraine had become a signatory in 1997, and by the principles of EU regional policy, including decentralisation and subsidiarity. Ukraine's political leadership already had aspirations to eventual EU membership following affirmation of the country's 'European Choice' through the Partnership and Cooperation Agreement (PCA) with the EU.[4] The Government of Ukraine was also aware that regional policy was potentially one of the most fruitful areas of financial assistance from the European Community, providing the country's political structures and administrative practices could be harmonised with those of the EU.

It was in the Concept of State Regional Policy that the argument was first made for a better integrated and less centralised approach to government intervention in the regions, and it was in the preparation of the Concept document that a key pro-reform actor within the state apparatus was to make his first appearance. This official, Serhiy Romaniuk from the Ministry of Economy, was later to play an important role in partnerships with programmes of international technical assistance in support of regional policy reform.

## The Emergence of a Pro-Reform Enclave in the Ministry of Economy

The following account documents the emergence of a small bureaucratic enclave of state officials acting on their own initiative to bring about change in the Government of Ukraine's approach to addressing the problem of regional disparities and stimulating more balanced social and economic development. There are close parallels here with the Budget Code reform discussed in chapter III.

---

[4] The Partnership and Cooperation Agreement came into force in 1998.

First, the existing mechanisms for providing state budget support to regional development were not only very highly centralised but also opaque and subject to manipulation or *'ruchnoe upravlenie'* ('steering by hand'). As a consequence there was little year-to-year stability in the level of state investment a region could expect to receive. Secondly, it could be confidently predicted that there would be powerful interests opposed to any reform which might threaten to make this process more objective and transparent. What distinguishes the experience of the officials in the Ministry of Economy from those in the Ministry of Finance who argued for the reform of intergovernmental finance is, as the following account shows, the degree to which the reform initiative remained confined to this small group of Ministry of Economy officials who were able to make only limited headway in attracting support from other domestic actors. The case study findings presented below are based on interviews with the leading actors in the Ministry of Economy and with independent Ukrainian experts on regional policy. They also draw on the evidence of official documents from Ukrainian and donor sources.

*The Concept of State Regional Policy 2001*

The first evidence of a new approach to regional policy appeared with the publication of a State Concept document. Following the enactment of the PCA between Ukraine and the EU in March 1998 and a Presidential decree entitled 'Strategy on Ukraine's Integration with the European Union'[5] in June of the same year, Leonid Kuchma established a working group to prepare a State Concept of Regional Policy, which he instructed should be in harmony with European approaches to regional development and thus reflect Ukraine's long-term ambition of joining the EU.

Membership of the working group was drawn not only from state service but also from Ukrainian academics and independent experts – the donor community was not invited to participate – and its work was one of the first examples, together with Anatoliy Maksiuta's approach to the Budget Code

---

[5] Strategy on Ukraine's Integration with the European Union. Decree of the President of Ukraine, 615/98, 11 June 1998.

reform, of 'public policy-making in a European style'.[6] It was also described as 'the first Ukrainian government document to show an understanding of regional policy as seen by the European Union.'[7]

Even so the international community gave a cool reception to the final Concept document when it was adopted by Presidential decree in May 2001.[8] It was dismissed by the World Bank as 'a long list of actions that might have some effect rather than coordinated strategy that clearly sets prioritisation and sequencing' and as 'a vertical approach to regional development in which regions are acted upon, as opposed to being critical agents in their own development' (2002b: 24). Members of the working group themselves had misgivings about the Concept, regarding it as largely in the Soviet tradition of designating dozens of priorities covering all possible sectors,[9] and as the outcome of compromises and trade-offs between competing interpretations of the purpose of regional policy (Romaniuk 2002: 181).

Any serious prospect of implementation of the Concept was considerably weakened by the perceived shortcomings of the finished document, and its adoption by Presidential decree rather than through legislation passed by the *Verkhovna Rada* was a further indication of the limited political support for the Concept's recommendations.[10] Nevertheless the criticisms of international and Ukrainian experts alike tend to overlook the boldly innovatory nature of parts of the document.

The Concept shows evidence of changing thinking about the relationship between national and sub-national governments in Ukraine and suggests the influence of the new paradigm of a more decentralised approach to regional policy. For example, section I strongly endorses the principle of susidiarity

---

[6] Interview with Serhiy Maksymenko, independent expert on regional policy and member of the working group, Kyiv, 22 March 2013.

[7] Interview with Serhiy Romaniuk, Kyiv, 23 March 2013. In 1999 Serhiy Romaniuk was Deputy Minister of Economy and a member of the working group.

[8] Decree of the President of Ukraine, 341/2001, 25 May 2001.

[9] Interview with Serhiy Maksymenko, Kyiv, 22 March 2013.

[10] Interview with Serhiy Romaniuk, Kyiv, 23 March 2013.

and the focusing of state resources on the resolution of problems of a national character only (Concept of State Regional Policy 2001: 2), while section III identifies a key task of state regional policy as support to independent decision-making by local self-government on priorities for regional and local development (Concept of State Regional Policy 2001: 7-8). In a notably radical step, section IV of the Concept proposes that future state capital investment grants to the regions should be determined on a competitive, transparent basis (Concept of State Regional Policy 2001: 10).

An influential figure in shaping the conclusions of the working group was Serhiy Romaniuk, recruited to the Ministry of Economy as a deputy minister in January 1999 from Vinnyts'ka region where he had been a deputy governor. In March 2000, following a reorganisation in the Ministry and a reduction in the number of deputy ministers, Romaniuk was appointed to the new post of Director of the Department of Regional Policy. Later the same year a Presidential decree accorded lead responsibility in government for regional policy to the Ministry of Economy and Romaniuk became Ukraine's most senior state servant advising on relations between national and sub-national levels of government.[11]

At this time Serhiy Romaniuk's ideas on reforming Ukraine's approach to regional policy and regional development were in the process of being crystallised through his participation in the Fellowship Programme of the Local Government and Public Service Initiative (LGI) in Budapest,[12] in which he was mentored by Gerard Marcou, a professor at the University of Sorbonne and an expert on local and regional government for the Council of Europe. This was a seminal period for Romaniuk and he regards Marcou's influence on his thinking as highly significant for his future development, a '*tolchok*' (a 'push' or 'shove') for much of the work on regional policy reform he was to do in the decade that followed.[13]

---

[11] Decree of the President of Ukraine, 1159/2000, 23 October 2000.

[12] The Local Government and Public Service Initiative was a project of the Soros-funded Open Society Institute.

[13] Interviews with Serhiy Romaniuk, Kyiv, 23 March 2013 and 26 July 2014.

In a published monograph he prepared for the Budapest programme under Marcou's guidance, Romaniuk argues that 'direct budget support for all regions is impossible, and sources of growth need to be found at the local level…..consequently regional and local communities should be transformed from objects of development into subjects of development.' Also that 'mobilization of social capital in the region….as a partnership of local government and non-governmental organizations' is the surest way to overcome the current obstacles to regional development posed by a 'closed, immoveable elite, which manages considerable political, institutional and financial resources' in the region. For the first time Romaniuk also proposes a 'contract system of relations' between central government and elected regional councils as a partnership of equals to promote regional development (2002: 189, 195).

Serhiy Romaniuk was about to emerge as the key figure, frequently almost a lone voice, in subsequent attempts to reform Ukraine's regional policy, and the lead government partner to all five major international donor programmes on regional policy to work in Ukraine between 2000 and 2012.

*The 2005 State Law and the 2006 State Strategy*

The principal pieces of state legislation and government policy on regional development to appear in the case study period were the 2005 State Law 'On the Stimulation of Regional Development'[14] and the 2006 'State Strategy for Regional Development to 2015'.[15] They were prepared as a follow-up to the 2001 Concept document and continue to adhere closely to a European Union oriented understanding of regional policy. The relatively short framework law of 2005 summarises in under ten pages the foundations of a reformed approach to relations between Kyiv and the regions, and is followed by the far more detailed State Strategy document which 'for the first time systematically, and taking into account the experience of the European Union',

---

[14] *Zakon Ukrainy 'Pro Stimuliuvannia Rozvitku Rehioniv'*, no. 2850-VI, passed 8 September 2005. Available at: http://me.kmu.gov.ua/ [Accessed 22 August 2014]

[15] *'Derzhavna Stratehia Rehional'novo Rozvitku na Period do 2015 Roku'*, resolution no. 1001 of the Cabinet of Ministers of Ukraine, 21 July 2006.

elaborates the principles, goals and strategic tasks of Ukraine's regional policy (Romaniuk 2013: 218).

Thus the State Law (art. 1) equates Ukraine's existing administrative regions or *oblasts* broadly with the EU's NUTS 2 categorisation for member states,[16] while the fundamentals of regional development as the balancing of national, regional and local interests, the establishment of partnership relations between national and sub-national authorities, the devolution of responsibility for service provision to the level closest to the service user (reflecting the EU principle of subsidiarity), and a targeted and competitive approach to the allocation of state investment funds to the regions (art. 2).

The Law also introduces into Ukrainian legislation as 'a new instrument of state policy' (Romaniuk 2013: 217) the concept of a contract or agreement (*ugoda*) between national and sub-national levels of government, based on mutually agreed priorities for regional development (arts. 4 & 5), making it the first occasion on which Ukrainian legislation identifies the organs of self-government at regional and local level as equal partners with state authorities in the development their territory. It also marks the introduction of the discipline of strategic, goal-oriented planning at all levels following accepted good practice in EU states (Romaniuk 2013: 217).

Much of the remainder of the Law (arts. 6-11) is taken up with measures to address the issue of depressed territories and to provide a procedure for securing budget support to poorer regions which would reduce the influence of political lobbying and the ad hoc decision-making which often followed it. According to Serhiy Romaniuk, who was largely responsible for drafting and leading consultations on the Law, the plight of depressed areas was to receive greater prominence in the final draft approved by the *Verkhovna Rada* than it had in earlier versions which, in the spirit of the new paradigm of regional policy in European Union states, had sought to shift the emphasis towards opportunity rather than disparity. This is evident from successive drafts of

---

[16] Nomenclature of Territorial Unit of Statistics. The NUTS 2 category applies to territories with populations of 800,000 to 3 million.

the Law. In original drafts the preamble refers only to the 'stimulation of development of the regions' while in the final version the phrase 'overcoming (*podolannia*) the depression of territories' was added following representations by parliamentary deputies and a number of regional governors.[17]

The State Strategy of 2006 also appears to make concessions to the traditional view of regional policy as being principally concerned with compensating for disparities in wealth, in declaring in its opening paragraphs that 'inequality in regional development and a significant differentiation of living standards across Ukraine create the preconditions for social tension, present a threat for the territorial integrity of the country, hinder the dynamics of social and economic growth, and slow down and reduce the effectiveness of market reforms' (GoU SSRD 2006: 2). In evidence the Strategy points to the problems arising from the concentration of half the country's wealth on five regions,[18] and contrasts this with the situation in around 1200 villages across the country where residents are still living without a regular water supply of acceptable drinking quality (GoU SSRD 2006: 7,10).

In its heavy emphasis on the question of inter-regional disparity the Strategy is to some extent dissonant with the arguably more balanced approach of the 2001 Concept, but Romaniuk explains that this was the result of the continuing and unequal impact of market transformation across the regions which had in turn created political pressure for stronger national government policies of equalisation (2013: 221).

In other respects however the Strategy marks a significant break with the past. Even while acknowledging the need to address disproportionality in the development of regions, the Strategy asserts that the solution to this lies in the increased competitiveness of regions leading to higher living standards overall and not, by implication, in a policy limited to providing state subsidies to regions in decline (GoU SSRD 2006: 2). This point is reinforced later in a reference to the 'creation of growth pole regions' (*'formuvannia opornykh*

---

[17] Interview with Serhiy Romaniuk, Kyiv, 26 July 2014.
[18] Donets'ka, Dnipropetrovs'ka, Zaporiz'ka and Poltavs'ka *oblasts*, and Kyiv City.

*rehioniv'*) as a guiding principle of the Strategy alongside balanced development, subsidiarity and partnership. These are faster growing regions able to act as Ukraine's locomotives of innovation and development.

The largest cities of Donets'k, Dnipropetrovs'k, Kyiv, L'viv, Odesa, and Kharkiv are singled out as focal points of economic and scientific innovation in a position to stimulate growth in their surrounding regions and beyond (GoU SSRD 2006: 24, 29-30). And while the two are not explicitly linked in the Strategy document, there is a strong indication that these growth pole regions will be the first to benefit from the introduction of the proposed contracts with national government which are to be introduced 'gradually… depending on the state of readiness of central and local authorities' (GoU SSRD 2006: 42).

Central to the future success or failure of the proposed agreements would be the availability of budget finance, and crucial in this regard is the Strategy's assertion that regional development will have its own budget heading within the annual state budget, distinct from equalisation and subvention payments and in addition to the multitude of existing sectoral ministry programmes (GoU SSRD 2006: 43). Ominously, while article 12 of the 2005 State Law states that the budget for stimulating regional development and supporting depressed territories should be no less than 0.2% of the annual State budget, this clause was amended by the *Verkhovna Rada* in late 2005 and in the State Strategy the 0.2% figure is ring-fenced to financial assistance to depressed territories (GoU SSRD 2006: 44). This was an early sign of the coming resistance to the fundamental reform of relations between national and sub-national government which was implicit in the principal of regional contracts.

*Contracts for Regional Development*

The proposed contract for regional development or *ugoda* was the most radical innovation of the 2005 State Law (arts. 4 & 5). Comparable in its boldness to the replacement of the *Matryoshka* system of intergovernmental finance by formula-based transfers (chapter III), it was a direct challenge to the existing top-down approach to the economic development of regions. The principal purpose of the contract was to strengthen the role of cities and regions in determining their own growth trajectory and to indicate a step-change 'from a paternalistic to a partnership relationship' between national and sub-national tiers of government.[19]

The idea of a regional contract had its origins in the decentralisation of public administration in France during the 1980s, as a result of which self-government at regional and local levels was granted a much greater degree of independence from the previously highly centralised French state. The first *Contrats de Plan Etat-Regions* were agreed for the period 1984-1988 and have been renewed every 4-6 years since, the most recent being for 2007-13. The key document is a State-Region Plan Convention which sets out a series of policies and programmes which will be financed jointly by national, regional and local tiers of government, with the details of the purpose of each measure and the financial commitment of each party to the agreement.[20] In the view of the World Bank the introduction of contract plans in France resulted in a shift away from the top-down imposition of plans from the centre towards a much more participatory approach based on the endogenous potential of each region (World Bank 2002b: 32).

The principal architect of the regional contract proposal was Serhiy Romaniuk from the Ministry of Economy. As already noted, Romaniuk had become acquainted with the French experience of regional contracts as a result of his work with Professor Gerard Marcou in the Fellowship Programme in Budapest in 2000-2001, and had been persuaded of their potential value for post-communist Ukraine. Marcou argues that one of the key functions of contractual agreements is to 'legitimise' national government authority in a context where command relations are no longer acceptable, and that 'contractual arrangements offer an opportunity to governments to submit their policies to the agreement of other authorities which will eventually be asked to comply with them, and to re-legitimate their authority through the process of negotiation.'[21] Ukrainian sources have commented similarly on the

---

[19] Interview with Serhiy Romaniuk, Kyiv, 26 July 2014.

[20] Background on French Regional Contracts provided in interview with Council of Europe expert Professor Gerard Marcou, University of the Sorbonne, Paris, 22 November 2013.

[21] Interview with Professor Gerard Marcou, Paris, 22 November 2013.

wider significance of establishing contractual rather than hierarchical relations between levels of authority, based on principles of negotiation and transparency, and on the integrating and stabilising function this has which may even transcend the benefits derived from the contract itself (Maynzyuk 2008: 2; Maynzyuk & Dzhygyr 2008: 11).

Despite all the difficulties which were to follow, the introduction of the regional contract in the 2005 State Law is an achievement which Romaniuk describes as 'my work, and something I'm still proud of.'[22] In this he cooperated closely with Olena Nyzhnyk, who had replaced him as Director of the Department of Regional Policy in the Ministry of Economy in December 2001 after Romaniuk was promoted back to the position of deputy minister. While Romaniuk took the leading role in securing the adoption of both the 2005 State Law and the 2006 Strategy, it is clear that he and Nyzhnyk held similar views on the need to reform Ukraine's regional policy and to harmonise it as much as possible with practice in EU member states. This was to prove quite a challenge and Olena Nyzhnyk herself acknowledges that she and Romaniuk were 'more or less isolated' in their shared goal, even within their own Ministry, and that there was a 'lack of support and a poor understanding of what regional policy meant among other members of the Cabinet of Ministers.'[23]

*Implementing the Regional Contract*

Implementation of the bold new policy got off to a reasonable enough start. The first regional contract was signed with Donets'ka *oblast* on 15 September 2007 for the period 2007-2011, and subsequent agreements were made with the regions of L'vivs'ka (2009-2013), Khersons'ka (2010-2013), Volyns'ka (2010-2014), Vinnyts'ka (2010-2015) and Ivano Frankivs'ka (2011-2015). Contracts were signed by the Prime Minister on behalf of the Government of Ukraine and by the chair of the relevant *oblast rada* as the representative of self-government at regional level. This deliberately gave regional contracts a different and more elevated status from that of sectoral ministry programmes

---

[22] Interview with Serhiy Romaniuk, Kyiv, 26 July 2014.
[23] Interview with Olena Nyzhyk, Kyiv, 29 March 2013.

to the regions, in that the *ugoda* were to be prepared, agreed and implemented by the most senior executive organ at the heart of government, the Cabinet of Ministers (Romaniuk 2013: 244).

The choice of Donets'ka and L'vivs'ka as the first regions was in part political - the two *oblasts* were at opposite poles of the country both geographically and historically and Viktor Yanukovych, who had become Prime Minister in August 2006, was a former governor of Donets'ka *oblast* – and in part because of their contrasting economic profiles and the 'difference in mentality' of their populations.[24]

The consultation process prior to the signing of any contract was very extensive, with Serhiy Romaniuk often leading a delegation of up to 17 Kyiv ministries to the region to negotiate the package of projects to be included in the agreement.[25] The final content of the contract was to comprise a series of joint actions by national and regional or local governments, reflecting on one side priorities of national importance as identified in the 2006 State Strategy for Regional Development, and on the other a set of priority objectives resulting from the region's own medium-term development strategy for the forthcoming 3-5 years.

All proposals for joint financing were to be supported by an economic or social impact analysis, and by measurable indicators against which the success of the action could be judged. Indicators were expected to demonstrate the extent to which successful completion of a programme of work would improve access to public services.[26] Agreement to the financing of any proposal from the state budget was conditional on a signed undertaking to provide co-finance by the regional or local government concerned (Romaniuk 2013: 245-6).

According to documents prepared in the Ministry of Economy, both the

---

[24] Interview with Serhiy Romaniuk, Kyiv, 26 July 2014.

[25] Interview with Serhiy Romaniuk, Kyiv, 26 July 2014.

[26] Serhiy Romaniuk also looked for evidence that implementation of the proposal would involve local enterprise and business as partners. Interview, Kyiv, 26 July 2014.

Donets'ka and L'vivs'ka contracts had four broadly similar 'priority directions'. The Donets'ka document identifies as its priorities the 'development and reconstruction of the region's coal industry,' 'a reliable and effective system of utilities and communal services for population centres,' 'the creation of an effective system of environmental protection,' and 'the development of the region's infrastructure.' The second and third priorities in the L'vivs'ka contract are identical to those of Donets'ka, while the first is 'the reconstruction and development of the region's industrial base' and the fourth 'the preservation of the region's historical and cultural heritage.' The Donets'ka contract has 13 joint operational programmes stemming from its four priority directions and 51 discrete tasks to be completed in the four year timeframe, while the corresponding figures for the L'vivs'ka contract are 14 and 82.

The statistics for the execution of these first two contracts make sorry reading. Of the 51 discrete tasks identified in the Donets'ka contract, only 23% were assessed as completed at the end of the four year term. In L'vivs'ka the figure was only a little better at 25%. A shortfall in finance from all sources appears to have been the main cause, with only 49.4% of the agreed overall budget realised in Donets'ka and 60.6% in L'vivs'ka. In Donets'ka it was said that overwhelming priority in construction work in the region was necessarily diverted to preparation for the 2012 European Football Championship, with an inevitable knock-on effect to other capital projects.

A Ministry of Economy review document, while pointing to a limited number of successes such as the provision of round-the-clock water supply to the city of L'viv and the construction of solid waste recycling sites in two cities in the Donets'ka region, acknowledges that there had been a serious failure on all sides to come forward with the promised financing. The problem had been compounded by a lack of effective monitoring and control from the centre, and major organisational weaknesses in the regions leading to delays in the tendering process. Overall, there had been little or no connection between strategic planning at national and regional levels and the operation of the regional contract mechanism.[27]

*Reform Champions or Voices in the Wilderness?*

The transparency and predictability offered by the contracts for regional development represented a genuine break with past practice, and for Romaniuk and Nyzhnyk as champions of the reform, the mutually binding agreements had been the flagship policy of both the 2005 State Law and the 2006 State Strategy. But they had clearly not been able to persuade their ministry and other colleagues to their point of view. Olena Nyzhnyk comments that during the process of preparing and consulting on the idea of a regional contract Cabinet of Ministers colleagues 'did not interfere, even if they were not actively helpful', but once the idea was enshrined in legislation it became obvious that most Cabinet members, including the Minister of Economy himself, had little real understanding of the policy. Nyzhnyk admits that at times she was 'on the point of giving up and was so tired of explaining, arguing, justifying.'[28]

However, the decisive factor in sealing the fate of the regional contract was the implacable opposition of the Ministry of Finance. The ministry successfully argued against having a separate line in the state budget for the financing of contracts, and against the whole principle of multi-year agreements between the Cabinet of Ministers and *oblast* councils. Instead the priorities identified in regional contracts should be financed from the existing top-down annual programmes of line ministries and, as with these, the endorsement of the Ministry of Finance and the Cabinet of Ministers as a whole would need to be sought every year. The distinctiveness of the regional

---

[27] Information on contract performance from documents provided by the Ministry of Economy, approved by the Cabinet of Ministers of Ukraine 16 November 2011, resolution no. 1187: (i) *ANALITYCHNA ZAPYSKA - shchodo rezul'tativ provedennia otsinky efektyvnosti zdiisnennia spil'nych zakhodiv, peredbachenikh ugodoiu shchodo rehional'novo rozvytku Donets'koi oblasti mizh Kabinetom Ministriv Ukrainy ta Donets'koiu Oblasnoiu Radoiu;* (ii) *ANALITYCHNA ZAPYSKA - shchodo rezul'tativ provedennia otsinky efektyvnosti zdiisnennia spil'nych zakhodiv, peredbachenikh ugodoiu shchodo sotsial'no-ekonomichnovo rozvytku L'vivs'koi oblasti mizh Kabinetom Ministriv Ukrainy ta L'vivs'koiu Oblasnoiu Radoiu.*

[28] Interviews with Olena Nyzhnyk, Kyiv, 29 March 2013 and 24 July 2014.

contract was immediately compromised and its founding principles of medium-term planning and partnership in the shared financing of regional investment projects effectively sabotaged.

As a result Serhiy Romaniuk, in leading delegations of ministry representatives to regions which might be candidates for contracts, was obliged to insist that the only projects eligible for conclusion in the agreement were those for which there was financing in line ministry budgets for the current year. The contract immediately lost any added value it might have over existing programmes, a position which in the opinion of one Ukrainian official was to have disastrous consequences for the way it was understood in the regions, and its relevance to any form of long-term planning. According to Olena Nyzhnyk, after the first two agreements in Donets'ka and L'vivs'ka, the regional contract rapidly became a 'political rather than an economic instrument.' Prime Minister Yulia Tymoshenko, when visiting a region to sign a memorandum of intention regarding a future contract, would often decide en route that the paperwork must be completed by ministry officials that day in order that she could sign the final agreement before leaving the region in the evening.[29] Any initial enthusiasm for the regional contract soon waned and, following an order from Prime Minister Azarov, no further agreements were signed after 2010.

Clearly short of allies in powerful positions, Romaniuk argues that he and Nyzhnyk at least had strong support among regional leaderships who saw the contract as a means of achieving predictability in the funding of capital projects, which until now had been subject to the vagaries of the annual budgeting process.[30] However once this principle had been dropped by the Cabinet of Ministers it is hard to see what advantages theses agreements offered an *oblast* governor over the existing way of doing things. It might even be worse if it resulted in less flexibility and less room for informal deals and negotiation.

---

[29] Interview with Olena Nyzhnyk, Kyiv, 24 July 2014.
[30] Interview with Serhiy Romaniuk, Kyiv, 23 March 2013.

More broadly the strength of support of regional leaderships for the contract, at least as originally conceived, must be open to doubt given the hybrid nature of Ukraine's system of regional government. Because an *oblast* administration is a form of deconcentrated state authority rather than decentralised self-government, regional contracts had to be agreed between the Cabinet of Ministers and the *oblast* council as the self-governing body representing the interests of urban and rural communities across the region. But under the hybrid system the key figure at *oblast* level is unquestionably the regional governor, appointed by the President, rather than the chair of the council, and in practice it was officials of the regional state administration who negotiated the terms of the contract with their colleagues in line ministries, to whom they were ultimately accountable. This was very far removed from Serhiy Romaniuk's original aspiration to a relationship based on partnership rather than paternalism.

Conclusions to Part I

The above account has followed the evolution of Ukraine's regional policy in the first decade of the new millennium, beginning with the Concept of State Regional Policy of 2001 and followed by the 2005 State Law on the Stimulation of Regional Development and the 2006 State Strategy for Regional Development to 2015. All three documents were much influenced by current international approaches to regional policy, in particular those of the European Union, and they should be understood in the context of Ukraine's 'European Choice' of the late 1990s and its long-term aspiration to membership of the EU.

They should also be seen more broadly as an attempt to depoliticise, even detoxify, the issue of regional policy, making it a matter for technocratic decision-making rather than conflict and political patronage. In this respect the most significant policy innovation to emerge in the period was the contract for regional development or *ugoda*, which aimed to remove state investment in the regions from the process of annual bargaining over the state budget and to introduce a greater measure of transparency and predictability in the allocation of capital grants for infrastructure development.

The driving force behind the drafting of the State Law, the State Strategy and the proposal for regional development contracts were two ambitious and well-placed state officials working in the Ministry of Economy. By their own admission, these officials were able to work with minimal bureaucratic interference or political oversight. Ironically the space provided by this relative autonomy was to be their eventual undoing, as they found themselves without sufficiently powerful allies to ensure the execution of policies which threatened entrenched practices and powerful interests. The proposed contracts for regional development, although enshrined in the 2005 legislation, foundered on the 'pervasive problem' of Ukraine's public administrative reform, its 'implementation weakness' (OECD 2014: 115).

Part II of the case study examines the role of the international donor community in assisting or otherwise the progress of this failed attempt at reform.

## Part II: International Advice and Regional Policy Reform

Introduction

At the end of the 1990s there was a fundamental change in approach by all international donors providing support to public administrative reform in Ukraine. Part II documents that change, which led to a new objective of long-term institution building in place of the skills and know-how sharing approach of the immediate post-independence period. In the area of regional policy, the focus of institution building was to be on assisting the Government of Ukraine to establish a stable framework of legislation and on strengthening its capacity to translate legislation into operational policy. The case study examines the contribution of technical assistance programmes in each of these areas and explores the nature and extent of the influence that international donors were able to bring to bear on the course of reform.

With regard to legislative reform the case study documents in particular the work of the most ambitious of the EU's interventions on regional policy, the Support to Sustainable Regional Development project, where the evidence suggests that the contribution of external advice had a disruptive impact on efforts to achieve political consensus in support of a framework of law governing regional policy. On the question of strengthening policy-making capacity Part II analyses the actions of donors in recommending policy models imported from good practice in public administration in Western Europe and North America and the extent to which Ukrainian recipients have found these applicable in their own contexts. The case study examines one policy model in particular, the preparation of medium-term strategies for municipal and regional development.

It will be argued that, largely due to factors on the donor side, agreement to adopt recommended imported practice has often been purely formal. In particular the short-term nature of technical assistance programmes has limited donor capacity to understand the institutional context in which their interventions take place and has compromised their ability to promote institutional change.

Institution Building: a New Priority for International Assistance to Ukraine

Between 2000 and 2012 there were five major technical assistance projects in support of the reform of Ukraine's regional policy, financed by three international donors. These were:

- UK Department for International Development (DFID) 'LARGIS',[31] 2000-2002
- EU 'Assistance to Regional Development', 2004-2006
- EU 'Support to Sustainable Local Development', 2007-2011
- EU 'Support to Sustainable Regional Development', 2008-2011
- Canadian Agency for International Development (CIDA) 'Regional Governance and Development', 2005-12

A sixth programme, the EU's 'Support to Ukraine's Regional Development Policy', began work in early 2013.

Lead partners to all but one of these projects were Serhiy Romaniuk and Olena Nyzhnyk in the Ministry of Economy. The exception was the EU's Support to Sustainable Regional Development project, which was partnered by the Ministry of Regional Development and Construction. However, here too Romaniuk and Nyzhnyk were to become lead partners to the project when they changed ministries in 2010.

Common to all five projects was a new focus on strengthening the capacity of Ukraine's institutions to formulate and deliver a coherent policy of regional development.[32] This reflected a wide concern in the donor community that the largely reactive training and know-how sharing content of much technical assistance to Ukraine in the 1990s had produced little obvious effect on the working of state institutions in general and the reform of public administra-

---

[31] Local and Regional Government Institutional Strengthening.

[32] The objective of the EU's Sustainable Local Development programme was to support municipal rather than regional development by assisting with the renovation of essential but run-down infrastructure services such as water supply and waste management. Since the intention was that the results would serve as a model for municipalities across Ukraine the project was partnered at national level by the Department of Regional Policy in the Ministry of Economy.

tion in particular (EU Commission 1998: 2, 7; Hamilton 2013: 155). With regard to relations between national and sub-national governments donors had come to the conclusion that it was only through proactive programmes of institutional development that the Government of Ukraine could be helped to establish a stable legislative and policy framework for reform and build a sufficient consensus at national and regional levels to ensure implementation.

Donor support for this approach is demonstrated in statements of broad strategy for future technical assistance to the Government of Ukraine and in the initial documentation for each of the five projects under consideration here. The project memorandum for DFID's LARGIS, which was the first intervention explicitly to prioritise institutional development, identifies as a major blockage to reform 'the institutional and structural defects' in the management of Ukraine's regional policy, the 'lack of [a] legislative base for decentralization' and the 'lack of adequate policy-making capacity.' The role of LARGIS would be to 'nurture the understanding and acceptance of regional government reform, through a consensus and support-building programme' (UK DFID 1999: 12, 4).

The EU was quick to follow suit and its Ukraine Country Strategy for 2002-2006 promised that future assistance would be 'progressively focused on a limited number of areas, in order to support institutional reforms….and achieve a systemic impact' (EU Commission 2001: 1). When the EU/Ukraine Action Plan 2005-2008 was signed in February 2005, a specific commitment was made to assist the Government of Ukraine to 'establish a legislative base for promotion of regional development' and to 'elaborate a draft state strategy for regional development to 2015' (EU/Ukraine Action Plan 2005: art. 23).

The terms of reference of the EU's first Assistance to Regional Development project 2004-2006, although drawn up just prior to the signing of the Action Plan, reflect this commitment. Support would be provided to the Ministry of Economy with the drafting and revision of legislation currently in preparation in the ministry, and to 'improve [the] capacity of national, regional and local authorities to formulate and implement regional development policies' (EU

TACIS ARD 2001: para. 2.2).

Five years later however the terms of reference for the Support to Sustainable Regional Development project note that there is still 'no comprehensive regional policy in place' in Ukraine. The new project needs to 'upgrade regional policy in Ukraine by extending the EU regional development policy' and 'strengthen the Ukrainian authorities' capacity in policy formulation and decision-making process for sustainable regional development' (EU ENPI SSRD 2006: paras. 2.1, 2.2).

CIDA's broad strategy towards Ukraine in this period was evolving in much the same way as those of DFID and the EU, with its Country Development Programme for 2002-2006 promising to 'refine and focus program activities more on governance institutions' and on the strengthening of 'governance structures and institutional capacity' (CIDA 2011: 18). The initial documentation from the contractor for the 2006-2012 Regional Governance and Development project refers to 'systemic challenges' emanating from the 'inadequate capacity of national and regional government structures, given the complexity of the reform effort required.' The project will assist its partner, the Ministry of Economy, to 'implement public engagement mechanisms' and to 'establish a participatory dialogue between ministerial and regional government representatives' on questions related to regional development policy (CUI RGD 2006: 6, 12, 17, 24).[33]

The stage now seemed set for co-ordinated and sustained support to the reform of Ukraine's regional policy on the part of donors. Moreover this was at a time when the Government of Ukraine appeared ready to respond to domestic pressure to introduce new measures to address the growing disparities in regional development and when there were well-placed pro-reform actors in a key ministry willing to be active partners to programmes of external assistance.

---

[33] There were no formal terms of reference from the donor as the project was part-financed by CIDA in response to the contractor's own proposal. This arrangement is known as 'responsive programming', where the contractor is required to make a financial contribution to the implementation of the project (CIDA 2011: 26).

Establishing a Stable Legislative Framework for Regional Policy

Whatever good intentions there may have been on the donor side, the reality was to prove very different. Whereas the input of international assistance to the key innovation of the Budget Code reform, the introduction of formula-based transfers, had been well coordinated, narrowly focused and influential, external advice on reforming legislation in the area of regional policy was characterised by discontinuity and inconsistency. At times donor assistance appeared directly to undermine the flagship policy of pro-reform elements in the Ministry of Economy, the contract for regional development.

At other times, despite the declared commitment of all donors to promoting systemic change through long-term institution building, the short-term nature of programmes of technical assistance fostered the use of imported, ready-made solutions to complex problems and the establishment of largely formal and superficial relationships with Ukrainian partners. These served merely to obscure the reality of the institutional challenges facing reform.

*Donor Assistance with the Preparation of the 2005 State Law*

The first draft of what was later to be the 2005 State Law on the Stimulation of Regional Development was ready at the end of 2002, at the time of the closure of the DFID LARGIS project. Within LARGIS, Serhiy Romaniuk had been able to continue to draw on the expertise of Professor Gerard Marcou, his mentor on contracts for regional development in the earlier Local Government and Public Service Reform Initiative (LGI) programme. In addition LARGIS had provided him with the opportunity to study the recent experience of Poland in introducing similar agreements, through contact with Professor Grzegorz Gorzelak from the University of Warsaw, an adviser on regional policy to the Polish government.

Romaniuk's intention was that regional contracts would form the centrepiece of the proposed new legislation and the subsequent State Strategy and he was anticipating further assistance from DFID in preparing the ground for what he knew would be a controversial measure. DFID's decision not to follow LARGIS with a similar programme in partnership with the Cabinet of

Ministers, as recommended by its Ukrainian Project Manager,[34] but to launch in its place two major regional projects with no national component, was therefore a source of considerable frustration to Romaniuk who was annoyed both by the lack of continuity in assistance to the Ministry of Economy and by the absence of any prior consultation.[35]

There would be a hiatus of eighteen months before the Ministry of Economy again had an international partner advising on the drafting of legislation. However, while strengthening the legislative base of regional policy is identified as a major task in the terms of reference of the EU's Assistance to Regional Development project (EU TACIS ARD 2001: para. 2.3), its final report makes only a general reference to experts preparing 'a number of analytical papers and recommendations' on draft legislative documents including the Law on the Stimulation of Regional Development.

The absence of constructive working relations with the Ministry of Economy is evident in the final report's comment that the project 'basically was on its own', and also in its observations on the ministry's draft State Strategy for Regional Development. The Strategy, in the project's view, 'does not develop visions and perspectives adapted to the various regions. The lack of concrete planning proposals at the central level adapted to the main economic spaces of Ukraine…..leaves each specific region free to plan its future, with no coordination with neighbouring regions' and 'the link between the national objectives and the regional and local priorities…..seems virtually non-existent' (EU TACIS ARD 2006: 53, 55).

There is no evidence that the project contributed in any way to the final draft of the State Law on Regional Development passed by the *Verkhovna Rada* in September 2005, or to discussions with the Cabinet of Ministers or members of Parliament prior to its adoption. Olena Nyzhnyk comments that the project team 'complained about lack of cooperation from the Ministry' and 'had no concrete outcomes' at national level, instead 'going off to Volyn region to do

---

[34] Towards European Standards of Public Administration in Ukraine (TESPA).
[35] Interview with Serhiy Romaniuk, Kyiv, 26 July 2014.

something or other.'[36] A Ukrainian specialist in regional policy who worked with the Assistance to Regional Development team described the project and its experts as 'wholly unmemorable.'

Whatever other factors may have been involved, it should be stressed that the Assistance to Regional Development project worked at a particularly difficult period, during and after the Orange Revolution of winter 2004/5, when cooperation with government institutions cannot have been straightforward. Unfortunately it was not possible to conduct any interviews with former project experts during the course of the case study in order to obtain a more balanced view. Contact was established but the expert concerned declined to be interviewed. Neither was it possible to gain access to the EU's own monitoring reports. Permission was requested but refused on the grounds of confidentiality. There are no on-line records of the project's work and the reports quoted were obtained from Ukrainian sources.

In summary the drafting of the 2005 State Law was a task largely undertaken by the Ministry of Economy itself, with initial advice from UK DFID's LARGIS project on the framing of the proposal for regional development contracts. The involvement in LARGIS of Professor Gerard Marcou, already known to Serhiy Romaniuk from the LGI programme, was particularly influential in helping to make this proposal the centrepiece of the legislation.

However DFID's decision not to extend LARGIS meant that the ministry had no access to external advice during the steering of the draft law through the Cabinet of Ministers and *Verkhovna Rada*. Despite its being identified as a priority task for the EU's Assistance to Regional Development programme, which followed LARGIS, the project appears to have made no input to the final draft of the law which was finally signed off by President Viktor Yushchenko on 8 September 2005.

---

[36] Interview with Olena Nyzhnyk, Kyiv, 29 March 2013

*Misdirected Assistance: the EU and the Ministry of Regional Development & Construction*

The EU's 'Support to Sustainable Regional Development' project began work in July 2008. It was the largest and most ambitious of the EU's programmes on regional policy to date, with a revenue budget of 6m EUR and an additional 9m EUR available for small-scale infrastructure projects in selected towns and cities. Unlike other EU programmes its lead partner was to be the new Ministry of Regional Development and Construction which had been established in May 2007 following the appointment of Viktor Yanukovych as prime minister. The Ministry of Economy was named in the project terms of reference only as one of seven 'intermediate beneficiaries' (EU ENPI SSRD 2006: para 4.1.3). Furthermore in what was to prove a significant omission the terms of reference, in commenting on the current status of regional policy in Ukraine, made no reference to either the 2005 State Law or the 2006 State Strategy.[37]

From the outset relationships between the Ministries of Economy and Regional Development had been strained, characterised by lack of cooperation, multiple conflicts and struggles for influence (Mrinska 2010: 11). There was confusion between the responsibilities of the new ministry and those of the Ministry of Economy, in particular the latter ministry's Department of Regional Policy. This was a source of continuing frustration to Vasil' Kuiybida, the first minister to be appointed to lead the Ministry of Regional Development and Construction, who lamented the failure of the Cabinet of Ministers to resolve the obvious duplication in roles[38] (Kuiybida et al. 2010: 41).

---

[37] The programme year for the Support to Sustainable Regional Development project was 2006. The project terms of reference are undated but must have been prepared later than 2006 as the project's main partner, the Ministry of Regional Development and Construction was not established until May 2007.

[38] According to resolution no. 750 of the Cabinet of Ministers on 16 May 2007, the tasks of the new ministry included 'participating in the formulation and ensuring the realisation of state regional policy', 'bringing forward proposals for the formulation of state regional policy', and 'participation in the preparation and implementation of measures.....for the stimulation of economic development in the regions and inter-regional co-operation.'(continued p156)

Lead partner or not, the initial reaction of the Ministry of Economy to the new EU programme was cautiously positive. Compared to the Assistance to Regional Development team, project experts 'did a lot and were much more active.' There were 'mountains of paper and reports and we found some of their analysis good and helpful.'[39] However, the new project inevitably brought with it a new managing consortium and a new expert team. According to Olena Nyzhnyk the EU expert team arrived with its own ideas and models for the reform of regional policy in Ukraine and appeared to have little understanding or institutional memory of what had gone before. Instead their preference was to start again 'from zero' (*vid nulya*).[40]

Among the first tasks the EU team undertook for the Ministry of Regional Development and Construction was to review existing government policy and legislation, starting with the 2005 State Law and the State Strategy of 2006. The advice of project experts was that neither offered any effective instruments for stimulating regional development. Too much attention was given to the problem of depressed territories and not enough to the potential of 'growth poles' as engines of economic development for other regions. Here the experts seem to have ignored one of the major themes of the State Strategy.

On contracts for regional development, the EU team argued that even a superficial analysis of the agreement with L'vivs'ka *oblast* showed that the measures identified as priorities for development were of a very general nature, applicable to almost any region in Ukraine and of little relevance to the real economic potential of the L'vivs'ka region. The fact that the regional contract model had been unable to attract ring-fenced state budget finance was testimony to its ineffectiveness and the lack of political commitment to

---

Meanwhile a parallel resolution no. 777 of 26 May 2007 included among the tasks of the Ministry of Economy 'formulating and ensuring, within the boundaries of its authority and related legislation, the realisation of state regional policy', and 'participation in the preparation and implementation of measures for the development of the infrastructure of regions and inter-regional cooperation' (Kuiybida et al. 2010: 42).

[39] Interview with Olena Nyzhnyk, Kyiv, 29 March 2013.
[40] Interview with Olena Nyzhnyk, Kyiv, 29 March 2013.

the idea (EU ENPI SSRD 2009: 13, 17; Kuiybida et al. 2010: 44-45; EU ENPI SSRD 2011: 13).

The EU team quickly set about advising the ministry on the preparation of new legislation entitled 'On the Principles of State Regional Policy' and intended to replace the 2005 law. A first draft of the law appeared in 2008, to be followed by numerous revisions before it was submitted to the Cabinet of Ministers in December 2009. Although the regional contract was retained in early drafts, later versions dispensed with it altogether, its place as the primary instruments of regional development being taken by a State Fund for Regional Development to be financed from a tax on enterprise profits and contributions from donors, international financial institutions and charitable sources (art. 21), and a proposed network of regional development agencies as a partnership between regional governments, business and the wider community (art. 16).[41]

A review of the draft law by Council of Europe experts commented that little consideration appeared to have been given to the work already carried out to develop an effective regional policy or to learning from the experience of implementing the 2005 legislation (Council of Europe 2008: 17-18), and one of these experts later commented in interview that in general he did not feel that successive re-workings of the proposed new law were 'in any way superior to the 2005 legislation.' Overall he 'had the impression overall that the new Ministry was not very interested in regional development as an issue, and had only a few people with a good understanding of regional policy. Their main interest was in municipal and communal services.'[42]

Understandably the Ministry of Economy was frustrated and annoyed that one group of international experts was now devoting its time to rewriting legislation that had been prepared in part with the assistance of experts from an earlier technical assistance programme. But their sharpest criticism was reserved for what they regarded as the inappropriateness of the EU expert models included in the draft legislation. These were felt to be imported from

---

[41] The full text of the December 2009 draft is reproduced in: Kuiybida et al. 2010: 195-216.
[42] Interview with Professor Gerard Marcou, Paris, 22 November 2013.

the experience of other European countries with very different political and economic contexts and, in their present form at least, were viewed by Serhiy Romaniuk and Olena Nyzhnyk as wholly unrealistic in Ukrainian conditions.

The project's proposal for a State Fund for Regional Development to provide multi-year funding for regional and inter-regional investment projects in accordance with the state strategy for regional development (art. 21 of the draft law) was in itself a useful idea. But the expert recommendation to establish the Fund as an arm's length bureau or agency, appointed by the Cabinet of Ministers and financed from the state budget but supervised independently by a management board including representation from business and civic organisations (art. 23), was naïve and 'dangerous in the Ukrainian reality.'[43]

Similarly the proposal to establish a network of regional development agencies as non-profit organisations bringing together local government, business and civic organisations in every region, with delegated and sole responsibility for preparing and executing projects financed through the State Fund (arts. 18 and 19), was inappropriate to a Ukrainian context where the risk of corruption was ever present.[44] When the draft legislation was presented to the Cabinet of Ministers in December 2009 it was successfully opposed by the Ministry of Economy.

Even so, according to Serhiy Romaniuk and Olena Nyzhnyk, EU experts continued their vocal opposition to the 2005 law and to the contracts for regional development. In their discussions with Romaniuk and Nyzhnyk 'they were inflexible and saw only one way' and when their recommendations were questioned they 'gave the impression that as experts they were right and ministry officials were fools.'[45]

---

[43] Council of Europe experts made a similar criticism of arrangements for supervising the proposed Fund at regional level, arguing that they were 'inappropriate and contrary to budgetary rules for the management of resources that will be uniquely public money, from national or foreign origin' (Council of Europe 2008: 30).

[44] Interview with Serhiy Romaniuk, Kyiv, 23 March 2013.

[45] Interviews with Serhiy Romaniuk and Olena Nyzhnyk, Kyiv, 23 & 29 March 2013.

Reflecting later on the role of the Ministry of Regional Development and Construction during the 2007-2010 period and the attempted replacement of the 2005 law, Romaniuk comments that 'they [the Ministry] had no understanding at all of the inter-ministerial, coordinating role of regional policy' and they set about re-drafting a basically sound piece of legislation simply 'because they were incapable of doing anything else.'[46] In 2012 responsibility for regional policy was removed from a renamed Ministry of Regional Development, Construction, Housing and Municipal Economy and returned to a similarly re-configured Ministry of Economic Development and Trade.

*Strengthening Policy-Making Capacity: Strategies, Strategies and More Strategies*

International donors concentrated much of their capacity building on interventions at regional and municipal level, and here the focus was largely on strengthening the capacity of state and local self-government officials to elaborate medium-term policies or strategies for regional or urban development. It is the impact of this activity that is examined here. Since the United States Agency for International Development (USAID) was so active in advising on strategy preparation at municipal level in this period, its programme of Local Economic Development is included in the account that follows.

Internationally, five to seven year strategies for development, prepared by local governments with the participation of the business, academic and wider community with the aim of improving the economic performance and investment attractiveness of a city or region, had become an increasingly popular instrument for sub-national governments in OECD states from the 1980s onwards. The inclusive nature of development strategy preparation was in tune with the thinking of the 'New Public Management' approach to public services which was finding favour with governments of many donor countries in the same period.[47]

---

[46] Interview with Serhiy Romaniuk, Kyiv, 26 July 2014.

[47] As discussed in chapter I, New Public Management became popular in many OECD countries in the 1980s and 1990s and is associated with the marketisation of public services through, for example, increased competition in service provision by contracting out to the private sector and the introduction of public-private partnerships in capital project construction.

The Ministry of Economy was keen to draw on this experience and at its request an agreement to assist Ukraine's regional authorities to prepare development strategies was specifically included at article 23 of the EU/Ukraine Action Plan of 2000. The medium-term strategic planning tool was attractive to Serhiy Romaniuk and Olena Nyzhnyk because it complemented their model of region-led, multi-year contract agreements between national and regional governments to take the place of the annual top-down programmes of line ministries. Under the terms of the 2005 State Law on the Stimulation of Regional Development and the State Strategy which followed in 2006, *oblast* authorities were required to prepare regional development strategies for periods up to seven years as a precondition for entering into negotiation for contract arrangements with the Cabinet of Ministers.[48]

In the period to 2012 the five projects in the present case study provided expert advice in the preparation of development strategies to 17 regional and local authorities. Two other programmes from UK DFID and one from the United Nations Development Programme (UNDP), all working exclusively at regional level, advised a further 12 regions, municipalities or districts.[49] By far the most far-reaching however was USAID's Local Economic Development project which, between 2004 and 2008, assisted with the preparation of municipal development strategies in up to 76 medium-sized towns across the whole of Ukraine (USAID LED 2009).

To date there has been no objective analysis of the outcome of this substantial input of donor resources, although donors themselves have made considerable claims. For example the final report on the first phase of CIDA's Regional Governance and Development project states that over 38,000 residents of its two partner regions, Zakarpats'ka and Zaporiz'ka, participated in the consultation and engagement activities of the strategic planning

---

[48] 2005 State Law article 4, 2006 State Strategy article 5, Section 2.

[49] **UK DFID LARGIS** – Kharkivs'ka region, city of L'viv, municipalities of Chuguyiv and Kupyans'k (Kharkivs'ka region); **EU Assistance to Regional Development** – Vinnyts'ka, Volyns'ka, Cherkas'ka regions; **EU Sustainable Local Development** - municipalities of Izium (Kharkivs'ka region), Pryluky (Chernihivs'ka), Romny (Sums'ka),

process, and that nearly 150 state servants were trained to prepare investment proposals related to plan implementation, as a result of which 5.5m USD of local, national and international financing was received by authorities and businesses in the two *oblasts* (CUI RGD 2010: paras. 4.1.3, 4.1.4). Similarly, USAID claims that as a result of its Local Economic Development project investments of 2 billion USD were received by its partner municipalities, resulting in the creation of up to 50,000 jobs and 4,600 new businesses (USAID LED 2009: 9, 16).

However, there is anecdotal and other evidence to suggest that while individual authorities may have benefited positively from donor assistance in the preparation of development strategies, the record on strategy implementation is far less impressive. An unpublished questionnaire survey of all regional administrations in 2007 was said to have found that only one *oblast* council had allocated finance for strategy implementation in its annual budget.[50] The OECD has also observed that regional strategies 'were not in fact working documents, and they were neither implemented nor funded as such. There were no operational plans binding on actors....and actual funding remained tied not to the strategies but to annual budget allocations for sectoral instruments – state and regional targeted programmes' (OECD 2014: 119-120). An EU expert report in 2011 also concluded that, in spite of the significant investment in training and capacity building, 'with very few exceptions [Ukrainian authorities] lack the institutional (and sometimes even technical) capabilities and budgets to implement their own policies' (EU ENPI SURDP 2011: 2).

---

Sverdlovs'k (Luhans'ka); **EU Support to Sustainable Regional Development** - Autonmous Republic of Crimea, Vinnyts'ka, Rivens'ka, Khmel'nits'ka regions; **CIDA Regional Governance and Development** – Zakarpats'ka, Zaporiz'ka regions. Other donor projects operating at a regional or municipal level only during this period included: **UK DFID Action Donbas** – Luhans'ka, Donets'ka regions; municipalities of Krasnodon, Severodonets'k and districts of Kremennaya, Perevals'k (Luhans'ka region); **UK DFID Lviv Development Project** (L'vivs'ka region: districts of Mostys'ka, Radekhiv, Sokal', Stryi); **United Nations Development Programme** (Autonmous Republic of Crimea).

[50] Unpublished survey by Professor Valentina Mamonova, Kharkivs'ka Regional Institute of Public Administration, 2007.

While both the OECD and EU expert analyses imply that the problem lies on the Ukrainian side, Ukrainian sources take an equally critical view of the short-termism of donor interventions and the imperative of technical assistance programmes to secure 'quick wins'. One expert described the result of a major donor programme in eastern Ukraine as 'fast food strategies', quickly prepared and immediately satisfying but made to a pre-set formula and of little practical value. Similarly another Ukrainian source argues that donors too often import their own home-grown models of strategic planning without sufficient regard to Ukrainian reality, and that this is why so many development strategies end up on the shelves of local authority leaders. Donors should avoid 'parachuting in' outside experts, should acquire a much deeper understanding of the local context and make better use of Ukrainian expertise (Mrinska et al. 2013: 299).

The experience of the EU's Support to Sustainable Local Development (SLD) project, described in Box II below, also suggests that failure to make the intended impact on policy-making capacity may have its origins in institutional factors on the donor side, related to the organisation and management of programmes of technical assistance. The objective of the project was to assist the municipal administrations of four medium-sized towns in central and eastern Ukraine with the renovation of essential but run-down infrastructure services such as water supply and waste management. The results should serve as a model for municipalities across Ukraine. The project budget included almost 13m EUR of capital expenditure for the purchase of equipment related to infrastructure improvement.

> **Box II**
> **EU 'Support to Sustainable Local Development' Project 2007-2011**
> 'The original plan in the terms of reference was to spend the first six months setting up the office and team and selecting the towns, and then the following six months working on development strategies before moving on to identifying the equipment to be purchased by the project which should reflect the priorities in the development strategies. However, within the first three months of set-up the EU Delegation informed me that since the TACIS timetable had slipped and the project was therefore late getting on the ground, and since the equipment finance had to be spent by the end of 2008 at the latest, the tendering process needed to be completed before the end of the first year, in other words before the strategies were prepared. Because of the change in the procurement deadline, there was a knock-on effect on the availability of the specialist EU experts in each utility area. The expectation had been that they would be needed most in the second year of the project, when equipment identification and tendering was to take place. Once this was shifted to year 1, problems arose with ensuring the input of these experts at the right time. Most of the four experts involved were already working in Ukraine, but on other programmes, and they could only be at the project's disposal in the regions or in Kyiv from time to time. So the process of agreeing what equipment was required was both rushed and patchy in quality.
>
> 'An information meeting was held in June or July of 2007 at which the equipment tenders for each municipality were explained. Towns were represented by their Mayors as this was a high-level meeting with the EU Delegation and Ministry representatives, and not by technical staff. Again because of the shortened timescale no critical eye on the Ukrainian side was passed over the tender documents. The municipality of Izium may be the clearest example of the negative consequences of this. The new boiler purchased for their district heating system was not compatible with the remainder of their existing network and could not be connected without renewing substantial parts of the network, for which there was no finance. Additionally, in the waste management area a bulldozer was bought for which the EU expert had overspecified the requirement. The maintenance costs of the vehicle - towns were responsible for all the maintenance costs which followed purchase of the capital equipment - were far higher than the Izium municipal budget could finance and they simply reverted to using the bulldozer they already had.'[51]

[51] Interview with Jean-Francois Devemy, EU Team Leader for the SLD Project from October 2006 to September 2007, Paris, 21 November 2013.

The above account highlights the irony of an international programme setting out to promote domestic institutional change but failing to achieve its objective as a result of institutional factors on the donor side. In this instance the timetable for spending EU funds was deemed to take precedence over the timetable agreed with the Ukrainian partner for determining how the funds should best be used. In such a situation partnerships inevitably become purely formal in nature and the commitment of either side to an outcome matching the original objective is reduced to a minimum.

As a result of problems with project implementation relations between team leader Jean-Francois Devemy and the EU Delegation became strained to breaking point and Devemy eventually left his post as team leader in September 2007. Nevertheless the documentation prepared at the time supports his version of events.

In an initial draft of the inception report written in May 2007, Devemy complains that the plans for project implementation have been affected by 'the EU Delegation's request to turn the initial planning upside down' and forecasts that there will be a decrease in interest in strategy preparation and the introduction of reforms once the equipment has been delivered (EU TACIS SLD 2007a: paras. 3.5, 3.6). The final edited draft of the inception report, submitted in July 2007, softens the tone of the original but nevertheless acknowledges the EU Delegation's requirement of 'speeding the procurement in order to respect the contracting deadline of the Action Programme 2005' (EU TACIS SLD 2007b: para. 3). A subsequent EU monitoring report confirms that for the time being municipal leaderships were asked to adopt what were now to be termed 'temporary territorial development strategies' (EU TACIS SLD 2008: para. 2, author's italics). According to the final report of the project work on these started in February 2007 with the adoption of full strategies coming much later, during 2008 (EU TACIS SLD 2010: para. 3).

By the autumn of 2007, less than a year into a four year project, it was evident that municipal leaderships had lost interest in the strategic planning process. After all the equipment had already been ordered and they had been told there was no additional financing available for strategy implementation.

Adoption of municipal strategies was therefore destined to be purely formal in nature and lacking local ownership.[52] The lessons learned section of the final project report of 2010, prepared by the replacement team leader, appears to confirm that there were serious problems at the implementation stage. With regard to local strategy implementation the report concludes that in future capital grants for equipment should not be paid in advance but rather 'to compensate expenses' and only after 'asking first [for evidence of] realization' (EU TACIS SLD 2010: para. 6).

It has been beyond the scope of the present study to examine the impact on individuals of donors' investment in building policy-making capacity through the process of strategic planning, though it seems highly probable that individual regional and local officials will have changed their attitudes and working practice as a result of their interaction with donor programmes. For example an independent evaluation of CIDA's Regional Governance and Development project found that in Zakarpats'ka and Zaporiz'ka regions 'stakeholders interviewed…..reported that public servants routinely are paying much more attention now to community identified priorities. The experience of community based planning has convinced them that their jobs can actually be made easier by adopting the new approach' (CIDA 2011: 25-26).

Asked for her view of the most useful contribution overall of donor technical assistance to the reform of Ukraine's regional policy, Olena Nyzhnyk also points to the increased capacity of middle-range regional state servants to conceptualise and prepare operational policies and projects to promote regional development. In the same interview however she notes somewhat sceptically that the new EU 'Support to Ukraine's Regional Development Policy' project is 'yet again busying itself with the preparation of regional development strategies,' underlining that the assistance required was with execution rather than design.[53]

---

[52] Interview with Tetyana Korneyeva, SLD Project Strategic Planning Lead Expert, Paris, 21 November 2013.

[53] Interview with Olena Nyzhnyk, Kyiv, 24 July 2014.

With regard to donors' stated objective of increasing policy-making capacity at an institutional level, perhaps the most telling comment is from Serhiy Romaniuk who argues that 'none of these projects stayed around long enough to see the process they had started through to a conclusion…the legacy of technical assistance to strategic planning in the regions is "dead human capital" (*'myortvyi chelovecheskyi kapital'*)…the inputs of training and capacity building have never been translated into continuing practice and regional and local governments carry on with their day-to-day business much as they always have.'[54]

The limited engagement of programmes of technical assistance and, as a consequence, the necessarily shallow understanding of the context in which they work, is further illustrated by the following two examples. Both are taken from interviews with Ukrainian informants.

*Understanding 'Ukrains'ka Real'nist'' (i): Zaporizhia's Golden Office*

The CIDA Regional Governance and Development project was unique among the five interventions in the case study in following up its advice to its regional partners in Zakarpats'ka and Zaporiz'ka on the preparation of development strategies with a year-long programme of capacity building in strategy implementation. The programme was felt to have been particularly effective in Zaporiz'ka where the CIDA project was proactive in helping its partners to attract loan finance from international finance organisations to support infrastructure development, and in the implementation of a programme to encourage growth in the small and medium-sized enterprise (SME) sector. Both had been included in the priorities identified in the Zaporiz'ka regional strategy to 2015, approved by the *oblast* council in 2008.[55]

On infrastructure improvement for example, the CIDA project was instrumental in training and mentoring the management of a number of Zaporizhia City's communal utilities to prepare investment proposals to an

---

[54] Interview with Serhiy Romaniuk, Kyiv, 26 July 2014. Mr Romaniuk was speaking in Russian and this is reflected in the transliteration of his remarks.

[55] A copy of the strategy can be accessed at <www.zoda.gov.ua>.

internationally recognised standard, as a direct result of which an agreement was reached between the European Bank for Reconstruction and Development and the city council to part finance modernisation of its district heating system. 18m EUR financing for the scheme, part-grant and part-loan, was confirmed in principle in 2012 (CUI RGD 2013: 5.2).

With regard to SME development, where the regional strategy's priorities included support to enterprises promoting innovation in the agrarian sector and to local producers providing goods for the home market, the CIDA project team advised on and part-financed a series of initiatives from the clustering of small agricultural machine-tool businesses in the city of Melitopol (CUI RGD 2010: para. 4.16) to a municipal government-backed programme in Zaporizhia City to raise the profile and competitiveness of local businesses selling regional products in the city's shops (CUI RGD 2010: annex C).

These activities appeared to be well received by the Zaporiz'ka *oblast* administration and an independent evaluation of the Regional Governance and Development project praised the expert team for having 'achieved more than was planned for a given budget'.[56] The account in Box III below contains revelations about Zaporizhia City's 'Golden Office' which invite a different interpretation of the project's accomplishments. Irina Lekh, founder of '*Porada*', a regional association of small businesses in Zaporiz'ka *oblast*, writes a regular blog on the activities of the office and also agreed to speak in interview.

---

[56] CIDA 2011: 26, citing Gombay, C., Hershkovitz, L. and Palyvoda, L., 2010: *Regional Governance & Development Project — Ukraine Evaluation Report*.

> **Box III**
> **Zaporizhia's 'Golden Office'**
>
> 'The 'Golden Office' – it gets its name from all the gold and the crystal chandeliers with which the building is crammed – is located in very heart of the city, not far from the Mayor's office. That is convenient because the Mayor is a regular visitor. Mostly if you want to see the Mayor you have to go to him, but not in the case of the Golden Office. He goes to them.
>
> 'The office is surrounded by a high fence and the sort of security cameras you only find at the President's Administration in Kyiv. This is the workplace of Yevgenii Anisimov, who formerly ran a waste metal business, but was appointed in 2011 by President Viktor Yanukovych's "family" as the "Smotryashchiy" for the Zaporiz'ka region. The term comes from the criminal world, where the Smotryashchiy is the person in a prison or a penal colony nominated by the criminal world to ensure that prisoners observe a set of codes and understandings governing how the prison functions, regardless of any formal rules of the prison authorities. The codes of course include the payment of regular dues to the Smotryashchiy. In the Soviet and post-Soviet periods he was a figure in the criminal world only, taking profits from drugs and prostitution. Since Viktor Yanukovych came to power the role has been imported into the informal structure of the state.
>
> 'I was unaware of this until, at a meeting of the Regional Council of Entrepreneurs in 2011, a member told us how for several months in succession she had been visited in her business by two men from the Golden Office pressuring her to join some non-governmental association or other to whom she should pay, in her words, "a crazy subscription fee." She had refused, after which they started to issue threats to her, to her colleagues and to her family. Immediately after the meeting I went to Kyiv, to the Council of Entrepreneurs of the Cabinet of Ministers. They wrote down all the facts, the names of the two men and so on and they promised to help. And then... nothing. To all my subsequent letters and questions, officials give the same reply every time – the facts have been checked but cannot be confirmed. Meanwhile the Golden Office continues to appropriate our businesses.
>
> 'The way the Smotryashchiy works is like this: in larger enterprises, including the communal enterprises which manage city utilities like water supply and heating, he prefers to put his own people in as managers. In smaller businesses like the

> ### Zaporizhia's 'Golden Office' cont'd
>
> *minibus taxis or high street kiosks and restaurants he might take them over completely if they are very small or else extract 50% of the profits. This has happened in several of the enterprises supplying fresh regional products to the city's shops, one of the priority areas in the regional strategy which the Canadian project helped with. Communal enterprises are particularly attractive to him because they put so much of their routine maintenance work out to tender. And you can make sure a tender is arranged so that the Golden Office takes a cut from the artificially inflated tender price. Managements of communal enterprises in Zaporozhzhia who refuse to cooperate are replaced.*
>
> *'In fact this is what happened to the director of the communal enterprise "Teploset" who was responsible for the successful loan negotiation with the European Bank. The Golden Office did not like the agreement because it would involve EBRD demanding transparency in the management of the enterprise, including its procedures for tendering. Representatives of the Golden Office instructed the director to withdraw from the negotiations. He refused and was forced out of his job into "retirement", to be replaced by one of the Golden Office's own appointees. Later on it was reported that the city had withdrawn from the loan agreement, supposedly because of the financial crisis.*
>
> *'The whole process has become quite open and blatant. It has the full cooperation of both the Regional Governor and the City Mayor, who both meet with Anisimov regularly. It has become like a parallel system of taxation, a shadow city administration, and its purpose is to ensure a steady flow of finance from the region up to Kyiv. It works through threats of harassment from the tax authorities or even criminal investigation and its favourite targets are complex projects with finance from different sources, including state and local budgets, where it is easier to lose money and not be noticed. It has also drained any available money from budgets from the region and city, including all finance for development. Sadly, all the funds and previous initiatives from the oblast administration to support the growth of small and medium-sized enterprises have simply dried up.'*[57]

---

[57] From interviews with Irina Lekh, Zaporizhia, 25 June 2013 and 21 October 2013, and Irina Lekh's blog at <irinaleh.com.ua>

*Understanding 'Ukrains'ka Real'nist'' (ii): Konvertatsionnyi Tsentr; Otkat*

The phenomenon of the *'Smotryashchiy'* is far from being unique to Zaporizhia, although it is apparently more usual for this figure to be the regional governor, who is also a Presidential appointee, than someone from the business sector. The so-called Conversion Centre (*Konvertatsionnyi Tsentr*) has also become a feature of all Ukraine's regions and large cities and, like the *Smotryashchiy*, plays a role in the life of small and medium-sized enterprises which is in direct contradiction to the reform-oriented objectives of strategies for regional development.

The conversion centre is a structure in the shadow economy consisting of a number of fictitious or 'shell' companies. The role of the centre is to assist local enterprises and banks to avoid the payment of tax, in particular value-added tax, and it can also help with the laundering of money by converting paper transfers into cash or, vice versa, by converting cash into hard-to-trace investments abroad. The centre also plays a key part in the payment of the obligatory backhander (*otkat*) to a state official for the awarding of a contract. Centres are said to have first appeared in Russia in the 1990s, in the period of economic reform following the dissolution of the Soviet Union, and they were already active in Ukraine in the early 2000s.[58] By 2010 it was estimated that in some regions there were up to 20 centres. In Kyiv the figure was closer to 100. It is claimed that when Viktor Yanukovych took office in 2010, he agreed with Prime Minister Mykola Azarov that if they could not eliminate conversion centres they should at least take them under their direct control.[59]

An interview was conducted with the owner of a small commercial cleaning company in city 'X', located in another of the regions where one of the five donor projects featured in the case study worked. In Box IV the entrepreneur, who preferred to remain anonymous, explains how the city conversion centre operates.

---

[58] http://www.companion.ua/articles/content?id=4861 (Site accessed 7 October 2014)

[59] http://www.economics.lb.ua/state/2014/06/23/270740_podatkoviy_kompromis_abo_yak.htms (Site accessed 7 October 2014)

## Box IV: The 'Conversion Centre'

'I run a business providing cleaning services to enterprises and offices in the city. Like most small businesses I must admit that I have used the conversion centre as a way of avoiding paying tax, especially value-added tax. Most businesses do it and if I did not I would quickly go out of business. In return for a fee which is now about 10% of any business transaction, which I pay them in cash, the centre provides me with a legal document which says I have met all my tax obligations connected with the transaction. They can do this because they are a legal entity, operating under the protection ("pod krishoi") of the regional tax inspectorate. They have a smart office on the main street and everyone knows what their business is about. The police do not interfere either because they also take a cut of the money received by the centre. When Yulia Tymoshenko was Prime Minister the number of these centres increased enormously, but when Viktor Yanukovych became President there was a process of drastic rationalisation. Now there are only two in this region. We all know where the money goes.

'The other side of the centre's business is the so-called "otkat" payment to officials in the city and regional administrations for the awarding of contracts to small businesses like mine. There is a kind of a play on words here since the word "konvert" in Russian also means an envelope, which is how the payment to the official is usually made. Under this system, if I win a tender valued at say 100,000 USD, the official with whom I am dealing will propose adding 20,000 USD to the total in respect of his "otkat" and his "help" in winning the tender. I go along to the conversion centre with my paper transfer from the city for the 120,000 USD and the centre converts this into cash for me. This is the only way in which I can get the hard cash. Otherwise the transfer's just a piece of paper which no one will honour. Not banks, no one. So you are trapped inside the process.

'The centre charges me a commission of 12,000 USD, in return for which I get a document certifying that I have paid all my due taxes, VAT included. This leaves me with 108,000 USD, 20,000 USD in cash for the official – it must always be cash – and rest is my payment for the cleaning service I provide. As far as I understand some of the centre's commission is supposed to go to the tax authorities, but most of it goes into people's pockets, and mainly to Kyiv. I do not much like the system, it's all wrong of course, but this is the only way in which my business can survive. If I refused to play along with it I would get no contracts at all. The city and regional authorities would see to that. 90% of businesses in the city who want to survive work this way.'[60]

---

[60] Interview with the owner of a small commercial cleaning company, city 'X', 17 August 2014.

*Two Parallel Realities*

There is nothing in the documentation of the 100 or so donor interventions to assist the preparation of regional or municipal development strategies which indicates an awareness of the 'Golden Office' or 'Conversion Centre' phenomena, though both are said by interviewees to have been a well-established practice in the regions and cities in which these strategies were designed.

On the contrary the final report of USAID's Local Economic Development project, which helped prepare strategies in 76 municipalities across Ukraine, records that 'for each partner city, the process resulted in a well-developed economic strategy and a new understanding of the value of public/private dialogue and collaboration in addressing business and social challenges' (USAID LED 2009: 4). CIDA's Regional Government and Development project final report similarly notes with satisfaction that its actions have sought to 'root economic activity in a given territory by tailoring it to local conditions and building on existing assets' and that it has helped its regional partners to promote 'alliances between local governments for local economic development. The private sector becomes the engine of economic growth, while local and regional governments work in tandem to become enablers by creating a policy, regulatory and program environment that stimulates private sector development while advancing the public interest' (CUI RGD 2013: para. 1.2).

The existence of Zaporizhia's Golden Office and the phenomenon of the Conversion Centre confirm at a regional level the finding that 'persistent state capture' by Ukraine's powerful business elites has allowed reform to proceed only so far as it does not conflict with the interests of business (Langbein & Wolczuk: 2012: 865). Optimistic final reports like those from USAID and CIDA above, written for donor governments who prefer good news to bad and understandably want to be assured their money is being well spent, either ignore or are simply unaware of the 'Ukrainian reality' in which projects like these work.

## Conclusions

The case study has charted the course of the Government of Ukraine's attempts to reform its regional policy and to fulfil its stated objective of bringing the policy into harmony with international, in particular European, practice. In common with the Budget Code reform, the story of the case study on regional policy combines efforts to change the relationship between Ukraine's national and sub-national governments in the direction of increased local autonomy, with a parallel attempt to bring greater financial discipline and transparency into the relationship and in so doing limit the opportunity for political patronage.

The evidence of the case study has again highlighted the central role of reform-minded officials being allowed the space to pursue a policy of convergence with EU practice without active encouragement or interference from the top echelons of their ministries. Unlike their counterparts in the Ministry of Finance however, the officials in the Ministry of Economy who were responsible for drafting the 2005 legislation, with its radical proposal of a contractual relationship between Kyiv and the regions, were unable to form any effective alliances in support of the reform.

Almost a decade later, while the 2005 law remains the principal legislation governing Ukraine's regional policy, its central objective of establishing a partnership relationship between the national and sub-national tiers of government in pursuit of a policy of region-led development remains unfulfilled and there has been little progress in building a political consensus on how this might be achieved.

The case study has also examined the impact of the five major programmes of international technical assistance which have set out to advise the Government of Ukraine on the establishment of a more settled legislative framework for regional development and on building capacity among state servants to support its implementation. The evidence has suggested that overall the influence of these programmes has been marginal, and on occasion even disruptive, to pro-reform initiatives. Above all the international community failed to provide consistent advice on the major innovation of the 2005 law, the contract for regional development, and appears to have merely added to the already complex problems of reaching political agreement in support of the reform.

With regard to capacity building, the pre-occupation of donors with the preparation of municipal and regional development strategies is indicative of the tendency to standardisation in the portfolios of technical assistance programmes noted by Carothers (2002: 18). Crucially, the short-term nature of these interventions and the resulting lack of attention to the issue of strategy implementation suggest that the institutional behaviour of donors themselves has played a not insignificant part in limiting the usefulness of their advice and the impact of their activities at national and sub-national level. This is in spite of the shared commitment of all donors to a longer-term strategy of institution building.

The shallow nature of donor engagement is further highlighted by the accounts of the role of the '*Smotryashchiy*' and the '*Konvertatsionnyi Tsentr*' at regional and city level. These are examples of Ukrainian reality in the form of the informal, hidden relationships which in practice shape the course of regional and urban development. They also limit the capacity of programmes of international technical assistance to exert more than a formal and superficial influence on the way things are done.

The relevance of these examples to the case study is that they indicate the complexity of the context in which external advisers operate and their apparent lack of awareness of the realities of the institutional environment in which they are working. There may be little in practice that programmes of international technical assistance can do to change this environment, but they need at least to be aware of the relationships involved and to understand their importance for the outcome of their interventions. There is nothing in the donor documentation which indicates that this is the case.

# CHAPTER V: ANALYSIS AND DISCUSSION - LINKING THE CASE STUDY EVIDENCE TO THEORY

Introduction

The analysis in the following chapter will examine the case study evidence from the perspective of four disciplines (see chapter I): Comparative Politics, Development Studies, Institutional Theory and EU Studies. It will be argued that international technical assistance to the reform of public administration in Ukraine is best conceptualised as an *isomorphic process* (Di Maggio & Powell 1991; Radaelli 2000; Andrews 2008), where a donor government or international organisation applies normative pressure to a recipient government to introduce models of economic and state institutions which the donor regards as good practice. The capacity to apply pressure follows from an asymmetry in relations between the two jurisdictions resulting either from the promise of grants, loans or other inward investment or, in the case of an international organisations like the European Union, the prospect of an offer of membership at some future date. The pressure may fall short of strict rules or conditionality but is explicitly normative in the sense that it relates to a prescribed set of norms and values concerning the 'right' institutional models to follow (Hughes et al. 2004: 13).

The two case studies in the thesis examine the introduction of institutional practices which have proved successful in donor countries, with the intention of redefining the relationship between national and sub-national government in Ukraine. Both cases concern reforms which were politically contested and neither gives an account of successful reform over the longer term or of significant donor influence on reform outcomes. However in the short term the two stories are sharply contrasting. In the case of fiscal decentralisation, major steps were taken in the direction of radical reform with the adoption of the 2001 Budget Code and the evidence suggests that technical assistance at this stage played an influential role in supporting pro-reform forces to achieve their objective. This was in spite of political opposition at the highest level. Attempts to 'Europeanise' Ukraine's regional policy, on the other hand, showed little real progress over the case study period in spite of the early introduction of reforming legislation. In this case relatively weak pro-reform forces failed to overcome powerful opponents in government and the regions and the influence of external advice on the progress of reform was minimal, even at times clearly unhelpful.

The contrast between the two accounts suggests that there are particular conditions in which the exercise of exporting policies and institutions through technical assistance may have a significant impact on the introduction of reform, in the short term at least, even when the reform is politically contentious. It will be argued that the most useful explanatory framework for these conditions is to be found in the concept of a *policy transfer network* (Evans & Davies 1999; Evans 2004a). The concept provides theoretical underpinning for the activity of the informal coalitions and alliances with domestic actors, which have been identified by previous empirical studies as prerequisites for external influence on the progress of reform (Jacoby 2006; Langbein & Wolczuk 2012).

In spite of the early triumph with the introduction of the 2001 Budget Code, the case study findings are that neither of the attempted reforms was successful over the longer term and, apart from the short-lived success with intergovernmental financial relations, external advice had limited influence on reform outcomes in either case. The analysis will suggest that the most convincing explanation for the failure of technical assistance programmes to make a significant and sustained impact on either fiscal decentralisation or regional policy reform is to be found in the *political economy analysis* of Development Studies. This argument follows from the adoption by international donors to Ukraine of a complex and open-ended strategy of institutional development to replace the more straightforward and finite task of sharing skills and know how which had been their policy through the 1990s. This step-change in direction had the effect of bringing the aims of technical assistance to Ukraine into the mainstream of international development and therefore susceptible to the critique of institution building interventions in developing countries in the wider development studies literature.

The discussion is arranged in the following way: in Part I international technical assistance is placed in a theoretical context and, in the light of this, a conceptual framework is proposed as an explanation for the short term success of the donor intervention on fiscal decentralisation; Part II draws on the political economy analysis of Development Studies to account for the longer-term failure of technical assistance to help the Government of Ukraine make substantial progress in either fiscal decentralisation or regional policy reform. The chapter concludes with a summary of the argument, comparing the evidence of the case studies with the findings of previous empirical research and placing it within a coherent theoretical framework.

# Part I: Theorising International Technical Assistance

Normative Institutional Isomorphism and Policy Transfer

The concept of institutional isomorphism is drawn from institutional theory (Di Maggio & Powell 1991) where it usually refers to the process of increasing homogenisation between organisations working in the same field. This may result either from competitive pressure or from attempts by an organisation to increase its legitimacy by imitating others which are perceived to be more powerful or influential. The related concept of *normative institutional isomorphism* is employed in a similar way to explain peer pressure in professional bodies to conform to a mutual understanding of behavioural norms which may be over and above any formal set of written rules (Di Maggio & Powell 1991: 70).

The concept of normative institutional isomorphism has also been applied to the behaviour of governments responding to pressure to adopt models of good practice in public administration employed in other countries (Andrews 2008: 381) or in policy-making processes which are dominated by imported specialist technical expertise (Radaelli 2000: 29). It is useful in the present analysis because it captures the inherent asymmetry of the donor-recipient relationship in technical assistance, particularly in contexts where there is no formal conditionality. The donor interventions examined in the two case studies were explicitly normative in nature, meaning that they set out to build new and 'better' social, political and economic institutions in place of the failed and discredited structures of the past (Offe 1996: 199), and to use as models examples of good practice from European and North American institutions. All the donors involved represent governments from whom the Government of Ukraine might hope to receive the promise of inward investment, grants or other financial assistance.

In the case of European Union programmes the declared goal of technical assistance programmes has been that of increasing approximation to EU norms and standards (EU Commission 2005b: 3; EU Commission 2007b: 14), and in view of Ukraine's longstanding aspiration to membership and the 'constructive ambiguity' of the EU's intentions in this regard, there is a good case for arguing that the Commission has been able to behave as a 'normative hegemon' in its one-way transfer of institutional norms and values (Huges, Sasse & Gordon 2004: 13; Haukkala 2009: 1762; Ganzle 2009: 1717; Boerzel 2010: 11; Korostoleva 2011: 6-8).

*Policy transfer* through programmes of technical assistance is one way in which donor governments set out to encourage recipient countries to adopt these norms of good practice. *Policy transfer* is defined by Dolowitz and Marsh (2000: 5) as a 'process by which knowledge about policies, administrative arrangements, institutions and ideas in one political system....is used in the development of policies, administrative arrangements, institutions and ideas in another political system'. The concept is commonly used as an umbrella term, embracing the related ideas of lesson drawing (Rose 1991) and social learning (Hall 1993) and not necessarily involving the active participation of a third party.

The notion of a 'negotiated' policy transfer identifies more clearly the role of a third party, usually a donor or international organisation, able to apply normative pressure on domestic actors to adopt a particular policy or institutional model. A process of exchange takes place but given the asymmetry of the donor-recipient relationship there is inevitably an element of implied or indirect coercion, even if it falls short of strict conditionality (Evans 2004a: 11).

Pro-Reform Enclaves and Informal Coalitions

The unfolding story of these two attempts at radical reform in the relations between national and sub-national levels of government in Ukraine provides sharply contrasting accounts of the interaction of international advisers and pro-reform domestic actors. The leading characters on the Ukrainian side in both case studies were middle-ranking state servants who had taken the initiative to pursue, but had yet to achieve, a particular institutional change. In both cases the direction of that change was politically contentious. It is argued that the findings of the case studies not only reinforce but provide substantial new insights over existing empirical research on the actions of pro-reform enclaves or constituencies within Ukraine's state bureaucracy (Jacoby 2004, 2006; Solonenko 2008; Wolczuk 2008, 2009; Langbein & Wolczuk 2012: 8-9).

In the case study on fiscal decentralisation pro-reform officials in the Ministry of Finance formed alliances with other domestic actors and external advisers, similar in nature to those Jacoby describes as 'informal coalitions' (2006: 625), and these alliances played a central role in overcoming powerful opponents and securing the reform. In contrast, the Ministry of Economy officials seeking regional policy reform were as isolated at the end of the case study period as they had been at the beginning. Somewhat ironically it was their ability to act with relative autonomy within the state bureaucracy which ultimately left them without the necessary allies to prevail over the resistance of other domestic actors.

The analysis which follows examines the differing outcomes of the two case studies in more detail with the aim of identifying the distinguishing features which enabled a small group of domestic actors in Ukraine's Ministry of Finance, supported by international advisers, to make significant if ultimately short-lived advances in an area of public administrative reform where there was as yet no political consensus on the need for change or the direction it should take.

The decisive factor appears to have been the establishment of a *policy transfer network* (Evans & Davies 1999; Evans 2004a) consisting of domestic and external supporters of the reform, sufficiently broadly based and influential to overcome domestic opposition forces. As discussed in chapters III and IV a network of this kind existed in the case of fiscal decentralisation and was notably absent in the area of regional policy. Generalising from this, the analysis draws provisional conclusions on the necessary conditions for programmes of technical assistance to a post-communist like Ukraine to exert influence on the progress of reform, where the nature of that reform is politically contested.

The analysis takes the form of an examination of the shared and distinguishing features of the interaction between external and domestic actors in the two case studies, followed by a discussion of the usefulness of the concept of a *policy transfer network* in explaining the differing outcomes.

## Shared Features of the Case Studies

The principal common features of the two case studies were:

- Frustrated attempts to increase the autonomy of sub-national government;
- Ambitious domestic actors within the state apparatus;
- Middle-level pro-reform enclaves in key ministries;
- Active 'champions' of reform.

These are discussed in turn below.

### *Frustrated Attempts to Increase the Autonomy of Sub-National Government*

The struggle to obtain greater powers of self-determination for regional and local government, having been at the centre of the constitutional arguments of the 1990s, was a recurring theme in both case studies. In the reform of intergovernmental financial relations the pressure for increased local autonomy was at its strongest from the larger cities, who were demanding greater independence in decision-making over spending and revenue-raising. In the case study on regional policy the aim of the contract for regional development was to establish a new relationship of partnership between the central and regional tiers of government over questions of state investment in capital infrastructure.

In both cases the effort to achieve greater autonomy for sub-national governments were largely thwarted. However the evidence of the case studies points to significant changes in the nature of the struggle for greater decentralisation from the form it had taken in the 1990s.

First, the campaign for the reform of intergovernmental finance challenged the concept of a homogenous meso-level political elite (Matsuzato 2000: 45) pressing for stronger regional autonomy. Since the reforms to local government of the late 1990s the interests of the leaderships of self-governing cites and state-appointed regional administrations have diverged, and in the arguments over the Budget Code reform they occupied sharply opposing positions. The relationship between locally accountable big city mayors and *oblast* governors continues to be a site of elite tensions today

Secondly however, apart from the budget reform there has been little evidence in the case study period of sustained pressures for decentralisation of powers away from national government. In the case study on regional policy, when the proposal was to change the relationship between Kyiv and the regions over the question of state investment grants, domestic pro-reform actors were unsuccessful in mobilising any effective regional support for their proposals. While this may in part have been the result of shortcomings in the final much diluted form of the proposed contract, it was also consistent with a wider pattern of weakly organised support for a number of decentralisation initiatives which came after the Budget Code reform.

As discussed in chapter IV there has been a series of draft proposals to strengthen the powers of local self-government since 2001, including the ambitious 'Reform for People' programme of the early period of Viktor Yushchenko's presidency which recommended fully self-governing status for *oblasts* and *raions*. None of these proposals has even reached the stage of being placed before the *Verkhovna Rada*, leading the Council of Europe to comment on the poor quality of draft legislation and the lack of any serious progress on the reform of local government despite 'ten years of cooperation' with its experts (Council of Europe 2010: 2). In 2012 intergovernmental relations remained as heavily weighted towards strong executive power in Kyiv as they had been at the end of the 1990s. Divergence in the interests of political elites at regional level, as noted above, has been an important factor in allowing this situation to continue without serious challenge.

*Ambitious Domestic Actors within the State Apparatus*

The leading domestic actors in the case studies, Anatoliy Maksiuta on fiscal decentralisation and Serhiy Romaniuk on regional policy reform, were recent recruits to their ministries from Zhytomyrs'ka and Vinnyts'ka regions respectively, each in mid-career and each with first hand experience from a regional perspective of the problematic relations between national and sub-national government. Both had also benefited from opportunities to travel in Western and Central Europe in the 1990s and were well informed on current international practice in their professional fields.

It is a reasonable inference from their accounts in interview that each had undergone a process of social learning during this period and had moved from a cognitive understanding of a particular policy employed elsewhere to a belief in its appropriateness to solve a domestic problem (Checkel 2005: 804). As noted in Chapter III Maksiuta regards his time in the Institute of Public Administration under the inspirational leadership of Bohdan Kravchenko, including study as an intern in a British local authority finance department, as a formative period in the development of his perspective on budget reform.

Similarly Serhiy Romaniuk identifies his relationship with Professor Gerard Marcou, his mentor in the Fellowship Programme of the Soros-funded Local Government and Public Service Initiative in Budapest, as the single most important influence on his thinking about regional policy. Under Marcou's guidance Romaniuk published a paper in which he for the first time set out his thinking on regions as the drivers of their own development and on the regional contract as a symbol of a partnership relationship between national and sub-national government.

As the case studies open therefore, both Maksiuta and Romaniuk have clear views about the direction reform should take and, as evidenced by their promotion to important jobs at ministry level, are already recognised as able and ambitious proponents of modern European thinking in their respective fields.

*Middle-Level Pro-Reform Enclaves in Key Ministries*

While Maksiuta and Romaniuk were later to hold senior positions as First Deputy Ministers of Finance and Economy respectively, at the time of their emergence as leading advocates of reform both occupied the middle-ranking post of department head, Maksiuta as Head of the Budget Department and Romaniuk as Head of the Department of Regional Policy. In Anatoliy Miarkovskyi and Olena Nyzhnyk, each was able to recruit as his deputy an equally ambitious professional, also from outside the ministry, who shared his thinking on the direction of reform.

The activism of this small group of officials first became apparent in 1999-2000 with the initial abortive attempt to introduce a formula approach to intergovernmental transfers and with the drafting of Ukraine's first 'European' Concept of State Regional Policy. Evidence from the case studies thus supports the findings of previous research that pro-reform enclaves in key ministries were already active during the presidency of Leonid Kuchma (Wolczuk 2008: 103), well before the Orange Revolution of 2004/5 and the signing of the first EU-Ukraine Action plan, events which have sometimes been misleadingly described as the main trigger for the mobilisation of pro-reform constituencies in Ukraine's state service (Solonenko 2008: 32).

It is also early evidence of the significant role of middle-level officials, acting largely on their own initiative and with few constraints from other domestic actors including their own managers. Both Anatoliy Maksiuta and Olena Nyzhnyk spoke in interview of their frequent feelings of isolation and vulnerability within their own ministries, where senior management tolerated rather than actively encouraged their pro-reform initiatives. As Checkel (2001: 573-574) has suggested it may be that the insulated nature of work in post-communist state institutions, with their formal hierarchies and weak horizontal networks a lasting legacy of the Soviet period, provides fertile ground for relatively autonomous activity with minimal supervision or active support.

*Active 'Champions' of Reform*

Jacoby (2006: 643) underlines the importance of international donors' correctly identifying and reaching 'pockets of reform' and it is apparent that both Maksiuta and Romaniuk were quickly adopted as reform champions by the international donor community. Maksiuta was explicitly identified as such by Deborah Wetzel, the World Bank's Chief Adviser on Budget Reform, and the fact that Serhiy Romaniuk and Olena Nyzhnyk were lead partners to all five of the case study programmes on regional policy suggests that the EU, DFID and CIDA took a similar view of their importance as individuals.

This reflects a wider tendency in international donor thinking, in developing and post-communist countries alike, that reform-minded figures in influential positions in government or politics are able to act as 'change agents' (Robison & Hout 2009: 198), making the kind of progress in public institutional reform which would be beyond the capacity of donors acting on their own. More realistically however it is highly unlikely that individuals, even in senior positions, will be able to bring about any lasting institutional change (Duncan & Williams 2012: 135). Focusing on individual personalities is too often simply the easy option for a donor programme, based on the mistaken assumption that reform can be achieved by supporting particular people.

In practice it may even have the opposite effect of narrowing the circle of potential allies and discouraging horizontal links between pro-reform actors (Wedel 1998: 188-190; Jacoby 2006: 642). The continuing isolation of the leading domestic actors throughout the period of the case study on regional policy suggests that all five technical assistance programmes paid too little regard to the need to broaden the base of domestic support for reform.

### Distinguishing Features of the Case Studies

Despite the above similarities, the case study findings differed in significant ways. The principal distinguishing features were:

- An active domestic constituency already pursuing reform;
- An alliance of donors;
- A clear template for reform;
- Argumentative and normative persuasion;
- An informal coalition of domestic and external actors.

These are discussed in turn below.

*An Active Domestic Constituency Already Pursuing Reform*

The case study findings support the view that the existence of a domestic faction of pro-reform movements, parties or sub-sets of officials is a prerequisite if external agents are to make a significant impact on the course of reform. Indeed the findings of the case studies go further than previous empirical research (Jacoby 2006) to suggest that, rather than a single faction, what is required is a broad base of domestic forces with similar objectives, even if initially these forces may not be working together in any form of alliance.

The decisive difference between the pro-reform enclaves in the Ministry of Finance and the Ministry of Economy was that while each was frequently isolated within its own ministry, domestic actors in the finance ministry were part of a much wider network. Even if it was rather fragile initially, as the case study demonstrates, this network extended beyond government to include leading political figures in the Budget Committee of the *Verkhovna Rada* and powerful big city mayors in the Association of Ukrainian Cities.

Both these domestic allies were at least as active as the Ministry of Finance and the tensions between the ministry and members of the Budget Committee were apparent in early meetings with donors. While international experts clearly regarded Maksiuta as the leading champion of reform, in the opinion of Budget Committee chair Yulia Tymoshenko and regional finance chiefs like Yuriy Balkoviy from Luhans'ka, Maksiuta and his ministry colleagues were if anything rather late converts to the cause.

The participants to this 'unique concurrence' of interests had different agendas. There was pressure on the Government of Ukraine from both the IMF and the World Bank to reform the state budget process overall as part of a package of measures agreed in return for loan support to Ukraine's spiralling budget deficit. However there does not seem to have been any conditionality attached specifically to the system of local government finance. The main concern of the Ministry of Finance was to bring order and control to an increasingly chaotic system of intergovernmental finance and to transfer responsibility, and with it the blame, for day-to-day budget decisions to locally elected city and district authorities.

The *Verkhovna Rada*'s Budget Committee must also have been aware of the pressure coming from the IMF and the World Bank, but the principal motivation of Yulia Tymoshenko, the committee chair and a recently elected and ambitious member of the Rada, was undoubtedly political. Tymoshenko's background was, like Maksiuta's, in the regions and she was aware of the frustration of local governments with the present financing arrangements. If she could deliver a programme of reform she would do much for her growing reputation and would secure a strong electoral base in the big industrial cities.

Lastly, the Association of Ukrainian Cities, increasingly powerful since the adoption of the 1996 Constitution and the 1997 State Law on Local Self-Government, had been campaigning since the mid-1990s for the removal of the authority of state-appointed *oblast* administrations to control the budgets of democratically mandated city councils. Not only did the Association have in its membership the elected mayors of all Ukraine's largest cities, but in its Deputy Director Pavlo Kachur it had the ear of the then Prime Minister. Kachur was one of Viktor Yushchenko's personal advisers and was in a position to secure his support at a time when the future of the reform was most under threat.

There was no comparable network in support of regional policy reform. Leading actors were not only isolated within their own ministry but also within government as a whole. There was little understanding in the Cabinet of Ministers for their flagship proposal, the contract for regional development, the central tenets of which were vehemently and successfully opposed by the Ministry of Finance. Further, instead of implementing the 2005 State Law on the Stimulation of Regional Development and the 2006 State Strategy, in 2007 the incoming government of Viktor Yanukovych established a new Ministry of Regional Development which quickly set about drafting replacement legislation.

The position outside Kyiv was no better. Romaniuk and Nyzhnyk might have looked to the powerful regional governors for support, particularly in relation to the regional contract which seemed to promise regions more stability and predictability in financial planning. But as unelected appointees of the President who could be recalled at any time, governors were never likely to be a strong lobby for reform in the balance of authority between Kyiv and the regions. A more promising reform constituency might have been the popularly elected leaderships of the major cities, but Romaniuk and Nyzhnyk were not helped in this by a ministry vertical which linked them directly with *oblast* administrations but made for much weaker functional and personal contacts with the self-governing cities. It may also be the case that with the introduction of the 2001 Budget Code reform the larger cities had got much of what they wanted (World Bank 2002a: 33-34) and were unlikely to be interested in being drawn into a further and potentially far more difficult struggle.

*An Alliance of Donors*

The strong trilateral relationship between the World Bank, USAID and DFID, where 'each of us had a comparative advantage that we drew on successfully to support reform' was described by one interviewee as 'one of my best experiences in working with others in trying to address policy issues.'[1] In what was a most unusual example of donor cooperation the role of the World Bank was to conduct what Wetzel describes as 'high level dialogue' with leading figures in the Government of Ukraine, including the application of pressure for overall budget reform in return for continued loan finance from the Bank and the IMF. In the process Wetzel herself became a trusted adviser to Yulia Tymoshenko.

Meanwhile DFID experts and USAID's Fiscal Analysis Office focused their attention on work with the Ministry of Finance and the Budget Committee respectively, and on different aspects of the transfer formula. As DFID's lead expert Professor Kenneth Davey observed, 'relations were remarkably

---

[1] E-mail correspondence from Deborah Wetzel, received 18 May 2014.

smooth.....the division [of work] was agreed from the beginning, at the very first meeting.'[2]

Again the contrast with donor behaviour in regional policy reform could hardly have been greater. Here three donors, managing five projects spanning a decade or more and working to broadly the same objectives, operated in apparent isolation from each other and at times at cross purposes. Each new team of experts arrived with their own ideas and little understanding or interest in what had gone before. In the case of the EU's Support to Sustainable Regional Development project this apparent determination to start from a blank page extended to a comprehensive critique and re-writing of legislation which had been prepared with the input of previous donor expertise.[3]

*A Clear Template for Reform*

Leading actors in the Ministry of Finance may already have been convinced of the need for reform and the appropriateness to Ukrainian conditions of the formula-based approach to intergovernmental transfers, but for others in the ministry task groups the model proposed by USAID and DFID experts was not only complex but also in sharp contradiction to years of practice. It was to the model's advantage therefore that, while the formula calculations themselves might be complicated, the fundamental principle of allocating finance transparently and on the basis of objective need, rather than as a result of lobbying and opaque negotiation, was straightforward and appealing to technical specialists in the ministry.

While the template for intergovernmental finance reform was clear and precise, easy to sign up to or reject on the Ukrainian side, issues of regional policy reform occupied a much broader canvas and the advice of international organisations was correspondingly less specific. For example, even in the earlier EU enlargement process the guidance on regional policy in Chapter 22 of the Acquis was deliberately general in recognition of the divergent

---

[2] Interview with Professor Kenneth Davey, Cheltenham, 27 August 2013.
[3] Interview with Olena Nyzhnyk, Kyiv, 29 March 2013.

models of sub-national government among member and accession states alike (Hughes et al. 2004: 68). Similarly, the EU-Ukraine Action Plan of 2005 contained only one short paragraph on regional policy with the broad commitment from the EU to assist with preparing a legislative base and state strategy for regional development (EU-Ukraine Action Plan 2005: para. 2.3).

As the case study findings indicate (chapter IV), the terms of reference for individual projects managed by all three donors, the EU, DFID and CIDA, were similarly all-embracing, with a repeated but broad emphasis on consensus building and increasing institutional capacity. As will be discussed in more detail later, objectives of this breadth and ambition do not marry easily with technical assistance programmes of three to four years' duration.

*Argumentative and Normative Persuasion*

Of equal importance with the clarity of the reform models proposed were the attitude and behaviour of external advisers. In the case study on budget reform the style in which experts offered their advice was remarked upon by both Anatoliy Maksiuta and Yuriy Hanushchak of the Association of Ukrainian Cities. Advisers were praised for their calm, non-didactic and authoritative manner, an approach conceptualised by Checkel as 'argumentative' or 'normative' persuasion (2001:562; 2005: 813).

Relationships based on trust and mutual respect were far less easily fostered in the context of the frequent turnover of visiting experts that was characteristic of donor interventions in the regional policy case study. Although there is little direct evidence on the quality of the interaction between domestic and external actors, it appears that the relationships with Ministry of Economy officials were at best distant in the EU's Assistance to Regional Development project, while in the Support to Sustainable Regional Development programme the attitude of EU advisers was described as often 'inflexible' and conveying the 'impression that they as experts were right and ministry officials were fools.'[4]

---

[4] Interview with Olena Nyzhnyk, Kyiv, 29 March 2013.

## An Informal Coalition of Domestic and External Actors

In the Budget Code reform at least, the factors were now present for the establishment of an informal, ad hoc coalition or alliance sufficiently strong and cohesive to overcome the expected resistance of powerful opposition players. This did indeed emerge in the shape of the President Kuchma himself and his appointed regional governors, the latter having the most to lose from the reform since they would have to give up their powers of patronage in the settling of annual budgets at city and district level.

The case study findings suggest that the importance of the input of the three international donors to the coalition was not only that it offered an appropriate policy solution communicated in a flexible and persuasive manner. As Association of Ukrainian Cities expert Yuriy Hanushchak comments, the 'most important contribution of donors was to provide a space where there could be an open dialogue about reform where key figures could speak openly without feeling under pressure' and to 'make it all sound possible and not overly complicated.'[5] This implies that advisers had a significant motivational role also. There are clear indications here of the mobilising effect of external actors and of the capacity of expert assistance to help formerly divergent domestic interests to coalesce into an effective force for reform.

## The Policy Transfer Network

### The Policy Transfer Network as Synthesis

The concept of a *policy transfer network* provides a useful synthesis of the key factors which enable a programme of international technical assistance to have a tangible influence on policy reform, even in circumstances where there is no political consensus on the direction the reform in question should take. Evans and Davies (1999: 376) describe such a network as an 'ad hoc, action-oriented phenomenon set up with the specific intention of engineering rapid policy change,' which functions only for the time the transfer of a particular policy idea is occurring. The policy transfer network consists of both domestic

---

[5] Interview with Yuriy Hanushchak, Kyiv, 21 March 2013.

and external agents and functions at a meso-level, between intergovernmental relations and donor programmes at the macro-level and the micro-level of individual domestic institutions where policy change is implemented. Once the transfer of policy has been secured the network has no further reason to exist.

The value of the policy transfer network concept to the present study is that it builds on earlier references to informal coalitions and ad hoc alliances in providing an insight into how endogenous and exogenous influences interact with one another to facilitate actual policy change. On the domestic side it underscores the importance of there being an alliance of interests, rather than a single domestic faction as Jacoby suggests (2006: 629), each with its own motivation for reform but prepared to work jointly for a finite period to achieve a common goal. In the case of the Budget Code reform there could hardly have been a more formidable network of domestic actors than one which involved senior politicians, well-placed and ambitious state servants, and a powerful lobby group representing big city interests.

The notion of a network also captures well the key role played by informal, interpersonal relationships as the basis for trust and communication between these differing, potentially conflicting, interests. The interpersonal relationships originating in Bohdan Kravchenko's seminal Insitute of Public Administration in the early 1990s were to play a pivotal role at critical points in the progress of the reform, including in securing the support of Prime Minister Viktor Yushchenko in the face of determined opposition from President Kuchma. No less crucially, external actors were able to become trusted members of this network themselves. Important though it was that the policy template for formula-based transfers was specific and comprehensible, the shared understanding between the three donors involved and the careful building of rapport with Ukrainian partners through the sensitive delivery of expert advice, were if anything even more decisive.

Most importantly, the findings of the case studies suggest that the role of such a network is particularly significant when there is powerful domestic opposition to a reform policy. For example it is highly probable that the transfer formula element of the 2001 Budget Code reform would have been thrown out but for the coordinated action of domestic and external actors working together, both formally and informally. It is equally clear that attempts to reform Ukraine's regional policy, including the intervention of five major donor projects, were constrained by the absence of an effective pro-reform lobby or network, broad-based enough to overcome the resistance of powerful opponents to reform in government and in the regions.

Jacoby's dismissive comment that the policy transfer model forces 'large numbers of contrasting motives and strategies into one overstuffed concept' (2004: 3) thus seems somewhat misjudged. On the contrary the Evans and Davies conceptualisation of a policy transfer network concept adds substantial explanatory power to Jacoby's original formulation of an informal coalition by providing a framework for examining indicating how such an alliance functions internally. It is the network's web of interpersonal relationships between domestic and external actors which enables it to achieve its key objectives of strengthening the commitment of supporters of reform and deterring opponents of change (Jacoby 2006: 625). It was the respectful, problem-solving approach of external advisers which allowed them full access to the network and which provided their Ukrainian partners with a clear reform policy around which to mobilise.

Conclusions to Part I

Part I of the chapter has introduced the concept of *normative institutional isomorphism* as a way to understand the export of institutional norms and practices from one jurisdiction to another through the process of international technical assistance. The evidence of the two case studies was examined with regard to the influence of this process on the reform of Ukraine's intergovernmental financial relations and regional policy.

In both cases there was evidence of pro-reform activism among middle-ranking state servants originating before contact was made with international donors. When technical assistance programmes began work in each area project experts were successful in identifying and establishing cooperation with these key domestic actors. However, only in the case of the Budget Code reform did this interaction lead to tangible progress with reform, the deciding factor being the establishment of a *policy transfer network*. The network was an alliance of domestic and external actors broadly based enough to overcome powerful political opposition to the Budget Code reform.

While the technocratic nature of expert-led technical assistance rests on the assumption that reform is a question which can be resolved through reason and consensus, the evidence of both case studies is that international donors were involved in reform processes which were strongly contested politically. The difference in outcome between the two, and the reason donors were able to influence the course of reform in one case and not the other, is explicable largely by the existence of the policy transfer network.

From the evidence presented in the case studies it is a reasonable inference that, where technical assistance programmes are working in areas of reform which are politically contested by powerful opposing forces, the establishment of a policy transfer network of pro-reform domestic and external actors is a likely prerequisite if international assistance is to exert influence on the course of reform. However as the case study on fiscal decentralisation has shown, the success of the Budget Code reform was short-lived for reasons which are discussed in Part II. Once the policy transfer network has fulfilled its purpose and disbanded, there is no guarantee that reform will be sustained over the longer term.

## Part II: Reform Failure and the Political Economy Analysis of Development Theory

Introduction

The second part of the analysis of the evidence from the two case studies sets out to explain how in the longer run both intergovernmental finance reform and the attempt to overhaul and Europeanise Ukraine's approach to regional policy were unsuccessful and the influence of external advice at best marginal. It will be argued that institutional factors on both sides played a central role in this, with those on the donor side no less important in contributing to the failure of technical assistance programmes to influence the reform process in the long term.

In the theoretical literature, the most persuasive explanation of the impact on reform of this interplay of domestic and external institutional forces is to be found in the *political economy analysis* of Development Studies.

The structure of the argument is as follows. First it is suggested that in making a step change from the relatively straightforward task of sharing know-how and skills with a post-communist country in transition to the more complex and developmental goal of building new state institutions, the objectives of technical assistance to Ukraine were brought into line with the aims of wider international aid policy towards developing countries. This is followed by a summary of the political economy analysis of the assumptions underlying much of the external advice given to the governments of those countries, in particular the belief that the relatively stable state institutions of developed OECD countries are an appropriate model for export to some of the world's poorest and least developed nations.

The relevance of this critique to the case study findings is then examined and it is argued that the problems arising in the attempt to transfer institutional arrangements from donor countries to Ukraine are analogous to those experienced in developing countries and may therefore help to explain the longer term failure of both case study reforms. Foremost among these problems is an inadequate appreciation on the part of the donor community of the *neo-patrimonial nature of the Ukrainian state* and its institutional relationships, a reality with which the formal government to government interventions of technical assistance projects find it difficult to engage. This proposition is supported by reference both to the case study evidence and to previous studies of the role of patronage and clientelism in countries of the former Soviet Union, including Ukraine.

From Know How Sharing to the Mainstream of International Development

There was a fundamental change in the objectives of international technical assistance to Ukraine at the turn of the millennium. The change, reflected in the programmes of all major donors advising on public administrative reform, was from the largely reactive and frequently ad hoc sharing of know-how and skills of the 1990s to the complex and strategic task of building institutional capacity. The effect of this re-think was to bring programmes of technical assistance to Ukraine firmly into the mainstream of international development policy. It represented a major shift from an approach which had stressed the 'finite nature' of the commitment to a state in transition and which was clearly distinguished from the 'deeper longer-term partnership' promised to the developing countries of Sub-Saharan Africa and South Asia (UK DFID 1997: 39-42).

Accordingly, the new vocabulary of institution building in Ukraine began to mirror the language of long-term development being used in the wider international aid community. Just as the World Bank was asserting that international aid to developing countries could be the 'midwife of good institutions' and that poor countries with sound policies and high quality institutions were able to grow more quickly than those without (1998: 83, 11), so donor government reports on Ukraine now referred to the need to address the country's 'institutional and structural defects' (UK DFID 1999: 12) and a commitment to 'support institutional reforms….and achieve a systemic impact' (EU Commission 2001: 1).

With regard to aid policy towards developing countries, the introduction of the ubiquitous and imprecise concept of 'good governance' (UK DFID 1997: 21; World Bank 1998: 23), and its identification with strong and accountable state institutions able to 'do well those things which governments must do' (World Bank 1998: 83), confirmed the implicitly normative nature of the institutional development project. The demanding, even idealised, standards prescribed in the good governance view of effective government are well captured in the following:

> It is small and limited in engagement, formalized in mission and process and drawing limited revenues primarily from domestic sources. High-quality personnel devise and implement needed programs and deliver efficient and effective services via participatory processes and through formalized, disciplined, efficient and targeted financial management. Responsiveness to the citizenry's changing needs is high, effected through transparent, decentralized and politically neutral structures; consistently, even during political instability, without impeding (even supporting) the private sector (Andrews 2008: 382).

Idealised it might be, but the same normative goal was now evident in the language of the country strategies of the major international donors working in Ukraine. 'Government institutions [which] are more effective, transparent and accountable' was identified as the strategic objective of future programmes of assistance (USAID 2002: 29), and the priorities for administrative and economic reform were to include the problems of 'unlimited centralised management' of the state apparatus and the lagging privatisation programme, both judged to be unfavourable to the growth of business and investment (EU Commission 2001: 8).

Improved standards of governance based on strengthened but also more responsive state institutions thus became the strategic goal of international donor programmes, and while the notion of Ukraine as a country 'in transition' continued to feature prominently in donor thinking,[6] the

---

[6] Ukraine is described as a state in transition 15 times in the EU's Country Strategy for 2002-2006 (EU Commission 2001) and 25 times in the USAID Country Strategy for 2003-2007 (USAID 2002).

commitment to provide assistance now appeared to have become open-ended and long-term rather than finite and transitory.

## Experts Bringing Solutions (i): Developing Countries & the Political Economy Analysis

The central argument of political economy analysis is that international donors in developing countries have interpreted the inherently political process of institution building as a problem which can be addressed by applying technical and managerial solutions. This approach rests on the false assumption that the stable institutions of OECD states are the result of rational choice rather than the outcome of a complex, long-term interaction and conflict between state and society, public and private actors, formal and informal institutions. In other words there is a failure to understand that what is known as 'good' governance is not the cause but rather the result of economic, social and political development (Chang 2002: 129, 139; Unsworth et al. 2010).

Starting from a default position that the objective is to align as far as possible the institutions of a developing country with those of a developed western economy, the 'whole institutional ethos' of international donors becomes one of 'experts bringing solutions' (Unsworth et al. 2010: 1; Unsworth 2009: 890). If the obstacles to improved governance are technical and managerial, then the remedies are to be found in adopting more effective policies and in building the capacity of the personnel who will be responsible for implementing them, and similar 'minor technocratic efforts' (Carothers 2002: 17).

All too often the result is a reliance on standardised, off-the-peg best practice solutions with limited relevance to what can be accomplished in practice, provided by supply-driven development agencies working to short time horizons (Fritz & Menocal 2007: 545, 549; Levy 2010: 1; Unsworth et al. 2010; Booth 2011a: S7). It is not uncommon for expert advice on best practice to be shaped more by vogue than by evidence, the attempts to export the fashionable ideas of New Public Management[7] being a case in point (Batley

---

[7] The ideas of New Public Management are explained in chapter I.

& Larbi 2004: 28-29; Fritz & Menocal 2007: 545).

Outcomes have hardly been encouraging. The World Bank's assessment of progress in introducing reforms to public administration through its own sponsored programmes in developing countries between 1998 and 2006 found that almost 60% had registered no gains at all, while only 10% had made significant advances (World Bank 2008: 46). The 'profound difficulties' experienced in good governance interventions in general had caused many leading donors to abandon them in favour of stipulating an already existing level of governance as a prerequisite for agreeing a package of aid (Hout & Robison 2009: 4).

Institutions are context specific and not amenable to a 'quick fix' (Williams et al. 2011: S33). The challenge for international donors in developing countries is to see problems rather than solutions as the starting point, and instead of advocating demanding and ill-fitting good practice from OECD country experience, to emphasise locally identified problems as a way of understanding the country context and opportunities for change (Andrews 2013: 217). Recognising what there is to build on can be the first step towards a development agency acting in a small way to promote reform by helping to improve what already exists. 'Good enough' governance and 'best fit' policies are more promising strategies for building the necessary consensus to ensure that reform policies are compatible with local circumstances and politics and have a realistic chance of being put into practice (Booth 2011a: S22; Grindle 2004, 2007; Williams et al. 2011: S53; Frodin 2011: S195).

Political economy analysis goes a step further in arguing that the overwhelming focus of donor attention on the strengthening of formal rule-based state institutions which reflect a clear separation between the public and private spheres, is misplaced in developing societies where weak governance and the prevalence of networks of patronage mean that the division is much more porous (Unsworth et al. 2010: 70-71). Donors are institutionally inclined to work from mental models of stable Western European and North American societies which are characterised by a relatively high degree of consensus about the 'rules of the game' (North 1990: 3), and where formal institutions have clearly defined and legally established boundaries to their authority (Malygina 2010: 11). In many developing countries the rules of the game are either not well established or are contested, and power is exercised through informal institutions and networks (Leftwich 2006: 3-4), where informal institutions are defined as 'socially shared rules, usually unwritten, that are created, communicated, and enforced outside officially sanctioned channels (Helmke & Levitsky 2004: 727).

What matters in political economy analysis is how formal and informal institutions interact which, it is argued, will be a key determinant of the course of development. Often in developing countries there is no shortage of well articulated formal laws and state institutions resembling Weberian models of bureaucracy. But more important than any formal arrangements are the informal realities of how they work in practice and the means by which informal rules are able to shape the decisions and outcomes of formal institutions. The disappointing outcomes of donor interventions aimed at institutional development follow directly from a neglect of the role of informal institutions (Leftwich & Sen 2010: 12; Duncan & Williams 2012: 134, 142; Unsworth et al. 2010: 889; Helmke & Levitsky 2004: 726).

What is needed is a more 'politically intelligent' approach by donors which looks at what is going on behind the façade of formal state institutions. There should be less focus on ambitious programmes to strengthen state capacity and more on the interests and informal relationships which underpin formal institutions. Above all perhaps, political economy analysis is an appeal to donors to improve their political awareness of the local situation and to make this the starting point of their interventions rather than a set of preconceived technical solutions. They must also accept the need for much longer-term perspective on change (Unsworth et al. 2010: 69; Unsworth 2009: 891-892; UK DFID 2003: 2).

There are major institutional barriers on the donor side which make this difficult territory to negotiate. The formal government-to government nature of interventions means that informal processes may be deliberately hidden from donors' view (Booth 2011a: S18), and development agencies have strong financial incentives to show tangible short-term progress and give their domestic taxpayers a straightforward and optimistic story which confirms the commitment of their partners. The alternative account of the depth and intractability of the challenge, and frequently the limited degree of local ownership other than in the formal sense, is a hard one for development agencies to admit to themselves let alone explain to their often sceptical sponsors at home (Unsworth 2009: 890; Duncan & Williams 2012: 198).

In the end the political economy analysis does not provide a fully convincing answer to the donors' dilemma. Observations such as 'informality, instead of being the main problem, could also be part of the solution', or that donors should see their role as 'convenors, facilitators and politically aware contributors to serious debate' (Unsworth et al. 2010: 70; Unsworth 2009: 891), are the worst kind of 'development speak'. Similarly DFID's 'Drivers of Change' policy, derived from a political economy analysis perspective, can only offer the vague notion of institutional change resulting from the 'interaction between structural features, formal and informal institutions, and individual agents' (UK DFID 2003: 3). It may be that the principal value of the political economy analysis lies less in its practical policy prescriptions than in its insights into the underlying reasons for the failure of so many donor interventions (Leftwich 2006: 17; Hout 2009: 36). The remaining part of the chapter will argue that this holds true as much for donor programmes in Ukraine as it does for those in developing countries.

## Internal Contradictions in Donor Policy towards Public Administrative Reform in Ukraine

The impact of programmes of international technical assistance in support of institutional reform in Ukraine's system of public administration has been compromised by internal contradictions in the policy of donors themselves. Ironically these are largely a reflection of institutional factors on the donor side.

On one hand the decision to the abandon the initial over-simplified strategy of transforming Ukraine's political economy through the sharing of skills and know-how, in favour of the far more complex and ambitious task of rebuilding the country's state institutions, appeared to reflect a re-set of western powers' early assumptions about the linear process of 'transition' taking place in post-communist countries. However the mechanism selected for the execution of the new strategy was to continue with short-term stand-alone projects, a model much better suited to the discarded assumptions of a finite period of transition rather than to a longer term process of development. Analysis of the problem may have changed but the means of addressing it were to remain the same.

The constraints imposed by the fixed-term project cycle have reinforced forms of donor behaviour which are characterised by short-termism and a default reliance on imported best-practice solutions of questionable relevance in the Ukrainian context. In addition, the technical 'projectification' of the development process in Ukraine has not only served to 'occlude' its essentially political nature (Swain 2007: 161, 165), but has also limited donors' ability to understand, let alone engage with, the underlying obstacles to reform. As noted in the two case studies the networks of patronage and neo-patrimonial relationships which both symbolise and reinforce Ukraine's institutional weakness have been left largely undisturbed by the interventions of international technical assistance.

## Institutional Development and the Project Cycle of Technical Assistance

There is an inherent tension between the complex long-term goal of institution building and what SIGMA[8] describes as the 'technocratic processes of [donor] project management technology and project cycles' (SIGMA 2006: 28). From the late 1990s both professional and academic opinion in the field of development assistance had moved away from individual project-based interventions in favour of a sector wide, rolling programme approach (UK DFID 1997; World Bank 1998; Bossuyt 2001; Killick 2004). The effectiveness of short-term 'techno-managerial' solutions was limited to 'very auspicious

---

[8] Support for Improvement in Governance and Management (SIGMA), a joint initiative of the OECD and the EU.

settings.....where there is a committed leadership [and] a broadly based coalition in favour of reform' (World Bank 2005: 298).

Every donor intervention in the two case studies was designed as a fixed-term project, generally of three to four years' duration. This included the DFID and USAID programmes which advised on fiscal decentralisation, and the DFID, EU and CIDA programmes whose brief was to assist with regional policy reform. Only one of the projects discussed in the case studies, CIDA's Regional Governance and Development programme, was extended for a further two years. However this was on condition that significant alterations to its terms of reference were accepted by the contractor, in effect turning the extension period into a new project.

The negative impact of the project cycle on programmes aimed at institutional change is a factor acknowledged by donors themselves. An evaluation of the EU's TACIS programme in the former Soviet Union, including Ukraine, found that its interventions on institutional and administrative reform consisted largely of 'stand-alone technical assistance projects [which] often achieve good results at project level, but have limited impact at sector and national policy level due to a lack of continuity and coherent long-term sector planning.' Because time horizons were so restricted there was a tendency to 'focus on outputs rather than outcomes and long-term objectives' (EU Commission 2006: x; EU Commission 2007b: 11).

Similarly an independent review of its Ukraine programme commissioned by CIDA concluded that 'while individual capacity can be built fairly readily, it is a much greater challenge to embed change in an institution' and that in relation to institutional capacity building, 'sustainability remained open to question' when activities had short time horizons (CIDA 2011: 63, 27). There is broad agreement in the donor community that, in the area of public administration particularly, 'successful reform requires sustained technical attention over many years' (SIGMA 2006: 28).

Two DFID experts with direct experience of work in Ukraine also point to what they regard as the conflict between the goal of institutional development and the constraints imposed by the project cycle. One, who was DFID's Ukraine Project Manager when the decision was taken in London, against her advice, to discontinue LARGIS at the end of its three-year term and therefore cease work on both fiscal decentralistion and regional policy reform, argues that 'progress in changing complex, interdependent systems' takes time and 'it doesn't happen in two to three years'.[9] The second, an experienced professional in international development and Governance Adviser to DFID's programme in Ukraine until 2001, takes a similar view that regrettably 'only lip service is paid to the need to engage in programmes of institutional development for periods of no less than ten years.'[10]

Experts Bringing Solutions (ii): Ukraine and the Output Culture of Technical Assistance

As Unsworth has remarked in relation to the advice offered to the governments of developing countries, donor governments and development agencies are not stupid and they are conscious that institution building is not a simple matter of importing unadapted OECD-style models of good government. Nevertheless the pressure to demonstrate short-term results to justify the funds they receive makes it hard for them to discard this approach (2009: 889; Unsworth et al. 2010: 1-2).

In Ukraine the temptation for donors to rely on 'best practice' models, which may or may not be suited to the local context, is reinforced by the limited time horizons imposed by the fixed-term project cycle. Programme terms of reference make liberal use of phrases like 'approximate the Ukrainian regional development framework to the European best practices' (EU TACIS ARD 2001:7) or 'support Ukraine in developing a regional development policy compatible with European best practice' (EU ENPI SSRD 2006: 23). CIDA's Country Strategy for Ukraine claims that the Canadian agency has 'become a leader in building capacity and transferring best practices' (CIDA 2009: 2).

---

[9] Interview with Olga Sandakova, Kyiv, 17 October 2013.
[10] Interview with Garth Glentworth, London, 18 February 2014.

The outcome is often frustration on the Ukrainian side. In the case study on regional policy reform for example, Ministry of Economy officials were sharply critical of the efforts of EU project experts to transfer inappropriate models of a State Fund for Regional Development and a nationwide network of regional development agencies into Ukrainian legislation. Both proposals as presented to the Ministry were considered to be out of touch with Ukrainian reality but the project team was nevertheless unwilling to show flexibility on the question of adapting them to local conditions. Here was a textbook example of experts taking short-cuts and designing new institutions on behalf of their partners (Crawford & Lijphart 1995: 196).

Failure to adjust a best practice model to one which is closer to 'best fit' can lead to a partial or incomplete reform which is not sustainable. In the case study on fiscal decentralisation, the introduction of formula-based transfers for the financing of Ukraine's local government, an approach based largely on British and Western European models, was initially hailed as a bold and successful reform. However, the reform quickly ran into difficulty because it resulted in two incompatible systems operating alongside one another: a formula-based approach which allocated state funds for education, health and social care between sub-national governments on a relative needs basis determined by the finite resources available, leaving local councils with discretion over actual expenditure decisions; and a historical and still centralised norm-based system, supported by legislation, which required local government to finance a prescribed level of staffing and set of budget institutions[11] per head of population.

DFID and USAID project experts themselves recognise that insufficient attention was given to the inconsistencies and contradictions arising from the reform.[12] By the time these became fully apparent both donors' interventions on fiscal decentralisation had reached the end of their preordained project

---

[11] Institutions identified in the annual budget of a unit of local government on the basis of ministry norms.

[12] Interviews with Pawel Swianiewicz, Warsaw, 12 October 2013, and Wayne Thirsk, Kyiv, 27 November 2012, 29 November 2012, 28 March 2013.

cycles and external advice was no longer available to help put right the anomalies inadvertently created by the introduction of a reform solution which addressed only part of the original problem.

Short time horizons also lead to a reliance on formulaic solutions driven more by the 'standardised portfolios' of contractors (Carothers 2002: 18) than by an analysis of needs on the ground. In the case study on regional policy the proliferation of regional and municipal development strategies, very few of which were ever to reach the implementation stage, is indicative of the one-size-fits-all supply-driven approach of development agencies highlighted by political economy analysis critique (Fritz & Menocal 2007: 548). It suggests a project environment where short-term visible activity is allowed to take precedence over longer-term objectives which are more challenging to achieve, and where there is pressure to 'focus on outputs rather than outcomes' (EU Commission 2006: x).

The reporting requirements of the EU in particular foster this culture of short-termism. The final report of the Assistance to Regional Development project itemises 38 individual outputs (EU TACIS ARD 2006), the Support to Sustainable Local Development 51 'deliverables' (EU TACIS SLD 2010), and the Support to Sustainable Regional Development a massive 74 outputs (EU ENPI SSRD 2011). Examples of outputs are said to include 'drafted legal frameworks, tools, models, guidelines, methods, case studies, knowledge, or recommendations that can be taken up by the beneficiary' (EU ENPI SSRD 2011: 33). A reporting culture which focuses on project outputs is one where the reported achievements of projects become little more than a reflection of the activities of the project contractor and 'their particular accountability arrangements' (SIGMA 2006: 28), and have little relevance to outcomes which might be of benefit to the Ukrainian partner.

Behind the Façade of Ukraine's Formal Institutions: the Political Intelligence Deficit

The relations of government to government technical assistance to countries such as Ukraine are by definition based on agreements with formal institutions and implicitly reflect what Hyden calls a consensual view of politics on the part of the donor (Hyden 2008: 262-263), rather than a recognition that the process of reform invariably involves a clash of interests (Roland 2002: 31).

The details are spelled out in memoranda of understanding, joint action plans and individual project terms of reference. As an instrument international technical assistance is therefore not well equipped to deal with situations where the direction of reform is politically contested, other than in the narrow circumstances described in Part I of the chapter where gains may be possible in the short run.

Over the longer term, public administrative reform in particular has been 'a casualty to bitter political in-fighting' (Youngs 2009: 905) because of the threat it poses for many deeply entrenched interests. The weakly developed political antennae of international donors have habitually failed to anticipate how these interests are able to re-assert themselves behind the façade of change at the level of formal institutional arrangements. When in 2002 DFID took the decision to discontinue work with the Ministry of Finance following the successful adoption of the Budget Code, and to concentrate instead on establishing two regional partnerships with Donets'ka and L'vivs'ka *oblasts*, Peter Fortune was one of the DFID advisers in London responsible for the decision. According to Fortune:

> 'London had control over all decisions. Ukrainian staff were regarded as administrators of the programme and not taken very seriously in the professional sense. This was probably a legacy of colonial days, extending to the dominance of the English language. I can say quite clearly that when the decision was taken to work exclusively in the regions no one, including myself, really understood the role of *oblast* state administrations. But there were no objections among the other advisers in London to stopping work with the ministries. If there were objections from our Ukrainian staff in Kyiv – I don't recall if there were - these probably would not have

been taken that seriously, for the reason I have already given.'[13]

Better political intelligence might have helped DFID in London to understand that, because of Ukraine's system of 'dual subordination' where deconcentrated education, health and social care departments at *oblast* level are responsible not only to the regional governor but also to ministries in Kyiv, it was *oblast* officials who presided over the contradiction between formula-based budget transfers and norm-based obligations with regard to the level of service. Far from being by-passed in the budget transfer process, as the reform of intergovernmental finance had intended, regional administrations which had consistently opposed the new Budget Code were now in a position to exploit one of its major weaknesses.

The significance of this lay less in the formal ability of *oblast* departments to require districts and municipalities to adhere to norms in their spending decisions, and more in the space it opened up for the continuation of the practice of patronage which the dismantling of the *Matryoshka* pyramid had been intended to end. As the case study on fiscal decentralisation suggests, the most vulnerable to this practice were the poorer municipal and district authorities where norm-based staffing and facility costs accounted for a high percentage of annual budgets.

As the thick fog of patronage began to obscure the intended transparency and simplicity of local transfer calculations, so local executors of delegated functions soon found that in spite of the reform they were to 'remain total hostages' ('*polnost'iu ostaiutsia zalozhhikami*') to arbitrary decision-making from above (Maynzyuk & Dzhygyr: 2008/9: 5) .

In the case study on regional policy the assistance given by EU project experts to the newly established Ministry of Regional Development and Construction in the re-writing of the 2005 Law on the Stimulation of Regional Development was another, more serious, example of poor political intelligence. In this instance it resulted in the contribution of the project being unknowingly 'in-

---

[13] Interview with Peter Fortune, DFID Adviser on Private Sector Development 1999-2008, London, 16 April 2013.

strumentalised' by vested interests rather than providing support to the emergence of stable institutions (SIGMA 2006: 28).

The Ministry of Regional Development and Construction had been created in the spring of 2007 nine months after Viktor Yanukovych succeeded Yulia Tymoshenko to the post of Prime Minister. Serhiy Romaniuk, at that time First Deputy Minister of Economy with lead responsibility in government for regional policy, describes the decision as 'purely political' in nature.[14] Certainly the decision to transfer the responsibility for the allocation of state capital grants or subventions to the regions from the Ministry of Economy to the new Ministry of Regional Development and Construction had all the appearance of a spoiling strategy to bypass the greater transparency required in the contract for regional development, the major innovation in the 2005 law.

The 'cult of targeted subventions'(chapter III), payments to assist regions or cities with current maintenance and repairs to schools, polyclinics and other community facilities, refers to the growing use of one-off grants to regional and local governments approved individually by the Cabinet of Ministers. There had already been a sharp rise in these under the premiership of Yulia Tymoshenko, but the establishment of the new ministry allowed the practice to be institutionalised. Targeted subvention payments were a means of subjective 'steering by hand' (*'ruchnoe upravlenie'*) and took place outside the normal budget process. Generally they would appear as a single line in the state budget, specifying only a very broad purpose such as the socio-economic development of a given region.[15] In 2007 alone the Ministry of Regional Development and Construction awarded 421 of these single payments on the authority of the Cabinet of Ministers, ranging in size from 1.6m UAH to 200m UAH, provoking criticism by the government's own Accounting Chamber (*Rakhunkova Palata*) as being in breach of the 2001 Budget Code (Romaniuk 2013: 256).

---

[14] Interview with Serhiy Romaniuk, Kyiv, 23 March 2013.
[15] Interview with Ihor Shpak, former expert with the USAID-funded Fiscal Analysis Office, Kyiv, 20 March 2013.

The practice of *ruchnoe upravlenie* not only undermined the guiding principle of the regional contract, that there should be a single transparent mechanism for the allocation of all state capital grants, but also reduced the finance available for use on infrastructure development and other strategic purposes. Infrastructure-related payments fell from a high of 27.4% of all subventions in 2006 to 15.9% in 2010 and 11.3% in 2012 (Romaniuk 2013: 254). Meanwhile the first contracts for regional development, agreed with Donets'ka and L'vivs'ka *oblasts*, were faltering and losing credibility due to a lack of finance.

As had been the case with the Budget Code reform, the practice of 'steering by hand' provided an ideal opportunity for the continued exercise of patronage in the allocation of funds from the state budget, which the introduction of contracts for regional development had threatened to make more problematic. In their cooperation with the new ministry in the discrediting of the 2005 legislation, and in particular the provision for regional contracts, EU experts had become unwitting allies in the process of keeping the patronage door firmly open.

## Ukraine as a Neo-Patrimonial State

As noted in chapter I a number of scholars have drawn attention to the neo-patrimonial nature of post-independence Ukraine and other states of the former Soviet Union. The case study on regional policy has provided detailed empirical data on how this manifests itself at a regional and city level, and how little understanding of the phenomenon there is in the donor community.

Malygina (2010: 10) defines a neo-patrimonial state as one where the public and private spheres are *de jure* separated, but *de facto* the differentiation does not exist. Its main features are appropriation of the public realm by private interests, with networks of patronage able to flourish at the intersections between state institutions, as in the manipulation of intergovernmental transfers and state capital grants described above, and at intersections between the state and the economy, typically the activities of 'Conversion Centres' and Zaporizhia City's 'Golden Office'.

In the case study on regional policy all donor programmes were actively supporting their regional or municipal government partners in working more effectively with economic actors, particularly through the collaborative preparation of local strategies for social and economic development. For example, promotion of a strong private business sector, with an improved regulatory climate which would be attractive to domestic and foreign investors, was the principal goal of USAID's Local Economic Development (LED) programme, and a strategic priority of the Zaporiz'ka Regional Development Strategy prepared with the help of CIDA's Regional Governance and Development project.[16]

However, there is nothing in the written reports of either of these two programmes, including in independent evaluations, which suggests any awareness of influences on the outcome of their interventions beyond the relationships with their formal partners at municipal and regional level.

For example an analysis of USAID's LED programme prepared by external consultants states simply that in the 76 municipalities in which project experts worked the strategic planning process had 'spawned.....public-sector commitment to improving the physical and regulatory business environment [and] strategic thinking about growing jobs and investment', leading to the creation of an estimated 1600-4600 new small and medium-sized businesses (USAID LED 2009: 16, 20). The conclusions of CIDA's Regional Governance and Development (RGD) project in Zaporiz'ka are more optimistic still. The contractor's final report states that 'a full-cycle model of.....strategic planning, implementation, and monitoring for regional economic development is now institutionalized in Zaporiz'ka *oblast* [including] establishment of a transparent and competitive funding mechanism to access financing from the state budget for strategic priority projects.....Zaporiz'ka has become an experimental ground for showing all the other *oblasts* how a regional development strategy can be formulated, implemented, monitored and evaluated with significant public engagement' (CUI RGD 2013: para. 3.1.4). The case study evidence of the presence of so-called Conversion Centres in many of Ukraine's towns and cities and the shadowy influence of the

---

[16] A copy of the strategy can be accessed at <www.zoda.gov.ua>.

'*Smotryashchiy*' figure in Zaporizhia City throws a different light on the realism of these judgements and suggests that they are in need of fundamental reappraisal.

The case study findings are consistent with previous studies of the increasingly neo-patrimonial nature of post-independence Ukraine (Fisun 2003; Fritz 2004, 2005, 2007; Haukkala 2008; Wolowski 2008; Malygina 2010) and of former Soviet Union states more generally (Linz & Stepan 1997; Roland 2002; Wedel 2003; Gel'man 2004; Franke et al. 2009; Whitmore 2010; Stewart et al. 2012). While the events of 2013/14 have demonstrated a particular association between the presidency of Viktor Yanukovych and the rise of neo-patrimonial relations in the government and economic management of Ukraine, the evidence of these studies is that the phenomenon has been pervasive since Leonid Kuchma's second term as president between 1999 and 2004 (Fritz 2007: 57; Malygina 2010: 12).

Although it has been suggested that this is best explained as the re-emergence of relationships that are a legacy of the Soviet past and therefore 'deeply embedded in [Ukraine's] political culture' (Malygina 2010: 12; Granovsky & Nanivska 2010: 16), it was argued in chapter II that a more persuasive analysis places it in the context of the state fragmentation and de-institutionalisation that occurred in other post-Soviet states in the 1990s. This was significantly greater than any comparable process in the countries of Central and Eastern Europe in the same period (Linz & Stepan 1997: 449; Roland 2002: 40; Gel'man 2004: 1028; Fritz 2007: 4).

If legacy had a part to play in this, it was arguably more in the erosion and hollowing out of the legitimacy of state institutions in the late Soviet period (Shlapentokh 1989; Fritz 2007: 41-42), followed in Ukraine's case by a protracted and contested process of state building. This opened the way for the emergence in the 1990s of what Fritz (2004: 11) describes as 'opaque groups', more or less invisible networks of patronage and clientelism operating between the state and private sectors whose power was not offset either by more visible organised interests or by the still weak institutions of the state (Wedel, 2003: 428; Haukkala 2008: 1614).

As the new millennium began, this 'modernised' form of neo-patrimonialism (Fisun 2003: 3), operating behind the façade of now stronger and superficially modern state institutions, was able to shape the choices available to economic and political actors and to determine *de facto* the new rules of the game (Gel'man 2004: 1028; Fritz 2007: 57). Ironically it was only at this point that programmes of international assistance began to take a belated interest in the functioning of Ukraine's public institutions.

For reasons analogous to those discussed in the literature of development theory the issue of neo-patrimonialism is difficult for international donors in Ukraine to confront. It challenges the fundamental assumptions on which donor programmes base their partnerships with formal state institutions at national and sub-national levels. This dilemma is sharpened by the fixed-term project model of technical assistance in Ukraine, where the transitory nature of project interventions and regular turnover of external advisers mean that individual programmes have neither the opportunity nor the incentive to look beyond the façade of the ministries or regional administrations with whom they work. In the words of one DFID project manager, technical assistance programmes and their Ukrainian partners 'inhabit two parallel institutional worlds.'[17]

Conclusions

The aim of this chapter has been to locate international technical assistance to public administrative reform in Ukraine in an appropriate theoretical framework by reference to the evidence of two empirical case studies on changing the relationship between national and sub-national tiers of government. Beyond this, its purpose has been to draw on theory to explain the degree of influence programmes of technical assistance are able to exert over the outcome of reform processes in a post-communist state like Ukraine. The analysis has employed theoretical concepts from three disciplines: Institutional Theory, Comparative Politics and Development Studies.

---

[17] Michael Chambers, Project Manager DFID 'Action Donbas', staff training session, Donets'ka, June 2007.

It has been argued that international assistance to the reform of public administration in Ukraine is an isomorphic process, involving the deliberate transfer of models of state institutions from donor countries where they are regarded as good practice. The concept of *normative institutional isomorphism* is drawn from Institutional Theory, particularly the work of Di Maggio and Powell (1991) and is used because it captures both the idea that the institutions that are 'right' in one setting can be transferred to another, and the inherent asymmetry in the donor-recipient relationship where transfers take place in one-direction only. This imbalance is usually underpinned by parallel negotiations for loans, grants or inward investment, or for future membership of an international organisation such as the European Union.

Although the reform of public administration is invariably a politically contested process involving a clash of economic and political interests, technical assistance – as its name implies – has been seen by donors as a neutral, technocratic exercise which does not engage with the politics of reform. Comparing the findings of the two case studies, on fiscal decentralisation and the approximation of Ukraine's regional policy to that of the European Union, it has been argued that there is a narrow set of conditions under which this technocratic solution to a political problem has yielded tangible results in the form of donor influence, albeit only in the shape of a short-term advance in the cause of reform.

The concept of a *policy transfer network*, drawn from the literature of Comparative Politics, was used to explain the productive alliance between domestic and external actors which resulted in the Budget Code reform of 2001 despite powerful political opposition. The concept adds useful substance to previous empirical research of the role of informal coalitions between endogenous and exogenous forces. This chapter has argued that the existence of a policy transfer network is a prerequisite for technical assistance programmes to exert an influence on the outcome of reforms which are politically contested. However it does not provide a guarantee that reform will be sustained over the longer term.

Taking the case study period 2000-2012 as a whole neither of the attempted reforms was successful and the influence of international donors was correspondingly marginal, even at times unhelpful. The chapter has argued that the most satisfactory explanatory framework for this absence of impact can be found in the *political economy analysis* of Development Studies. Ukraine is not a developing country in the conventional sense of the term, but a fundamental shift in the strategy of the international donor community towards Ukraine at the start of the new millennium meant that its interventions became susceptible to development theory analysis. It was at this time that the objective of technical assistance switched from finite support to a post-communist country 'in transition' to the more complex and open-ended goal of institution building.

Applying the political economy analysis of Development Studies to the findings of the two empirical studies it has been argued that the longer term failure of technical assistance projects successfully to support reform in either case was due largely to institutional factors on the donor side. First, the continuing reliance on the transfer of best practice models through fixed-term projects was incompatible with the changed, developmental objective of institution building. Secondly, the technocratic nature of programmes of technical assistance limited their engagement with the political realities of reform processes. In common with many developing countries, and also a number of post-communist states of the former Soviet Union, present day Ukraine displays the characteristics of a *neo-patrimonial state*, where informal relationships of patronage and clientelism are able to shape the actual outcomes of reform as much as the decisions of the formal institutions of the state. Evidence was presented from the case studies to explain how networks of patronage were able to determine the fate of both attempts at reform.

For international donors there are no straightforward answers to this problem, whether in developing countries or in post-communist states like Ukraine, since it challenges the basic assumptions of their relationship with partner governments. Clearly a less supply-driven and more problem-oriented, politically intelligent approach to the task of institutional development would be a positive first step.

# CHAPTER VI: CONCLUSIONS

Although the international community has been providing expert advice to the post-communist countries of Central and Eastern Europe and the former Soviet Union for a quarter of a century or more, there has been no systematic research on the interactions between donors and recipients and their consequences for reform outcomes. In the quest for a coherent theoretical framework to explain these, this study has explored the relevant literature of Comparative Politics, EU Studies, Development Studies and International Theory. The results are summarised and discussed below.

As noted in chapter I there is consensus among domestic and international observers that progress in reforming Ukraine's system of public administration, in other words the machinery of the Ukrainian state, has been minimal in the twenty years since the constitutional settlement of 1996. This is despite legislation in the late 1990s aimed at clarifying the relationship between the national and sub-national tiers of government and numerous failed reform initiatives since then, two of which have been examined in this study. The powerful vested interests which benefit from the web of clientelist and patronage relationships at every level of administration in Ukraine have successfully resisted any serious attempt at reform.

The case studies at chapters III and IV document two frustrated attempts at reform to the relationship between Kyiv and the regions, both of which were in large part driven by the desire to introduce greater transparency into these relations and eliminate or at least reduce the scope for political and bureaucratic patronage. While it has been customary to lay the blame for these and other failures at the door of Ukrainian political and business elites, the thesis has argued that the problem lies also with systemic weaknesses in the provision of reform advice through programmes of international technical assistance. These are summarised below, with reference as appropriate to the research questions identified in chapter I and the theoretical analysis set out in chapter V. This is followed by a discussion of the broader implications of the research for the role of the international community in shaping the course of reform in Ukraine.

*Technical Assistance, Isomorphism and Partial Reform*

When programmes of international technical assistance began work in Ukraine in the early 1990s their mission was regarded as relatively straightforward. Like other post-communist and post-Soviet states Ukraine had embarked on a course of transition to a liberal market democracy and required practical advice and know how from the West on the building of the necessary economic and political institutions to achieve this. Politically the incentive for supporting this process was that successful transition in an independent Ukraine would provide a useful counterweight to Russian power in the post-Soviet region (Hamilton 2013: 121). Institutional isomorphism, where institutional forms from an external source are copied because they are deemed to have greater legitimacy than those which currently exist, was implicit in technical assistance. It was argued in chapter I that the low esteem in which public institutions of the late Soviet period were held and the endogenous pressure for change on the Ukrainian side meant that there were ample numbers of willing partners amongst the political and bureaucratic classes.

This was evidently the situation with regard to the attempted reforms of intergovernmental financial relations and regional policy, where ambitious reformers in the state apparatus were enthusiastic advocates of harmonisation with international good practice and looked to programmes of technical assistance for support in overcoming the resistance of those whose interests were threatened by reform. As the two case studies have shown, this support was forthcoming in the area of budget reform but only erratically so in the case of regional policy.

The introduction of formula-based transfers in the financing of sub-national government is a reform in which the influence of external advice through technical assistance played a significant role. Furthermore it is a reform which, as noted in the conclusion to chapter III, has remained in place even if its original intentions have been much compromised. However, it would be too strong a claim to suggest that the reform is entirely attributable to external influence through technical assistance. The findings of the case study point to the central role played by pro-reform elements within the state apparatus, the parliament and the leaderships of Ukraine's largest cities. The role of external advice in this situation was to provide a realistic reform proposal around which this potentially divergent group of interests could coalesce. It was argued in chapter V that this was achieved through the mechanism of a policy transfer network, a theoretical representation of the alliance of domestic and external actors which was able to overcome opposition at the highest level and secure adoption of the 2001 Budget Code.

This finding is consistent with previous studies of the influence of international advice in areas of reform that are politically contested, which have pointed to the importance of coalitions with domestic actors and the role of external assistance as a catalyst for cooperation (Jacoby 2006; Wolczuk 2009). However, the present study has gone considerably further in arguing in chapter V that the policy transfer network concept provides the framework for an empirical examination of how such coalitions function internally in order to achieve their objective, and in hypothesising that the existence of such a network is a necessary precondition for the influence of technical assistance on the course of domestic reform which is politically contested.

Despite its initial success the contribution of technical assistance to the reform of intergovernmental financial relations was to be unfinished business from the Ukrainian point of view. By 2004 the benefits of the new Budget Code had begun to unravel and the momentum of reform had been lost. Meanwhile, in the words of one Ukrainian expert, technical assistance projects on fiscal decentralisation had 'left like an Englishman,'[1] leaving behind a position of 'partial reform equilibrium' (Hellman 1998: 228, cited in Vachudova 2005: 14), where comprehensive reform has stalled and the practice of patronage and the extraction of rents continue unabated.

---

[1] 'Leaving like an Englishman' is a Ukrainian or Russian expression meaning leaving without saying goodbye.

## Technical Assistance and Institutional Development

The major constraint on the influence of international assistance to public administrative reform in Ukraine follows from an imbalance between the ambitious rhetoric of its objectives and the modesty of what Carothers describes as its 'minor technocratic efforts' on the ground (2002: 17). As was argued in chapter II, motivated by a poorly informed judgement that any reduction in the scale of the post-Soviet state was to be welcomed, international donors largely ignored the increasing fragmentation and dysfunction in Ukraine's public institutions which occurred during the 1990s, particularly at sub-national level. It was to be almost ten years after independence before programmes of assistance to Ukraine would make an abrupt change in policy and begin to speak the language of institution building and development. These are concepts which figure prominently in the terms of reference of all donor interventions in this study.

What was to remain wholly unchanged however would be the delivery mechanism for this new and more complex objective. And it was not long before the constraints imposed by the continued adherence to the fixed-term project approach of the 1990s led to problems similar to those in identified in the political economy analysis of the management of international aid in developing countries. The pressure to demonstrate positive achievements and quick wins, aggravated by the ubiquitous use of results-based management technology, produces an approach to external advice where offering ready-made solutions takes precedence over problem-solving. As both case studies demonstrate, external actors who are driven by short time horizons too often fall back on imported institutional models of doubtful relevance in the Ukrainian context.

More problematic still, given the revised objective of institution building, has been donors' weak understanding of the institutional environment in which they work. The constraints of the project cycle, combined with the conventions of technical assistance, mean that the focus of programmes of technical assistance has been on developing the capacity of the state institutions with whom they are formally partnered. On the evidence of the case studies, where two separate attempts to introduce greater transparency into the financial relationship between national and sub-national government were defeated by the political and bureaucratic elites most threatened by such reforms, donors need to look beyond those formal partnerships.

However, technical assistance programmes have little or no contact with, or understanding of, the informal neo-patrimonial relationships which determine the outcomes of the 'good governance' reforms which they promote. Indeed those relationships are very likely to be deliberately concealed from them. And while it can be argued that Ukraine's formal state institutions, like those of Russia, cannot be dismissed as merely as a 'façade' (Whitmore 2010: 1002), for the incurious project manager in a hurry to produce the next benchmarking report for Brussels or Washington the façade and the reality are all too often indistinguishable.

The latter point may be amplified by the observation that the author of the present study, despite having worked for ten or more years in senior positions in programmes of technical assistance to Ukraine, including on fiscal decentralisation and regional policy reform, had little understanding of the manner in which these reforms were systematically undermined by dense networks of patronage invisible to most outsiders, and no knowledge at all of phenomena such as the 'Golden Office' and the 'Conversion Centre'. It was only through the process of research for the two case studies that this failure to appreciate '*Ukrains'ka Real'nist*'' was to some extent rectified.

*The Wider Context: Exporting 'Good Governance'*

The promotion of good governance through the building of effective and accountable public institutions has been the underlying theme of international aid management since the late 1990s. It has applied equally to donor assistance in developing countries and to the policy of institution building adopted by the international community in Ukraine at the beginning of the new millennium. One of international development's more unsatisfactory 'plastic' concepts (Sogge 2002: 131-2), criticised for its 'dangerous isomorphism' (Andrews 2008: 380), the export of good governance through normative power has nevertheless also been central to the strategy of the EU's Neighbourhood Policy and Eastern Partnership. On the evidence of the present study, which has examined the two major donor interventions in the field of public administration in the decade or so after 2000, the policy of exporting models of good governance to Ukraine has met with little success. Correspondingly, the influence of technical assistance on the course of public administrative reform, including in the area of relations between national and sub-national government, has been negligible. This is notwithstanding the short-term success achieved in the intervention on budget reform.

The wider problem here derives from the assumptions implicit in the use of the good governance concept. As argued in chapter V, the term itself is imprecise and idealised with no clear relationship to institutional relationships that exist on the ground. More importantly the notion of importing good governance is unconvincing as a theory of institutional change, implying as Chang has observed, that the institutions of good governance are a matter of rational political choice or agency rather than the outcome of structural influences, both external and domestic (2002: 139). These include history, geography, economic power and geopolitical relationships, and longer-term struggles among social and political institutions (Hout 2009: 38).

Seen from this perspective it is hardly surprising that the weak and inherently flawed instrument of technical assistance, based as it is on assumptions about rational political choice and the agency of key domestic actors, has failed to deliver what was asked of it. Whether more was expected of it is less clear. Looked at from a Ukrainian point of view the answer is almost certainly in the affirmative. Being a partner to a technical assistance programme requires a considerable investment of time and trust, and the author's impression from the interviews undertaken for this study is that pro-reform actors in Ukraine have given generously of both, and continue to do so. Donors' view of this has only partly been addressed by the present research, for reasons outlined in chapter I, but is a topic meriting further investigation.

However the shortcomings and short-termism of the project approach to expert technical assistance, and the superficiality of engagement with complex problems which unavoidably follows, are far from counter-intuitive. As this study has shown they have been understood and analysed exhaustively in the scholarship of Development Studies, and it is both puzzling and a matter for regret that there has not been more cross-referencing between disciplines. Nevertheless it must be abundantly clear to all international donors to Ukraine, and in particular to the European Union, that the continued provision of stand-alone programmes of technical assistance will do little to assist the cause of reform unless it is accompanied by external incentives which more decisively empower pro-reform domestic actors. A credible offer of future EU membership is the obvious example. Even then a radically different approach is needed which avoids the discontinuities and the resort to clumsy isomorphism which have been features of the two case studies.

In the meantime the picture of a confused and ambivalent approach to international assistance to Ukraine which emerges from this research may be no more than a reflection of the muddled view of the international community with regard to its longer term economic and political relations with the country.

# Bibliography

Amis, P., Green, L., Hubbard, M., 2005. Measuring Aid Costs: What Has Been Learnt and What Still Needs to be Learnt? *Public Administration and Development*, 25, (5), 373-378.

Andrews, M., 2008. The Good Governance Agenda: Beyond Indicators without Theory. *Oxford Development Studies*, 36, (4), 379-407.

Andrews, M., 2010. Good Government Means Different Things in Different Countries, *Governance*, 23, (1), 7-35.

Andrews, M., 2013. *The Limits of Institutional Reform in Development: Changing Rules for Realistic Solutions*. Cambridge: Cambridge University Press.

Ashworth, R., Boyne, G., Delbridge, R., 2009. Escape from the Iron Cage? Organizational Change and Isomorphic Pressures in the Public Sector. *Journal of Public Administration Research and Theory*, 19, 165-187.

Aslund, A., Paskhaver, O., 2010. *Proposals for Ukraine: 2010 – Time for Reforms*. Kyiv: Independent International Experts Commission.

Batley, R., Larbi, G., 2004. *The Changing Role of Government: The Reform of Public Services in Developing Countries*. England: Palgrave Macmillan.

Bennett, C., 1991. How States Use Foreign Evidence. *Journal of Public Policy*, 11, (1), 31-54.

Bennett, C., 1997. Understanding Ripple Effects: The Cross-National Adoption of Policy Instruments for Bureaucratic Accountability. *Governance*, 10, (3), 213-233.

Birch, S., 2000. Interpreting the Regional Effect in Ukrainian Politics. *Europe-Asia Studies*, 52, (6), 1017-1041.

Booth, D., 2011a. Aid, Institutions and Governance: What Have We Learned? *Development Policy Review*, 29, (S1), S5-S26.

Booth, D., 2011b. Turning Governance Upside Down. Book Review Article. *Development Policy Review*, 29, (1), 115-124.

Boerzel, T., 2010. The Transformative Power of Europe Reloaded: The Limits of External Europeanization. *KFG Working Paper Series*, 11, February.

Bossuyt, J., 2001. Mainstreaming Institutional Development: Why is it Important and How Can it be Done? *European Centre for Development Policy Management*, Maastricht.

Bourdieu, P., 1992. *The Logic of Practice*. Cambridge: Polity Press.

Bova, R., 1991. Political Dynamics of the Post-Communist Transition: A Comparative Perspective. *World Politics* 44, (1), 113-138.

Brett, E., 2009. *Reconstructing Development Theory: International Inequality, Institutional Reform and Social Emancipation*. England: Palgrave Macmillan.

Brown, T., 2001. Contracting Out by Local Governments in Transitioning Nations: The Role of Technical Assistance in Ukraine. *Administration & Society*, 32, (6), January, 728-755.

Bulmer, S., Padgett, S. 2005. Policy Transfer in the European Union: An Institutionalist Perspective. *British Journal of Political Science*, 35, (1), 103-126.

Bunce, V., 1995. Should Transitologists be Grounded? *Slavic Review*, 54, (1), 111-127.

Campbell, A., 1995. Regional and Local Government in Ukraine. In: Coulson, A., ed., *Local Government in Eastern Europe: Establishing Democracy at the Grass Roots*. Aldershot, England: Edward Elgar, 115-127.

Campbell, A., Coulson, A., 2006. Into the Mainstream: Local Democracy in Central and Eastern Europe. *Local Government Studies*. 32, (5), 543-561.

Carothers, T., 2001. Democratic Conditionality for Development Assistance? Presentation to Carnegie Endowment for International Peace, 27 June.

Carothers, T., 2002. The End of the Transition Paradigm. *Journal of Democracy*, 13, (1), January, 5-21.

Chang, H., 2002. *Kicking Away the Ladder: Development Strategy in Historical Perspective*. London: Anthem Press.

Checkel, J., 2001. Why Comply? Social Learning and European Identity Change. *International Organization*, 55,(3), 555-588.

Checkel, J., 2005. International Institutions and Socialization in Europe: Introduction and Framework. *International Organization*, 59, (4), 801-826.

CIDA 2011. *Evaluation of CIDA's Ukraine Program 2004-2009; Synthesis Report*. Quebec: Canadian International Development Agency.

Concept of State Regional Policy 2001. *Kontseptsia Derzhavnoi Rehional'noi Polytyky*, 2001. Available at: http://rada.gov.ua/ (Accessed 20 August 2014)

Copsey, N., Mayhew, A., 2006. *Wider Europe: European Neighbourhood Policy, Ukraine and the European Union*. In: Copsey, N., Mayhew, A., eds., European Neighbourhood Policy: the Case of Ukraine. Sussex European Institute, 4-6.

Council of Europe 2008. *Appraisal of the Draft Law on the Principles of State Regional Policy of Ukraine*. (RF/ns – CEAD 23562). Directorate General of Democracy and Political Affairs, Strasbourg, September.

Council of Europe, 2010. *Appraisal of the Draft Law on Local Self-Government in Ukraine*. (DPA/LEX 7/2010). Directorate General of Democracy and Political Affairs, Strasbourg, October.

Council of Europe 2011. *Policy Advice: Comments on the Proposals for Improving the Territorial Organisation of Power*. (DPA/PAD 5/2011). Directorate General of Democracy and Political Affairs, Strasbourg, July.

Crawford, G., 2003, Promoting Democracy from Without – Learning from Within, Part I. *Democratization*, 10 (1), 77-98.

Crawford, B., Lijphart, A., 1995. Explaining Political and Economic Change in Postcommunist Eastern Europe: Old Legacies, New Institutions, Hegmonic Norms, and International Pressures. *Comparative Political Studies*, 28, (2), 171-199.

Cremona, M., Hillion, C., 2007. Potential and Limitations of the European Neighbourhood Policy as an Integrated EU Foreign and Security Policy, in A. Mayhew, N. Copsey, eds., *European Neighbourhood Policy: The Case of Ukraine*. Sussex European Institute, SEI Seminar Papers Series 1, 20-44.

Cresswell, R., 2003. *Research Design: Qualitative, Quantitative, and Mixed Methods Approaches*. London: Sage.

CUI RGD 2006. *Regional Governance and Development (RGD) – Ukraine: Project Implementation Plan*. Toronto: Canadian Urban Institute.

CUI RGD 2010. *Regional Governance and Development (RGD) – Ukraine: Project Narrative for the Period April 1, 2005 – July 26, 2010*. CIDA Project Z020640. Toronto: Canadian Urban Institute.

Curtis, D., 2004. 'How Do We Think They Think? Thought Styles in the Management of International Aid. *Public Administration and Development*. 25, (1), 1-9.

Dangerfield, M., 2009. The Contribution of the Visegrad Group to the European Union's 'Eastern' Policy: Rhetoric or Reality? *Europe-Asia Studies*, 61, (10), 1735-1755.

Daniels, R., Trebilcock, M., 2004/5. The Political Economy in Rule of Law Reform in Developing Countries. *Michigan Journal of International Law*, 26, 99-140.

D'Anieri, P., 2007. Ethnic Tensions and State Strategies: Understanding the Survival of the Ukrainian State. *Journal of Communist Studies and Transition Politics*. 23, (1), 4-29.

Denscombe, M., 2009. *Groundrules for Social Research: Guidelines for Good Practice*. Maidenhead: Open University Press.

De Vaus, D., 2001. *Research Design in Social Research*. London: Sage.

DiMaggio, P., Powell, W., 1991b. The Iron Cage Revisited: Institutional Isomorphism and Collective Rationality in Organizational Fields. In: Powell, W., DiMaggio, P., eds., *The New Institutionalism in Organizational Analysis*. Chicago & London: University of Chicago Press, 63-82.

Dimitrova, A., Dragneva, R., 2009. Constraining External Governance: Interdependence with Russia and the CIS as Limits to the EU's Rule Transfer in the Ukraine. *Journal of European Public Policy*, 16, (6), 853-872.

Dolowitz, D., Marsh, D., 1996. Who Learns What from Whom? : A Review of the Policy Transfer Literature. *Political Studies*, XLIV, 343-357.

Dolowitz, D., March, D., 2000. Learning from Abroad: The Role of Policy Transfer in Contemporary Policy Making. *Governance*, 13, (1), January, 5-24.

Dragneva, R., Wolzcuk, K., 2012. EU Law Export to the Eastern Neighbourhood. In Cardwell, P., ed., *EU External Relations, Law and Policy in the Post Lisbon Era*. TMC Asser Press.

Duncan, A., Williams, G., 2012. Making Development Assistance More Effective through Using Political Economy Analysis: What Has Been Done and What Have We Learned? *Development Policy Review*, 30, (2), 133-148.

EBRD, 1995. *Transition Report 1995*. London: European Bank for Reconstruction and Development.

Emerson, M., 2004. *European Neighbourhood Policy: Strategy or Placebo?* Centre for European Policy Studies Working Document, 215, November.

EPRC 2001. Where is Regional Policy Going? Changing Concepts of Regional Policy. *Twenty-second meeting of the Sponsors of the European Policies Research Centre*. Ross Priory, Loch Lomondside, Scotland 8-9 October 2001.

Available at: http://www.eprc.strath.ac.uk/eorpa/Documents/ EoRPA_01_Papers/EoRPA_01-5.pdf (Accessed 25 August 2014)

EU Commission 1997a. *Tacis Interim Evaluation: Synthesis Report*. Brussels: European Commission.

EU Commission 1997b. *Final Report: Evaluation of the Phare and Tacis Democracy Programme 1992-1997*. Brussels: European Commission.

EU Commission 1998. *Ukraine – Evaluation of EC Country Programme. Final Report, Volume 1*. Brussels: European Commission.

EU Commission 2001. *Country Strategy 2002-2006. National Indicative Programme 2002-2003. Ukraine*. Brussels: European Commission.

EU Commission 2003. *Wider Europe – Neighbourhood: A New Framework for Relations with our Eastern and Southern Neighbours*. (Com[2003] 104 final). Brussels: European Commission.

EU Commission 2004. *European Neighbourhood Policy: Strategy Paper*. (Com[2004] 373 final). Brussels: European Commission.

EU Commission 2005a. *EU/Ukraine Action Plan 2005*. Available at: http://www.enpi-info.eu/library/content/eu-ukraine-action-plan-0 (Accessed 23 August 2014)

EU Commission 2005b *Draft Action Programme for Ukraine 2005*. (AIDCO/135/05/EN-Orig). Brussels: European Commission.

EU Commission 2006. *Evaluation of Council Regulation 99/2000 (TACIS) and its Implementation*. Brussels: European Commission.

EU Commission 2007a. *TACIS in Tables*. Brussels: European Commission.

EU Commission 2007b. *European Neighbourhood and Partnership Instrument: Ukraine Country Strategy Paper 2007-2013*. Brussels: European Commission.

EU ENPI SSRD 2006. *EU Support to Sustainable Regional Development: Terms of Reference*. EuropeAid/125234/C/SER/UA. Brussels: European Commission.

EU ENPI SSRD 2009. *EU Support to Sustainable Regional Development: Regional Development Position Paper*.

EU ENPI SSRD 2011. *EU Support to Sustainable Regional Development: Regional Development. Exit Report*.

EU ENPI SURDP 2011. 'Support to Ukraine's Regional Development Policy.' Action Fiche for EuropeAid Project CRIS: ENPI/2011/022-825. Brussels: European Commission.
Available at:
http://ec.europa.eu/europeaid/documents/aap/2011/af_aap_2011_ukr_p2.pdf (Accessed 20 August 2014)

EU ENPI SURDP 2013. *Support to Ukraine's Regional Development Policy: Inception Report*.

EU TACIS ARD 2001. *EU Assistance to Regional Development in Ukraine: Terms of Reference*. (EuropeAid 114674/C/SV/UA). Brussels: European Commission.

EU TACIS ARD 2006. *EU Assistance to Regional Development: Final Report*. November.

EU TACIS SLD 2004. *EU Support to Sustainable Local Development: Terms of Reference*. (EuropeAid/122411/C/SV/UA). Brussels: European Commission.

EU TACIS SLD 2007a. *Sustainable Local Development in Ukraine: Draft Inception Report*. (EuropeAid/122411/C/SV/UA). May.

EU TACIS 2007b. *Sustainable Local Development in Ukraine: Final Inception Report*. (EuropeAid/122411/C/SV/UA). July.

EU TACIS SLD 2008. *Monitoring Report, Ukraine, Sustainable Local Development*. (MR-40566.02). Brussels: European Commission.

EU TACIS SLD 2010. *EU Assistance to Regional Development: Final Report*. December.

Evans, M., 2004a. Understanding Policy Transfer. In: M. Evans, ed., *Policy Transfer in Global Perspective*. England: Ashgate, 10-42.

Evans, M., 2004b. In Conclusion - Policy Transfer in Global Perspective. In: M. Evans, ed., *Policy Transfer in Global Perspective*. England: Ashgate, 210-226.

Evans, M., Davies, J., 1999. Understanding Policy Transfer: A Multi-Level, Multi-Diciplinary Perspective. *Public Administration*, 77, (2), 361-385.

Faint, T., 2004. *Review of DFID/ODA's Programmes in Accession Countries*. UK Department for International Development Evaluation Report, EV 650, July.

Fiscal Analysis Office 1998. *Recent Developments in Ukrainian Intergovernmental Finance. First Quarter 1998 Budget & Fiscal Review*. Kyiv: Fiscal Analyisis Office of the *Verkhovna Rada* Sub-Committee on Taxation.

Fisun, O.,2003. Developing Democracy or Competitive Neopatrimonialism? The Political Regime of Ukraine in Comparative Perspective. *Presentation in Centre for Russian and East European Studies, University of Toronto, Canada*, October.

Foster, M., 2000. New Approaches to Development Cooperation: What Can We Learn from Experiences with Implementing Sector-Wide Approaches? *Overseas Development Institute*, Working Paper, (140), October.

Franke, A., Gawrich, A., Alakbarov, G., 2009. Kazakhstan and Azerbaijan as Post-Soviet Rentier States: Resource Incomes and Autocracy as a Double 'Curse' in Post-Soviet Regimes. *Europe-Asia Studies*, 61, (1), 109-140.

Frenz, A., 2007. The European Commission's TACIS Programme 1991-1996: A Success Story. *Report Prepared for the European Commission.*

Freyburg, T., Lavenex, S., Schimmelfennig, F., Skripka, T., Wetzel, A., 2009. EU Promotion of Democratic Governance in the Neighbourhood. *Journal of European Public Policy*, 16, (6), 916-934.

Fritz, V., 2004. State Weakness in Eastern Europe; Concept and Causes. *European University Institute,* Working Paper RSCAS 2004/35.

Fritz, V., 2005. New Divisions in Europe? East-East Divergence and the Influence of Euroepan Enlargement. *Journal of International Relations and Development*, 8, 192-217.

Fritz, V., 2007. *State Building: A Comparative Study of Ukraine, Lithuania, Belarus and Russia.* Budapest: Central European University Press.

Fritz, V., Menocal, A., 2007. Development States in the New Millennium: Concepts and Challenges for a New Aid Agenda. *Development Policy Review*, 25, (5), 531-552.

Frodin, O., 2011. Generalised and Particularistic Thinking in Policy Analysis and Practice: the Case of Governance Reform in South Africa. *Development Policy Review,* 29, (S1), S179-S198.

Frumkin, P., Galaskiewicz, J., 2004. Institutional Isomorphism and Public Sector Organizations. *Journal of Public Administration and Theory*, 14, (3), 283-307..

Ganzle, S., 2009. EU Governance and the European Neighbourhood Policy: A Framework for Analysis. *Europe-Asia Studies,* 61, (10), 1715-1734.

Gel'man, V., 2004. The Unrule of Law in the Making: The Politics of Informal Institution Building in Russia. *Europe-Asia Studies*, 56, (7), 1021-1040.

George, A., Bennett, A., 2005. Case Studies and Theory Development. In: *Case Studies and Theory Development in the Social Sciences*. Cambridge, Mass.: MIT Press.

Gheciu, A., 2005. Security Institutions as Agents of Socialization? NATO and the 'New Europe'. *International Organization*, 59, Fall, 973-1012.

Glentworth, G., 1995. *Ukraine: Support for Public Sector Reform. Good Government and Regional and Economic Development*. London: UK Joint Assistance Unit (East). (Internal Memorandum).

Goldsmith, A., 2010. Governance and the Depoliticisation of Development. Book Review Article. *Governance*, 23, (2), 368-370.

Gorzelak, G., 1992. Dilemmas of Polish Regional Policies During Transition. In: Gorzelak, G., Kuklinski, A., eds. *Dilemmas of Regional Policies in Eastern and Central Europe*. Warsaw: University of Warsaw European Institute for Regional and Local Development, 18-38.

GoU SSRD 2006. *Derzhavna Stratehia Rehional'novo Rozvytku na Period do 2015 Roku* Government of Ukraine State Strategy for Regional Development to 2015. Accessible at: http://me.kmu.gov.ua/ (Accessed 20 August 2014)

Grabbe, H., 2001. How Does Europeanization Affect CEEC Governance? Conditionality, Diffusion and Diversity. *Journal of European Public Policy*, 8, (6), 1013-1031.

Grabbe, H., 2006. *The European Union's Transformative Power: Europeanization through Conditionality in Central and Eastern Europe*. London: Palgrave.

Granovsky, V., Nanivska, V., 2010. Eurointegration: Reset. *Inside Ukraine #11*. Kyiv: International Centre for Policy Studies.

Grindle, M., 2004. Good Enough Governance: Poverty Reduction and Reform in Developing Countries. *Governance*, 17, (4), 525-548.

Haas, P., 1992. Introduction: Epistemic Communities and International Policy Coordination. *International Organization,* 46, 1, 1-35.

Hague, J., Rose, A., Bojcun, M., 1995. Rebuilding Ukraine's Hollow State: Developing a Democratic Public Service in Ukraine. *Public Administration and Development*, 15, 417-433.

Hakim, C., 2000. *Research Design: Successful Designs for Social and Economic Research.* London: Routledge.

Hall, P., 1993. Policy Paradigms, Social Learning and the State. *Comparative Politics*, 25, 275-296.

Hall, P. Taylor, R., 1996. Political Science and the Three New Institutionalisms. *Political Studies*, 44, 936-957.

Hamilton, K., 2013. *Transformational Diplomacy after the Cold War: Britain's Know How Fund in Post-Communist Europe*, 1989-2003. London and New York: Routledge.

Haukkala, H., 2008. The European Union as a Regional Normative Hegemon: The Case of the European Neighbourhood Policy. *Europe-Asia Studies*, 60, (9), November, 1601-1622.

Haukkala, H., 2009. Lost in Translation? Why the EU has Failed to Influence Russia's Development. *Europe-Asia Studies*, 61, (10), 1757-1775.

Healey, N., Leskin, V., Svetsov, A., 1999. The Municipalization of Enterprise-Owned 'Social Assets' in Russia. *Post-Soviet Affairs.* 15, (3), 262-280.

Hellman, J., 1998. Winner Takes All: The Politics of Partial Reform in Postcommunist Transitions. *World Politics*, 50, (2), 203-234.

Helmke, G., Levitsky, S., 2004. Informal Institutions and Comparative Politics; A Research Agenda. *Perspectives on Politics*, 2, (4), 725-740.

Heretier, A., Knill, C., Mingers, S., 1996. *Ringing the Changes in Europe: Regulatory Competition and the Redefinition of the State.* Berlin: Walter de Gruyter.

Hildreth, P., 2009. Understanding 'New Regional Policy': What is Behind the Government's Sub-National and Economic Development Policy for England? *Journal of Urban Regeneration and Renewal,* 2, (4), 318–336.

Hout, W., 2009. Development and Governance: An Uneasy Relationship. In: Hout, W., Robison, R., eds., *Governance and the Depoliticisation of Development.* Abingdon: Routledge, 29-43.

Hout, W. Robison, R., 2009. Development and the Politics of Governance: Framework for Analysis. In: Hout, W., Robison, R., eds., *Governance and the Depoliticisation of Development.* Abingdon: Routledge, 1-11.

Hudson, R., 2007. Regions and Regional Uneven Development Forever? Some Reflective Comments upon Theory and Practice. *Regional Studies,* 41, (9), 1149-1160.

Hughes, J., Sasse, G., Gordon, C., 2004. *Europeanization and Regionalization in the European Union's Enlargement to Central and Eastern Europe. The Myth of Conditionality.* England: Palgrave.

Hyden, G., 2008. After the Paris Declaration: Taking on the Issue of Power. *Development Policy Review,* 26, (3), 259-274.

IBRD 2012. *Final Report of the Public Finance Modernization Project, No. 4882-UA.* ( Project of World Bank) Vienna: ATC Consultants.

Ivanova, V., Evans, M., 2004. Policy Transfer in a Transition State: The Case of Local Government Reform in the Ukraine. In: Evans, M., ed., *Policy Transfer in Global Perspective.* England: Ashgate, 95-112.

Jacoby, W., 1999. Priest and Penitent: The European Union as a Force in the Domestic Politics of Eastern Europe. *East European Constitutional Review*, 8, 62-67.

Jacoby, W., 2002. Talking the Talk and Walking the Walk: The Cultural and Institutional Effects of Western Models. In: Bonker, F., Muller, K., Pickel, A., eds., *Postcommunist Transformation and the Social Sciences: Cross-Disciplinary Approaches*. Boulder, CO: Rowman and Littlefield, 129-152.

Jacoby, W., 2004. *The Enlargement of the European Union and NATO: Ordering from the Menu in Central Europe*. New York: Cambridge University Press.

Jacoby, W., 2006. Inspiration, Coalition, and Substitution: External Influences on Postcommunist Transformations. *World Politics*, 58, 623-651.

James, O., Lodge, M., 2003. The Limitations of 'Policy Transfer' and 'Lesson Drawing' for Public Policy Research. *Political Studies Review*, 1, 179-193.

Kelley, J., 2006. New Wine in Old Bottles: Promoting Political Reform through the New European Neighbourhood Policy. *Journal of Common Market Studies*, 44, (1), March, 29-55.

Kelley, J., 2004. International Actors on the Domestic Scene: Membership Conditionality and Socialization by International Institutions. *International Organization*, 58, 3, 425-457.

Kelley, J., 2006. New Wine in Old Bottles: Promoting Political Reform through the New European Neighbourhood Policy. *Journal of Common Market Studies*, 44, (1), March, 29-55.

Killick, T., 2004. Politics, Evidence and the New Aid Agenda. *Development Policy Review*, 22, (1), 5-29.

Kopstein, J., Reilly, D., 2000. Geographic Diffusion and the Transformation of the Postcommunist World. *World Politics*, 53, 1-37.

Korostoleva, E., 2011. The Eastern Partnership Initiative: A New Opportunity for Neighbours? *Journal of Communist Studies and Transition Politics*, 27, (1), 1-21.

Kuiybida, V., Tkachuk, A., Zabukovets'-Kovachich, T., 2010. *Rehional'na Polytyka: Pravove Rehuliuvannia. Svitovyi ta Ukrains'kyi Dosvid.*

Available at: http://www.csi.org.ua/www/wp-content/uploads/2010/03/reg_polit-prn.pd (Accessed 8 May 2012)

Landaburu, E., 2006. From Neighbourhood to Integration Policy: Are There Concrete Alternatives to Enlargement? *Centre for European Studies*, Policy Brief, 95, March.

Langbein, J., Wolczuk, K., 2012. Convergence Without Membership? The Impact of the European Union in the Neighbourhood. Evidence from Ukraine. *Journal of European Public Policy*, 19, (6), 863-881.

Lankina, T., Getachew, L., 2006. A Geographic Incremental Theory of Democratization. Territory, Aid, and Democracy in Postcommunist Regions. *World Politics*, 58, July, 536-582.

Lankina, T., Getachew, L., 2008. The Virtuous Circles of Western Exposure in Russian Regions: A Case for Micro-Polity Analysis of Democratic Change. *Journal of Communist Studies and Transition Politics*, 24, (3), 338-364.

Lavenex, S., 2008. A Governance Perspective on the European Neighbourhood Policy: Integration Beyond Conditionality? *Journal of European Public Policy*, 15, (6), 938-955.

Lavenex, S., Lehmkuhl, D., Wichmann, N., 2009. Modes of External Governance: A Cross-National and Cross-Sectoral Comparison, *Journal of European Public Policy*, 16, (6), 813-833.

Lavenex, S., Schimmelfennig, F., 2009. EU Rules Beyond EU Borders: Theorizing External Governanance in European Politics. *Journal of European Public Policy*, 16, (6), 796-812.

Leftwich, A., 2006. From Drivers of Change to the Politics of Development. Refining the Analytical Framework to Understand the Politics of the Places Where We Work. *University of York*, July.

Leftwich, A., 2007. The Political Approach to Institutional Formation and Change. *Improving Institutions for Pro-Poor Growth (IPPG) Discussion Paper Series*, 14, October.

Leftwich, A., 2011. Thinking and Working Politically: What Does it Mean, Why is it Important and How Do You Do It? *Development Leadership Program Working Paper*, March 10-11, Frankfurt, Germany.

Leftwich, A., Sen, K., 2010. *Beyond Institutions. Institutions and Organizations in the Politics and Economics of Poverty Reduction – a Thematic Synthesis of the Research Evidence.* Report of Research Programme on Improving Institutions for Pro-Poor Growth (IPPG). Manchester: University of Manchester.

Leigh, M.,2007. Making a Success of the ENP: Challenge and Response. In: Weber, K., Smith, M., Baun, M., eds., *Governing Europe's Neighbourhood: Partners or Periphery?* Manchester: Manchester University Press, 219-217.

Lewis, J., 2005. The Janus Face of Brussels: Socialization and Everyday Decision Making in the European Union. *International Organization*, 59, Fall, 937-971.

Levy, B., 2010. *Development Trajectories: An Evolutionary Approach to Integrating Governance and Growth.* Economic Premise. World Bank Poverty Reduction and Economic Management Network.

Libanova, E., 2009. Assessing Human Development in Ukraine's Regions. *Development and Transition*, 14, 28-30.

Linz, J., Stepan, A., 1997. *Problems of Democratic Transition and Consolidation: Southern Europe, South America and Post-Communist Europe.* Baltimore and London: John Hopkins University Press.

Maksiuta, A., et al. 2004. *Improving Intergovernmental Fiscal Relations in Ukraine.* Report of a Working Group for the World Bank Country Economic Memorandum of Ukraine, Vol. 2. December.

Malygina, K., 2010. Ukraine as a Neo-Patrimonial State: Understanding Political Change in Ukraine in 2005-2010. *SEER Journal for Labour and Social Affairs in Eastern Europe.* 1/2010, 7-27.

March, J., Olsen, P., 1989. *Rediscovering Institutions: The Organizational Basis of Politics.* New York: Free Press.

Martinez-Vasquez, J., Thirsk, W., 2010. *Fiscal Decentralization in Ukraine: Accomplishments and Challenges in the Transition.* New York: Nova Science.

Matsuzato, K., 2000. Local Reforms in Ukraine 1990-1998: Elites and Institutions. In: Ieda, O., ed., *The Emerging Local Governments in Eastern Europe and Russia: Historical and Post-Communist Developments.* Hiroshima: Keisuisha.

Maynzyuk, K., 2008. *Prychyni i Ryzky Nevyznachenosti Mizhbiudzhetnyukh Vidnosyn v Ukraini.* FISCO Consulting, Kyiv, Ukraine. Available at: www.fisco-id.com (Accessed 10 April 2014)

Maynzyuk, K., Dzhygyr, Y., 2008. *Positioning LGI/OSI Policy Dialogue to Support Decentralisation in Ukraine.* Budapest: Local Government and Public Service Reform Initiative/Open Society Institute. FISCO Consulting, Kyiv, Ukraine. Available at: http://www.fisco-id.com (Accessed 30 April 2012)

Maynzyuk, K., Dzhygyr, Y., 2008/9. *Prigovor k Svobode: Proshloe I Budushchee Mezhbiudzhetnikh Otnoshenii v Ukraine.* FISCO Consulting, Kyiv, Ukraine. Available at: www.fisco-id.com (Accessed 30 April 2012)

Maynzyuk, K., Dzhygyr, Y., 2011. *Questionnaire on Local Government: Responses to Recession Across Europe. Part II: Responses, Outcomes and Challenges.* FISCO Consulting, Kyiv, Ukraine. Available at: www.fisco-id.com (Accessed 30 April 2012)

Mendras, M., 1999. How Regional Elites Preserve their Power, *Post-Soviet Affairs*. 15, (4), 295-311.

Molenaers, N., Nijs, L., 2009. From the Theory of Aid Effectiveness to the Practice: The European Commission's Governance Incentive Tranche. *Development Policy Review*, 27, (5), 561-580.

Mrinska, O., 2006. The National Strategy for Regional Development in Ukraine: Squeezed Between Political Reforms and More Assertive Regional Elites? *Annual Conference of the Regional Studies Association*, Leuven, Belgium, June 2006. Unpublished Paper.

Mrinska, O., 2010. Between Confusion and Ignorance: Public Policy Responses to Growing Regional Divergence in Ukraine. *Annual Conference of the Regional Studies Association*, Pecs, Hungary, 2010. Unpublished Paper.

Mrinska, O., Gorzelak., G., 2002. *DFID LARGIS Final Report Regional Policy Component*. November. Unpublished Paper.

Mrinska, O., Tkachuk, A., Tretiak, Y., 2013. *Rehional'nyi Rozvytok ta Derzhavna Rehional'na Polityka v Ukraini: Stan i Perspektyvy Zmin u Konteksti Global'nykh Vyklykiv ta Evropeys'kikh Standartiv Polityky: Analitychnyi Zvit*. Available at: http://surdp.eu (Accessed 20 August 2014)

Nielson, K., Jessop, B., Hausner, J., 1995. Institutional Change in Post-Socialism. In: Hausner, J., Jessop, B., Nielson, K., eds., *Strategic Choice and Path Dependency in Post-Socialism: Institutional Dynamics in the Transformation Process*. Aldershot: Edward Elgar, 3-44.

North, D., 1990. *Institutions, Institutional Change, and Economic Performance*. Cambridge: Cambridge University Press.

Noutcheva, G., Emerson, M., 2007. Economic and Social Development. In: Weber, K., Smith, M., Baun, M., eds., *Governing Europe's Neighbourhood: Partners or Periphery?* Manchester: Manchester University Press, 76-96.

Oberemchuk, M., 1999. *Lyubit Mestnyi Biudzhety Stalo Modno*. Ukrainska Pravda, 24 November.

O'Dwyer, C., 2006. Reforming Regional Governance in East Central Europe: Europeanization or Domestic Politics as Usual? *East European Politics and Societies*, 20, (2), 219-253.

OECD 2014 (Organisation for Economic Cooperation and Development). *OECD Territorial Reviews: Ukraine 2013*. Paris: OECD Publishing. Available at: http://dx.doi.org/10.1787/9789264204836-en (Accessed 20 August 2014)

Offe, C, 1996. *Designing Institutions for East European Transitions*. Bremen: Center for Social Policy Research.

Radaelli, C., 2000. Policy Transfer in the European Union: Institutional Isomorphism as a Source of Legitimacy. *Governance*, 13, 25-43.

Ragin, C., 1989. *The Comparative Method: Moving Beyond Qualitative and Quantitative Strategies*. Berkeley: University of California Press.

Ritchie, J., Lewis, J., 2003. *Qualitative Research Practice: A Guide for Social Science Students and Researchers*. London: Sage.

Roland, G., 2002. The Political Economy of Transition. *Journal of Economic Perspectives*, 16, (1), 29-50.

Romaniuk, S., 2002. Policy of Regional Development in Ukraine: Current Situation and New Opportunities. In: Marcou, G., ed., *Regionalisation for Development for Accession to the European Union. A Comparative Perspective*. Budapest: LGI Fellowship Series, Local Government and Public Service Reform Initiative, Open Society Institute.

Romaniuk, S., 2013. *Rozvytku Regioniv u Vidkrytii Ekonomitsi: Teoria, Polityka, Praktyka*. Kyiv: National Academy of Public Administration under the President of Ukraine.

Rose, R., 1991. What is Lesson Drawing? *Journal of Public Policy*, 11 (1), 3-30.

Rose, R., 1993. *Lesson Drawing in Public Policy: A Guide to Learning across Time and Space.* New Jersey: Chatham House.

Ross, C., 1987. *Local Government in the Soviet Union: Problems of Implementation and Control.* New York, St. Martin's Press.

Ross, C., 2009. *Local Politics and Decentralization in Russia.* Oxford: Routledge.

Sakwa, R., 1996. Russian Studies: The Fractured Mirror. *Politics,* 16, (3), 175-186.

Sakwa, R., 1999. Postcommunist Studies: Once Again through the Looking Glass (Darkly)? *Review of International Studies,* 25, 709-719.

Sasse, G., 2001. The 'New' Ukraine: A State of Regions. *Regional & Federal Studies* 11, (3), 69-100.

Sasse, G., 2008. The European Neighbourhood Policy: Conditionality Revisited for the EU's Eastern Neighbours. *Europe-Asia Studies,* 60, (2), March, 295-316.

Schimmelfennig, F., 2005. Strategic Calculation and International Socialization: Membership Incentives, Party Constellations, and Sustained Compliance in Central and Eastern Europe. *International Organization,* 59, (4), 827-860.

Schimmelfennig, F., 2009. Europeanization Beyond Europe. *Living Reviews in European Governance,* 4, (3), 1-28.

Schimmelfennig, F. and Sedelmeier, U., 2004. Governance by Conditionality: EU Rule Transfer to the Candidate Countries of Central and Eastern Europe. *Journal of European Public Policy,* 11, (4), 661-679.

Schimmelfennig, F., Sedelmeier, U., 2005a. Introduction: Conceptualizing the Europeanization of Central and Eastern Europe. In: Schimmelfennig F., Sedelmeier, U., eds., *The Europeanization of Central and Eastern Europe.* Ithaca, N.Y.: Cornell University, 1-28.

Schimmelfenning, F. and Sedelmeier, U., 2005b. Conclusions: The Impact of the European Union on the Accession Countries. In: Schimmelfenning, F. and Sedelmeier, U., eds., *The Europeanization of Central and Eastern Europe*. Ithaca, N.Y.: Cornell University, 210-228.

Schmitter, P., Lynn Karl, T., 1994. The Conceptual Travels of Transitologists and Consolodologists: How Far to the East Should They Attempt to Go? *Slavic Review*, 53, (1), 173-185

Sedelmeier, U., 2007. The European Neighbourhood Policy: A Comment on Theory and Policy. In: Weber, K., Smith, M., Baun, M., eds., *Governing Europe's Neighbourhood: Partners or Periphery?* Manchester: Manchester University Press, 195-208.

Shlapentokh, V., 1989. *Public and Private life of the Soviet People*. New York: Oxford University Press.

SIGMA 2006. *Ukraine Governance Assessment*. Organisation for Economic Cooperation and Development/European Union.

Simmons, B., Dobbin, F., Garrett, G., 2006. The International Diffusion of Liberalism. *International Organization*, 60, October, 781-810.

Smith, K., 2005. The Outsiders: The European Neighbourhood Policy. *International Affairs*, 81, (4), 757-773.

Smith, A., Pickles, J., 1998. Introduction: Theorising Transition and the Political Economy of Transformation. In: Pickles, J., Smith, A., eds., *Theorising Transition: The Political Economy of Post-Communist Transformations*. London: Routledge.

Smith, A., Swain, A., 1998. Regulating and Institutionalising Capitalisms: the Micro-Foundations of Transformations in Eastern and Central Europe. In: Pickles, J., Smith, A., eds., *Theorising Transition: The Political Economy of Post-Communist Transformations*. London: Routledge, 25-53.

Smith, M., Weber, K., 2007. Governance Theories, Regional Intergration and EU Foreign Policy. In: Weber, K., Smith, M., Baun, M., eds., *Governing Europe's Neighbourhood: Partners or Periphery?* Manchester: Manchester University Press, 3-20.

Solonenko, I., 2008. European Neighbourhood Policy after Four Years: Has it Had Any Impact on the Reform Process in Ukraine? *International Issues and Slovak Foreign Policy Affairs*, XVII, (4), 20-40.

Sogge, D., 2002. *Give and Take: What's the Matter with Foreign Aid?* London & New York: Zed Books.

Stegniy, O., 2011. Ukraine and the Eastern Partnership: 'Lost in Translation'? *Journal of Communist Studies and Transition Politics*, 27, (1), 50-72.

Stewart, S., Klein M., Schmitz, A., Schröder, H, 2012. *Presidents, Oligarchs and Bureaucrats. Forms of Rule in the Post-Soviet Space.* German Institute for International and Security Affairs. Farnham: Ashgate.

Stone, D., 2000. Non-Governmental Policy Transfer: The Strategies of Independent Policy Institutes. *Governance*, 13, (1), 45-62.

Strauss, A., Corbin, J., 1990. *Basics of Qualitative Research: Grounded Theory Procedures and Techniques.* London: Sage.

Swain, A., 2006. Soft Capitalism and a Hard Industry: Virtualism, the "Transition Industry" and the Restructuring of the Ukrainian Coal Industry. *Institute of British Geographers*, NS 31, 208-223.

Swain, A., 2007. ed., *Restructuring the Post-Soviet Industrial Region: the Donbas in Transition.* London: Routledge.

Swianiewicz, P., 2006. Poland and Ukraine: Contrasting Paths of Decentralisation and Territorial Reform. *Local Government Studies* 32, (5), 599-622.

Unsworth, S., 2009. What's Politics Got To Do With It? Why Donors Find it So Hard to Come to Terms with Politics and Why This Matters. *Journal of International Development*, 21, 883-894.

Unsworth, S., et al., 2010. *An Upside Down View of Governance.* Centre for the Future State, Institute of Development Studies, University of Sussex.

Vachudova, M., 2005. *Europe Undivided: Democracy, Leverage and Integration after Communism.* New York: Oxford University Press.

UK DFID, 1997. *Eliminating World Poverty: A Challenge for the 21st Century.* (White Paper on International Development). (Cmnd. 3789). London: HMSO.

UK DFID, 1999. *Local and Regional Government Institutional Strengthening Project (LARGIS).* London: UK DFID EECAD. (Internal Memorandum).

UK DFID, 2003. *Drivers of Change.*
Available at: www.dfid.gov.uk/contracts/files/ojec_5512_background.pdf (Accessed 10 September 2010)

USAID 1996. *Municipal Finance and Management Training Assessment in Ukraine.* Research Triangle Institute. Available at: http://pdf.usaid.gov/pdf_docs/PNABY745.pdf (Accessed 12 January 2015)

USAID 2002. *USAID/Ukraine Country Strategic Plan for FY 2003-2007.* USAID Regional Mission for Ukraine, Belarus and Moldova.
Available at:http://pdf.usaid.gov/pdf_docs/Pdabx822.pdf (Accessed 12 January 2015)

USAID 2004. *Assistance in Fiscal Reform: Fiscal Decentralization in Ukraine.* Fiscal Reform in Support of Trade Liberalization Project. Available at: www.egateg.usaid.gov/sites/default/files/ukraine_intergovernmental_fiscal_relations.pdf (Accessed 31 March 2014)

USAID 2009. *Local Economic Development in Ukraine.* Washington: Unites States Agency for International Development.

Wallace, H., 2000. The Domestication of Europe and the Limits to Globalization. Paper presented at the International Political Science Association Meetings. Quebec, Canada, 1-5 August.

Wedel, J., 1998. *Collision and Collusion: The Strange Case of Western Aid to Eastern Europe*. New York: St Martin's.

Wedel, J., 2003. Clans, Cliques and Captured States: Rethinking "Transition" in Central and Eastern Europe and the Former Soviet Union. *Journal of International Development*, 15, 427-440.

White, H., 1998. British Aid and the White Paper on International Development: Dressing a Wolf in Sheep's Clothing in the Emperor's New Clothes? *Journal of International Development*, 10, 151-166.

White, P., 2009. *Developing Research Questions: A Guide for Social Scientists*. Basingstoke: Palgrave Macmillan

Whitmore, S., 2010. Parliamentary Oversight in Putin's Neo-patrimonial State. Watchdogs or Show-dogs? *Europe-Asia Studies*, 62, (6), 999-1025.

Williams, G., Duncan, A., Landell-Mills, P., Unsworth, S., 2011. The Rise and Transformation of Institutional Theory. *Development Policy Review*, 29, (S1), s29-s55

Wilson, A., 1997. *Ukrainian Nationalism in the 1990s: A Minority Faith*. Cambridge: Cambridge University Press.

Wolczuk, K., 2001. *The Moulding of Ukraine: The Constitutional Politics of State Formation*. Budapest: Central European University Press.

Wolczuk, K., 2002. Catching up with 'Europe'? Constitutional Debates on the Territorial-Administrative Model in Independent Ukraine. In: Batt, J, Wolczuk, K., eds., *Region, State and Identity in Central and Eastern Europe*. London: Frank Cass, 65-88.

Wolczuk, K., 2004. Integration without Europeanisation: Ukraine and its Policy towards the European Union. *EUI RSCAS Working Paper No 2004/15.*

Wolczuk, K., 2008. Ukraine and its Relations with the EU in the Context of the European Neighbourhood Policy. In: Fischer, S., ed., *Ukraine: Quo Vadis?* Institute for Security Studies, Chaillot Paper #108, February, 87-117.

Wolczuk, K., 2009. Implementation without Coordination: The Impact of EU Conditionality on Ukraine under the European Neighbourhood Policy. *Europe-Asia Studies,* 61, (2), 187-211.

Wolczuk, K., 2011. Perceptions of, and Attitudes Towards, the Eastern Partnership Amongst the Partner Countries' Political Elites. *Eastern Partnership Review,* 5.

Wolowski, P., 2008. Ukrainian Politics after the Orange Revolution – How Far from Democratic Consolidation? In: Fischer, S., ed., *Ukraine: Quo Vadis?* Institute for Security Studies, Chaillot Paper #108, February, 87-117.

World Bank 1998. *Assessing Aid: What Works, What Doesn't, and Why.* New York: Oxford University Press.

World Bank 2002a. *Ukraine: Review of the Budget Process. A Public Expenditure and Institutional Review.* Report No. 23356-UA, Country Unit and Poverty Reduction and Economic Management Unit, Europe and Central Asia Region. March 8. Washington DC: World Bank.

World Bank 2002b. *Ukraine: Moving Forward on Regional Development and Regional Policy.* Report No. 25945-UA, Country Unit and Poverty Reduction and Economic Management Unit, Europe and Central Asia Region. June 10. Washington DC: World Bank.

World Bank 2004. *Improving Intergovernmental Fiscal Relations in Ukraine.* Report of a Working Group for the World Bank Country Economic Memorandum of Ukraine, Vol. 2. December. Washington DC: World Bank.

World Bank 2005. *Economic Growth in the 1990s: Learning from a Decade of Reform.* Washington DC: World Bank

World Bank 2008. Ukraine: *Improving Intergovernmental Fiscal Relations and Public Health and Education Expenditure Policy: Selected Issues.* Report # 42450 – UA. Washington DC: World Bank.

Youngs, R., 2009. Democracy Promotion as External Governance? *Journal of European Public Policy,* 16, (6), 895-915.

Zabrowski, M., 2005. Westernizing the East: External Influences in the Post-Communist Transformation of Eastern and Central Europe. *Journal of Communist Studies and Transition Politics,* 21, (1), 16-32.

Zhovtiak, Y., 1998. *Za Mistsevi Biudzhety Zamovyty b Slovo.* Polityka, 2 March.

Zurn, M., Checkel, J., 2005. Getting Socialized to Build Bridges: Constructivism and Rationalism, Europe and the Nation-State. *International Organization,* 59, Fall, 1045-1079.

# List of Interviewees

Yuriy Balkoviy, *Director of Finance, Luhans'ka Oblast Administration,* Luhans'k, 27 June and 23 October 2013

Yuriy Dzhygyr, *Public Finance Expert, FISCO Consulting, Kyiv,* Kyiv, 29 November 2012 and 28 March 2013

Yevhen Fishko, *Formerly Director of the Department of Regional Policy, MRDC,* Kyiv, 1 July 2013

Vladymyr Glazunov, *Vice Rector, Zaporizhia Classical University,* Zaporizhia, 26 June 2013

Yuriy Hanushchak, *Formerly Consultant to the Association of Ukrainian Cities,* Kyiv, 21 March 2013

Pavlo Kachur, *Formerly Deputy Director of the Association of Ukrainian Cities,* Kyiv, 20 March 2013

Maya Koshman, *Deputy Head, Department of International Technical Assistance, MoE,* Kyiv, 24 May 2013

Svetlana Kruglyak, *Deputy Head of Department of Economy, Zaporiz'ka Oblast Administration,* Zaporizhia, 27 July 2014

Oleksey Kubar, *Strategic Planning Expert, Luhans'k,* Luhans'k, 28 June 2013

Irina Lekh, *Founder of 'Porada' Business Association, Civil Rights Activist, Zaporiz'ka,* Zaporizhia, 25 June and 21 October 2013

*Vitaliy Lysenko,* Strategic Planning Expert, Zaporizhia, Zaporizhia, 21 October 2013

Anatoliy Maksiuta, *First Deputy Minister of Economy, MoE,* Kyiv, 25 May 2013.

ASSISTING REFORM IN POST-COMMUNIST UKRAINE 2000-2012 249

Serhiy Maksymenko, *Regional Policy Expert, Kyiv*, Kyiv, 22 March 2013

Kataryna Maynzyuk, *Public Finance Expert, FISCO Consulting, Kyiv*, Kyiv, 29 November 2012 and 28 March 2013

Olga Mrinska, *Regional Policy Expert, Kyiv and London*, Kyiv, 11 October 2013

Vira Nanivska, *President, International Centre for Policy Studies, Kyiv*, Kyiv, 20 March 2013

Olena Nyzhnyk, *Director of Department of Regional Policy, MoE*, Kyiv, 29 March 2013 and 24 July 2014

Maria Popadinets, *Formerly Leader, CIDA Regional Gov'nance & Dev't Project, Zakarpats'ka*, Uzhgorod, 9 October 2013

Serhiy Romaniuk, *First Deputy Minister of Economy, MoE*, Kyiv, 23 March 2013 and 26 July 2014

Inna Samchinska, Andrey Kornienko, *Institute for Budgetary & Socio-Economic Research, Kyiv*, Kyiv, 28 March 2013

Ihor Sanzharovskiy, *Formerly Manager, CIDA Regional Governance & Development Project*, Kyiv, 16 October 2013

Irina Shcherbina, *Formerly Head of Institute for Budgetary & Socio-Economic Research, Kyiv*, Kyiv, 28 March 2013

Vladymyr Shevchuk, *Director of Vynogradiv Municipal Development Agency, Zakarpats'ka*, Uzhgorod, 9 October 2013

Ihor Shpak, *Formerly Public Finance Expert, Fiscal Analysis Office of Verkhovna Rada*, Kyiv, 20 March 2013

Oleksandr Sin, *Mayor of Zaporizhia City*, Zaporizhia, 26 June 2013

Anatoliy Tkachuk, *Formerly Deputy Minister, MRDC*, Kyiv, 15 October 2013

Yuriy Tretiak, *Regional Policy Expert, Kyiv*, Kyiv, 30 November 2012

Small Business Owner, City 'X', Ukraine, August 2014

Professor Kenneth Davey, *University of Birmingham, Formerly Senior Expert DFID LARGIS*, Cheltenham, 27 August 2013

Jean-Francois Devemy, *Formerly Team Leader, EU TACIS Support to Sustainable Local Development*, Paris, 21 November 2013

Peter Fortune, *Formerly DFID Adviser on Private Sector Development in Ukraine*, London, 16 April 2013

Garth Glentworth, *Formerly DFID Governance Adviser*, London, 18 February 2014

Tetyana Korneyeva, *Formerly Lead Project Expert on Strategic Planning, EU TACIS Support to Sustainable Local Development*, Paris, 21 November 2013

Professor Gerard Marcou, *University of the Sorbonne, Expert for the Council of Europe*, Paris, 22 November 2013

Dominik Papenheim, *Sector Manager, Regional Policy, EU Delegation, Kyiv*, Kyiv, 3 December 2012

Olga Sandakova, *Formerly DFID Project Manager Ukraine*, Kyiv, 17 October 2013

Professor Pawel Swianiewicz, *University of Warsaw, Formerly Project Expert DFID LARGIS*, Warsaw, 12 October 2013

Wayne Thirsk, *Formerly Public Finance Expert, Fiscal Analysis Office of Verkhovna Rada*, Kyiv, 27, 29 November 2012 and 28 March 2013.

Deborah Wetzel, *Formerly Chief Adviser on Budget Reform in Ukraine, World Bank*, e-mail, 18 May 2014

14 Nathan D. Larson
Alexander Solzhenitsyn and the
Russo-Jewish Question
ISBN 3-89821-483-4

15 Guido Houben
Kulturpolitik und Ethnizität
Staatliche Kunstförderung im Russland der neunziger Jahre
Mit einem Vorwort von Gert Weisskirchen
ISBN 3-89821-542-3

16 Leonid Luks
Der russische „Sonderweg"?
Aufsätze zur neuesten Geschichte Russlands im europäischen Kontext
ISBN 3-89821-496-6

17 Евгений Мороз
История «Мёртвой воды» – от страшной сказки к большой политике
Политическое неоязычество в постсоветской России
ISBN 3-89821-551-2

18 Александр Верховский и Галина Кожевникова (ред.)
Этническая и религиозная интолерантность в российских СМИ
Результаты мониторинга 2001-2004 гг.
ISBN 3-89821-569-5

19 Christian Ganzer
Sowjetisches Erbe und ukrainische Nation
Das Museum der Geschichte des Zaporoger Kosakentums auf der Insel Chortycja
Mit einem Vorwort von Frank Golczewski
ISBN 3-89821-504-0

20 Эльза-Баир Гучинова
Помнить нельзя забыть
Антропология депортационной травмы калмыков
С предисловием Кэролайн Хамфри
ISBN 3-89821-506-7

21 Юлия Лидерман
Мотивы «проверки» и «испытания» в постсоветской культуре
Советское прошлое в российском кинематографе 1990-х годов
С предисловием Евгения Марголита
ISBN 3-89821-511-3

22 Tanya Lokshina, Ray Thomas, Mary Mayer (Eds.)
The Imposition of a Fake Political Settlement in the Northern Caucasus
The 2003 Chechen Presidential Election
ISBN 3-89821-436-2

23 Timothy McCajor Hall, Rosie Read (Eds.)
Changes in the Heart of Europe
Recent Ethnographies of Czechs, Slovaks, Roma, and Sorbs
With an afterword by Zdeněk Salzmann
ISBN 3-89821-606-3

24 Christian Autengruber
Die politischen Parteien in Bulgarien und Rumänien
Eine vergleichende Analyse seit Beginn der 90er Jahre
Mit einem Vorwort von Dorothée de Nève
ISBN 3-89821-476-1

25 Annette Freyberg-Inan with Radu Cristescu
The Ghosts in Our Classrooms, or: John Dewey Meets Ceauşescu
The Promise and the Failures of Civic Education in Romania
ISBN 3-89821-416-8

26 John B. Dunlop
The 2002 Dubrovka and 2004 Beslan Hostage Crises
A Critique of Russian Counter-Terrorism
With a foreword by Donald N. Jensen
ISBN 3-89821-608-X

27 Peter Koller
Das touristische Potenzial von Kam''janec'–Podil's'kyj
Eine fremdenverkehrsgeographische Untersuchung der Zukunftsperspektiven und Maßnahmenplanung zur Destinationsentwicklung des „ukrainischen Rothenburg"
Mit einem Vorwort von Kristiane Klemm
ISBN 3-89821-640-3

28 Françoise Daucé, Elisabeth Sieca-Kozlowski (Eds.)
Dedovshchina in the Post-Soviet Military
Hazing of Russian Army Conscripts in a Comparative Perspective
With a foreword by Dale Herspring
ISBN 3-89821-616-0

29  Florian Strasser
    Zivilgesellschaftliche Einflüsse auf die
    Orange Revolution
    Die gewaltlose Massenbewegung und die
    ukrainische Wahlkrise 2004
    Mit einem Vorwort von Egbert Jahn
    ISBN 3-89821-648-9

30  Rebecca S. Katz
    The Georgian Regime Crisis of 2003-
    2004
    A Case Study in Post-Soviet Media
    Representation of Politics, Crime and
    Corruption
    ISBN 3-89821-413-3

31  Vladimir Kantor
    Willkür oder Freiheit
    Beiträge zur russischen Geschichtsphilosophie
    Ediert von Dagmar Herrmann sowie mit
    einem Vorwort versehen von Leonid Luks
    ISBN 3-89821-589-X

32  Laura A. Victoir
    The Russian Land Estate Today
    A Case Study of Cultural Politics in Post-
    Soviet Russia
    With a foreword by Priscilla Roosevelt
    ISBN 3-89821-426-5

33  Ivan Katchanovski
    Cleft Countries
    Regional Political Divisions and Cultures in
    Post-Soviet Ukraine and Moldova
    With a foreword by Francis Fukuyama
    ISBN 3-89821-558-X

34  Florian Mühlfried
    Postsowjetische Feiern
    Das Georgische Bankett im Wandel
    Mit einem Vorwort von Kevin Tuite
    ISBN 3-89821-601-2

35  Roger Griffin, Werner Loh, Andreas
    Umland (Eds.)
    Fascism Past and Present, West and
    East
    An International Debate on Concepts and
    Cases in the Comparative Study of the
    Extreme Right
    With an afterword by Walter Laqueur
    ISBN 3-89821-674-8

36  Sebastian Schlegel
    Der „Weiße Archipel"
    Sowjetische Atomstädte 1945-1991
    Mit einem Geleitwort von Thomas Bohn
    ISBN 3-89821-679-9

37  Vyacheslav Likhachev
    Political Anti-Semitism in Post-Soviet
    Russia
    Actors and Ideas in 1991-2003
    Edited and translated from Russian by Eugene
    Veklerov
    ISBN 3-89821-529-6

38  Josette Baer (Ed.)
    Preparing Liberty in Central Europe
    Political Texts from the Spring of Nations
    1848 to the Spring of Prague 1968
    With a foreword by Zdeněk V. David
    ISBN 3-89821-546-6

39  Михаил Лукьянов
    Российский консерватизм и
    реформа, 1907-1914
    С предисловием Марка Д. Стейнберга
    ISBN 3-89821-503-2

40  Nicola Melloni
    Market Without Economy
    The 1998 Russian Financial Crisis
    With a foreword by Eiji Furukawa
    ISBN 3-89821-407-9

41  Dmitrij Chmelnizki
    Die Architektur Stalins
    Bd. 1: Studien zu Ideologie und Stil
    Bd. 2: Bilddokumentation
    Mit einem Vorwort von Bruno Flierl
    ISBN 3-89821-515-6

42  Katja Yafimava
    Post-Soviet Russian-Belarussian
    Relationships
    The Role of Gas Transit Pipelines
    With a foreword by Jonathan P. Stern
    ISBN 3-89821-655-1

43  Boris Chavkin
    Verflechtungen der deutschen und
    russischen Zeitgeschichte
    Aufsätze und Archivfunde zu den
    Beziehungen Deutschlands und der
    Sowjetunion von 1917 bis 1991
    Ediert von Markus Edlinger sowie mit einem
    Vorwort versehen von Leonid Luks
    ISBN 3-89821-756-6

44  *Anastasija Grynenko in Zusammenarbeit mit Claudia Dathe*
Die Terminologie des Gerichtswesens der Ukraine und Deutschlands im Vergleich
Eine übersetzungswissenschaftliche Analyse juristischer Fachbegriffe im Deutschen, Ukrainischen und Russischen
Mit einem Vorwort von Ulrich Hartmann
ISBN 3-89821-691-8

45  *Anton Burkov*
The Impact of the European Convention on Human Rights on Russian Law
Legislation and Application in 1996-2006
With a foreword by Françoise Hampson
ISBN 978-3-89821-639-5

46  *Stina Torjesen, Indra Overland (Eds.)*
International Election Observers in Post-Soviet Azerbaijan
Geopolitical Pawns or Agents of Change?
ISBN 978-3-89821-743-9

47  *Taras Kuzio*
Ukraine – Crimea – Russia
Triangle of Conflict
ISBN 978-3-89821-761-3

48  *Claudia Šabić*
"Ich erinnere mich nicht, aber L'viv!"
Zur Funktion kultureller Faktoren für die Institutionalisierung und Entwicklung einer ukrainischen Region
Mit einem Vorwort von Melanie Tatur
ISBN 978-3-89821-752-1

49  *Marlies Bilz*
Tatarstan in der Transformation
Nationaler Diskurs und Politische Praxis 1988-1994
Mit einem Vorwort von Frank Golczewski
ISBN 978-3-89821-722-4

50  *Марлен Ларюэль (ред.)*
Современные интерпретации русского национализма
ISBN 978-3-89821-795-8

51  *Sonja Schüler*
Die ethnische Dimension der Armut
Roma im postsozialistischen Rumänien
Mit einem Vorwort von Anton Sterbling
ISBN 978-3-89821-776-7

52  *Галина Кожевникова*
Радикальный национализм в России и противодействие ему
Сборник докладов Центра «Сова» за 2004-2007 гг.
С предисловием Александра Верховского
ISBN 978-3-89821-721-7

53  *Галина Кожевникова и Владимир Прибыловский*
Российская власть в биографиях I
Высшие должностные лица РФ в 2004 г.
ISBN 978-3-89821-796-5

54  *Галина Кожевникова и Владимир Прибыловский*
Российская власть в биографиях II
Члены Правительства РФ в 2004 г.
ISBN 978-3-89821-797-2

55  *Галина Кожевникова и Владимир Прибыловский*
Российская власть в биографиях III
Руководители федеральных служб и агентств РФ в 2004 г.
ISBN 978-3-89821-798-9

56  *Ileana Petroniu*
Privatisierung in Transformationsökonomien
Determinanten der Restrukturierungs-Bereitschaft am Beispiel Polens, Rumäniens und der Ukraine
Mit einem Vorwort von Rainer W. Schäfer
ISBN 978-3-89821-790-3

57  *Christian Wipperfürth*
Russland und seine GUS-Nachbarn
Hintergründe, aktuelle Entwicklungen und Konflikte in einer ressourcenreichen Region
ISBN 978-3-89821-801-6

58  *Togzhan Kassenova*
From Antagonism to Partnership
The Uneasy Path of the U.S.-Russian Cooperative Threat Reduction
With a foreword by Christoph Bluth
ISBN 978-3-89821-707-1

59  *Alexander Höllwerth*
Das sakrale eurasische Imperium des Aleksandr Dugin
Eine Diskursanalyse zum postsowjetischen russischen Rechtsextremismus
Mit einem Vorwort von Dirk Uffelmann
ISBN 978-3-89821-813-9

60  Олег Рябов
    «Россия-Матушка»
    Национализм, гендер и война в России XX века
    С предисловием Елены Гощило
    ISBN 978-3-89821-487-2

61  Ivan Maistrenko
    Borot'bism
    A Chapter in the History of the Ukrainian Revolution
    With a new introduction by Chris Ford
    Translated by George S. N. Luckyj with the assistance of Ivan L. Rudnytsky
    ISBN 978-3-89821-697-5

62  Maryna Romanets
    Anamorphosic Texts and Reconfigured Visions
    Improvised Traditions in Contemporary Ukrainian and Irish Literature
    ISBN 978-3-89821-576-3

63  Paul D'Anieri and Taras Kuzio (Eds.)
    Aspects of the Orange Revolution I
    Democratization and Elections in Post-Communist Ukraine
    ISBN 978-3-89821-698-2

64  Bohdan Harasymiw in collaboration with Oleh S. Ilnytzkyj (Eds.)
    Aspects of the Orange Revolution II
    Information and Manipulation Strategies in the 2004 Ukrainian Presidential Elections
    ISBN 978-3-89821-699-9

65  Ingmar Bredies, Andreas Umland and Valentin Yakushik (Eds.)
    Aspects of the Orange Revolution III
    The Context and Dynamics of the 2004 Ukrainian Presidential Elections
    ISBN 978-3-89821-803-0

66  Ingmar Bredies, Andreas Umland and Valentin Yakushik (Eds.)
    Aspects of the Orange Revolution IV
    Foreign Assistance and Civic Action in the 2004 Ukrainian Presidential Elections
    ISBN 978-3-89821-808-5

67  Ingmar Bredies, Andreas Umland and Valentin Yakushik (Eds.)
    Aspects of the Orange Revolution V
    Institutional Observation Reports on the 2004 Ukrainian Presidential Elections
    ISBN 978-3-89821-809-2

68  Taras Kuzio (Ed.)
    Aspects of the Orange Revolution VI
    Post-Communist Democratic Revolutions in Comparative Perspective
    ISBN 978-3-89821-820-7

69  Tim Bohse
    Autoritarismus statt Selbstverwaltung
    Die Transformation der kommunalen Politik in der Stadt Kaliningrad 1990-2005
    Mit einem Geleitwort von Stefan Troebst
    ISBN 978-3-89821-782-8

70  David Rupp
    Die Rußländische Föderation und die russischsprachige Minderheit in Lettland
    Eine Fallstudie zur Anwaltspolitik Moskaus gegenüber den russophonen Minderheiten im „Nahen Ausland" von 1991 bis 2002
    Mit einem Vorwort von Helmut Wagner
    ISBN 978-3-89821-778-1

71  Taras Kuzio
    Theoretical and Comparative Perspectives on Nationalism
    New Directions in Cross-Cultural and Post-Communist Studies
    With a foreword by Paul Robert Magocsi
    ISBN 978-3-89821-815-3

72  Christine Teichmann
    Die Hochschultransformation im heutigen Osteuropa
    Kontinuität und Wandel bei der Entwicklung des postkommunistischen Universitätswesens
    Mit einem Vorwort von Oskar Anweiler
    ISBN 978-3-89821-842-9

73  Julia Kusznir
    Der politische Einfluss von Wirtschaftseliten in russischen Regionen
    Eine Analyse am Beispiel der Erdöl- und Erdgasindustrie, 1992-2005
    Mit einem Vorwort von Wolfgang Eichwede
    ISBN 978-3-89821-821-4

74  Alena Vysotskaya
    Russland, Belarus und die EU-Osterweiterung
    Zur Minderheitenfrage und zum Problem der Freizügigkeit des Personenverkehrs
    Mit einem Vorwort von Katlijn Malfliet
    ISBN 978-3-89821-822-1

75  *Heiko Pleines (Hrsg.)*
Corporate Governance in post-
sozialistischen Volkswirtschaften
ISBN 978-3-89821-766-8

76  *Stefan Ihrig*
Wer sind die Moldawier?
Rumänismus versus Moldowanismus in
Historiographie und Schulbüchern der
Republik Moldova, 1991-2006
Mit einem Vorwort von Holm Sundhaussen
ISBN 978-3-89821-466-7

77  *Galina Kozhevnikova in collaboration
with Alexander Verkhovsky and
Eugene Veklerov*
Ultra-Nationalism and Hate Crimes in
Contemporary Russia
The 2004-2006 Annual Reports of Moscow's
SOVA Center
With a foreword by Stephen D. Shenfield
ISBN 978-3-89821-868-9

78  *Florian Küchler*
The Role of the European Union in
Moldova's Transnistria Conflict
With a foreword by Christopher Hill
ISBN 978-3-89821-850-4

79  *Bernd Rechel*
The Long Way Back to Europe
Minority Protection in Bulgaria
With a foreword by Richard Crampton
ISBN 978-3-89821-863-4

80  *Peter W. Rodgers*
Nation, Region and History in Post-
Communist Transitions
Identity Politics in Ukraine, 1991-2006
With a foreword by Vera Tolz
ISBN 978-3-89821-903-7

81  *Stephanie Solywoda*
The Life and Work of
Semen L. Frank
A Study of Russian Religious Philosophy
With a foreword by Philip Walters
ISBN 978-3-89821-457-5

82  *Vera Sokolova*
Cultural Politics of Ethnicity
Discourses on Roma in Communist
Czechoslovakia
ISBN 978-3-89821-864-1

83  *Natalya Shevchik Ketenci*
Kazakhstani Enterprises in Transition
The Role of Historical Regional Development
in Kazakhstan's Post-Soviet Economic
Transformation
ISBN 978-3-89821-831-3

84  *Martin Malek, Anna Schor-
Tschudnowskaja (Hrsg.)*
Europa im Tschetschenienkrieg
Zwischen politischer Ohnmacht und
Gleichgültigkeit
Mit einem Vorwort von Lipchan Basajewa
ISBN 978-3-89821-676-0

85  *Stefan Meister*
Das postsowjetische Universitätswesen
zwischen nationalem und
internationalem Wandel
Die Entwicklung der regionalen Hochschule
in Russland als Gradmesser der
Systemtransformation
Mit einem Vorwort von Joan DeBardeleben
ISBN 978-3-89821-891-7

86  *Konstantin Sheiko in collaboration
with Stephen Brown*
Nationalist Imaginings of the
Russian Past
Anatolii Fomenko and the Rise of Alternative
History in Post-Communist Russia
With a foreword by Donald Ostrowski
ISBN 978-3-89821-915-0

87  *Sabine Jenni*
Wie stark ist das „Einige Russland"?
Zur Parteibindung der Eliten und zum
Wahlerfolg der Machtpartei
im Dezember 2007
Mit einem Vorwort von Klaus Armingeon
ISBN 978-3-89821-961-7

88  *Thomas Borén*
Meeting-Places of Transformation
Urban Identity, Spatial Representations and
Local Politics in Post-Soviet St Petersburg
ISBN 978-3-89821-739-2

89  *Aygul Ashirova*
Stalinismus und Stalin-Kult in
Zentralasien
Turkmenistan 1924-1953
Mit einem Vorwort von Leonid Luks
ISBN 978-3-89821-987-7

90  Leonid Luks
    Freiheit oder imperiale Größe?
    Essays zu einem russischen Dilemma
    ISBN 978-3-8382-0011-8

91  Christopher Gilley
    The 'Change of Signposts' in the
    Ukrainian Emigration
    A Contribution to the History of
    Sovietophilism in the 1920s
    With a foreword by Frank Golczewski
    ISBN 978-3-89821-965-5

92  Philipp Casula, Jeronim Perovic
    (Eds.)
    Identities and Politics
    During the Putin Presidency
    The Discursive Foundations of Russia's
    Stability
    With a foreword by Heiko Haumann
    ISBN 978-3-8382-0015-6

93  Marcel Viëtor
    Europa und die Frage
    nach seinen Grenzen im Osten
    Zur Konstruktion ‚europäischer Identität' in
    Geschichte und Gegenwart
    Mit einem Vorwort von Albrecht Lehmann
    ISBN 978-3-8382-0045-3

94  Ben Hellman, Andrei Rogachevskii
    Filming the Unfilmable
    Casper Wrede's 'One Day in the Life
    of Ivan Denisovich'
    Second, Revised and Expanded Edition
    ISBN 978-3-8382-0044-6

95  Eva Fuchslocher
    Vaterland, Sprache, Glaube
    Orthodoxie und Nationenbildung
    am Beispiel Georgiens
    Mit einem Vorwort von Christina von Braun
    ISBN 978-3-89821-884-9

96  Vladimir Kantor
    Das Westlertum und der Weg
    Russlands
    Zur Entwicklung der russischen Literatur und
    Philosophie
    Ediert von Dagmar Herrmann
    Mit einem Beitrag von Nikolaus Lobkowicz
    ISBN 978-3-8382-0102-3

97  Kamran Musayev
    Die postsowjetische Transformation
    im Baltikum und Südkaukasus
    Eine vergleichende Untersuchung der
    politischen Entwicklung Lettlands und
    Aserbaidschans 1985-2009
    Mit einem Vorwort von Leonid Luks
    Ediert von Sandro Henschel
    ISBN 978-3-8382-0103-0

98  Tatiana Zhurzhenko
    Borderlands into Bordered Lands
    Geopolitics of Identity in Post-Soviet Ukraine
    With a foreword by Dieter Segert
    ISBN 978-3-8382-0042-2

99  Кирилл Галушко, Лидия Смола
    (ред.)
    Пределы падения – варианты
    украинского будущего
    Аналитико-прогностические исследования
    ISBN 978-3-8382-0148-1

100 Michael Minkenberg (ed.)
    Historical Legacies and the Radical
    Right in Post-Cold War Central and
    Eastern Europe
    With an afterword by Sabrina P. Ramet
    ISBN 978-3-8382-0124-5

101 David-Emil Wickström
    Rocking St. Petersburg
    Transcultural Flows and Identity Politics in
    the St. Petersburg Popular Music Scene
    With a foreword by Yngvar B. Steinholt
    Second, Revised and Expanded Edition
    ISBN 978-3-8382-0100-9

102 Eva Zabka
    Eine neue „Zeit der Wirren"?
    Der spät- und postsowjetische Systemwandel
    1985-2000 im Spiegel russischer
    gesellschaftspolitischer Diskurse
    Mit einem Vorwort von Margareta Mommsen
    ISBN 978-3-8382-0161-0

103 Ulrike Ziemer
    Ethnic Belonging, Gender and
    Cultural Practices
    Youth Identitites in Contemporary Russia
    With a foreword by Anoop Nayak
    ISBN 978-3-8382-0152-8

104  Ksenia Chepikova
'Einiges Russland' - eine zweite
KPdSU?
Aspekte der Identitätskonstruktion einer
postsowjetischen „Partei der Macht"
Mit einem Vorwort von Torsten Oppelland
ISBN 978-3-8382-0311-9

105  Леонид Люкс
Западничество или евразийство?
Демократия или идеократия?
Сборник статей об исторических дилеммах
России
С предисловием Владимира Кантора
ISBN 978-3-8382-0211-2

106  Anna Dost
Das russische Verfassungsrecht auf dem
Weg zum Föderalismus und zurück
Zum Konflikt von Rechtsnormen und
-wirklichkeit in der Russländischen
Föderation von 1991 bis 2009
Mit einem Vorwort von Alexander Blankenagel
ISBN 978-3-8382-0292-1

107  Philipp Herzog
Sozialistische Völkerfreundschaft,
nationaler Widerstand oder harmloser
Zeitvertreib?
Zur politischen Funktion der Volkskunst
im sowjetischen Estland
Mit einem Vorwort von Andreas Kappeler
ISBN 978-3-8382-0216-7

108  Marlène Laruelle (ed.)
Russian Nationalism, Foreign Policy,
and Identity Debates in Putin's Russia
New Ideological Patterns after the Orange
Revolution
ISBN 978-3-8382-0325-6

109  Michail Logvinov
Russlands Kampf gegen den
internationalen Terrorismus
Eine kritische Bestandsaufnahme des
Bekämpfungsansatzes
Mit einem Geleitwort von
Hans-Henning Schröder
und einem Vorwort von Eckhard Jesse
ISBN 978-3-8382-0329-4

110  John B. Dunlop
The Moscow Bombings
of September 1999
Examinations of Russian Terrorist Attacks
at the Onset of Vladimir Putin's Rule
Second, Revised and Expanded Edition
ISBN 978-3-8382-0388-1

111  Андрей А. Ковалёв
Свидетельство из-за кулис
российской политики I
Можно ли делать добро из зла?
(Воспоминания и размышления о
последних советских и первых
послесоветских годах)
With a foreword by Peter Reddaway
ISBN 978-3-8382-0302-7

112  Андрей А. Ковалёв
Свидетельство из-за кулис
российской политики II
Угроза для себя и окружающих
(Наблюдения и предостережения
относительно происходящего после 2000 г.)
ISBN 978-3-8382-0303-4

113  Bernd Kappenberg
Zeichen setzen für Europa
Der Gebrauch europäischer lateinischer
Sonderzeichen in der deutschen Öffentlichkeit
Mit einem Vorwort von Peter Schlobinski
ISBN 978-3-89821-749-1

114  Ivo Mijnssen
The Quest for an Ideal Youth in
Putin's Russia I
Back to Our Future! History, Modernity, and
Patriotism according to Nashi, 2005-2013
With a foreword by Jeronim Perović
Second, Revised and Expanded Edition
ISBN 978-3-8382-0368-3

115  Jussi Lassila
The Quest for an Ideal Youth in
Putin's Russia II
The Search for Distinctive Conformism in the
Political Communication of Nashi, 2005-2009
With a foreword by Kirill Postoutenko
Second, Revised and Expanded Edition
ISBN 978-3-8382-0415-4

116  Valerio Trabandt
Neue Nachbarn, gute Nachbarschaft?
Die EU als internationaler Akteur am Beispiel
ihrer Demokratieförderung in Belarus und der
Ukraine 2004-2009
Mit einem Vorwort von Jutta Joachim
ISBN 978-3-8382-0437-6

117  Fabian Pfeiffer
Estlands Außen- und Sicherheitspolitik I
Der estnische Atlantizismus nach der
wiedererlangten Unabhängigkeit 1991-2004
Mit einem Vorwort von Helmut Hubel
ISBN 978-3-8382-0127-6

118  Jana Podßuweit
Estlands Außen- und Sicherheitspolitik II
Handlungsoptionen eines Kleinstaates im
Rahmen seiner EU-Mitgliedschaft (2004-2008)
Mit einem Vorwort von Helmut Hubel
ISBN 978-3-8382-0440-6

119  Karin Pointner
Estlands Außen- und Sicherheitspolitik III
Eine gedächtnispolitische Analyse estnischer
Entwicklungskooperation 2006-2010
Mit einem Vorwort von Karin Liebhart
ISBN 978-3-8382-0435-2

120  Ruslana Vovk
Die Offenheit der ukrainischen
Verfassung für das Völkerrecht und
die europäische Integration
Mit einem Vorwort von Alexander Blankenagel
ISBN 978-3-8382-0481-9

121  Mykhaylo Banakh
Die Relevanz der Zivilgesellschaft
bei den postkommunistischen
Transformationsprozessen in mittel-
und osteuropäischen Ländern
Das Beispiel der spät- und postsowjetischen
Ukraine 1986-2009
Mit einem Vorwort von Gerhard Simon
ISBN 978-3-8382-0499-4

122  Michael Moser
Language Policy and the Discourse on
Languages in Ukraine under President
Viktor Yanukovych (25 February
2010–28 October 2012)
ISBN 978-3-8382-0497-0 (Paperback edition)
ISBN 978-3-8382-0507-6 (Hardcover edition)

123  Nicole Krome
Russischer Netzwerkkapitalismus
Restrukturierungsprozesse in der
Russischen Föderation am Beispiel des
Luftfahrtunternehmens "Aviastar"
Mit einem Vorwort von Petra Stykow
ISBN 978-3-8382-0534-2

124  David R. Marples
'Our Glorious Past'
Lukashenka's Belarus and
the Great Patriotic War
ISBN 978-3-8382-0574-8 (Paperback edition)
ISBN 978-3-8382-0675-2 (Hardcover edition)

125  Ulf Walther
Russlands "neuer Adel"
Die Macht des Geheimdienstes von
Gorbatschow bis Putin
Mit einem Vorwort von Hans-Georg Wieck
ISBN 978-3-8382-0584-7

126  Simon Geissbühler (Hrsg.)
Kiew – Revolution 3.0
Der Euromaidan 2013/14 und die
Zukunftsperspektiven der Ukraine
ISBN 978-3-8382-0581-6 (Paperback edition)
ISBN 978-3-8382-0681-3 (Hardcover edition)

127  Andrey Makarychev
Russia and the EU
in a Multipolar World
Discourses, Identities, Norms
With a foreword by Klaus Segbers
ISBN 978-3-8382-0629-5

128  Roland Scharff
Kasachstan als postsowjetischer
Wohlfahrtsstaat
Die Transformation des sozialen
Schutzsystems
Mit einem Vorwort von Joachim Ahrens
ISBN 978-3-8382-0622-6

129  Katja Grupp
Bild Lücke Deutschland
Kaliningrader Studierende sprechen über
Deutschland
Mit einem Vorwort von Martin Schulz
ISBN 978-3-8382-0552-6

130  Konstantin Sheiko, Stephen Brown
History as Therapy
Alternative History and Nationalist
Imaginings in Russia, 1991-2014
ISBN 978-3-8382-0665-3

131 *Elisa Kriza*
Alexander Solzhenitsyn: Cold War
Icon, Gulag Author, Russian
Nationalist?
A Study of the Western Reception of his
Literary Writings, Historical Interpretations,
and Political Ideas
With a foreword by Andrei Rogatchevski
ISBN 978-3-8382-0589-2 (Paperback edition)
ISBN 978-3-8382-0690-5 (Hardcover edition)

132 *Serghei Golunov*
The Elephant in the Room
Corruption and Cheating in Russian
Universities
ISBN 978-3-8382-0570-0

133 *Manja Hussner, Rainer Arnold (Hgg.)*
Verfassungsgerichtsbarkeit in
Zentralasien I
Sammlung von Verfassungstexten
ISBN 978-3-8382-0595-3

134 *Nikolay Mitrokhin*
Die "Russische Partei"
Die Bewegung der russischen Nationalisten in
der UdSSR 1953-1985
Aus dem Russischen übertragen von einem
Übersetzerteam unter der Leitung von Larisa Schippel
ISBN 978-3-8382-0024-8

135 *Manja Hussner, Rainer Arnold (Hgg.)*
Verfassungsgerichtsbarkeit in
Zentralasien II
Sammlung von Verfassungstexten
ISBN 978-3-8382-0597-7

136 *Manfred Zeller*
Das sowjetische Fieber
Fußballfans im poststalinistischen
Vielvölkerreich
Mit einem Vorwort von Nikolaus Katzer
ISBN 978-3-8382-0757-5

137 *Kristin Schreiter*
Stellung und Entwicklungspotential
zivilgesellschaftlicher Gruppen in
Russland
Menschenrechtsorganisationen im Vergleich
ISBN 978-3-8382-0673-8

138 *David R. Marples, Frederick V. Mills (eds.)*
Ukraine's Euromaidan
Analyses of a Civil Revolution
ISBN 978-3-8382-0660-8

139 *Bernd Kappenberg*
Setting Signs for Europe
Why Diacritics Matter for
European Integration
With a foreword by Peter Schlobinski
ISBN 978-3-8382-0663-9

140 *René Lenz*
Internationalisierung, Kooperation
und Transfer
Externe bildungspolitische Akteure in der
Russischen Föderation
Mit einem Vorwort von Frank Ettrich
ISBN 978-3-8382-0751-3

141 *Juri Plusnin, Yana Zausaeva, Natalia Zhidkevich, Artemy Pozanenko*
Wandering Workers
Mores, Behavior, Way of Life, and Political
Status of Domestic Russian Labor Migrants
Translated by Julia Kazantseva
ISBN 978-3-8382-0653-0

142 *Matthew Kott, David J. Smith (eds.)*
Latvia – A Work in Progress?
100 Years of State- and Nation-building
ISBN 978-3-8382-0648-6

143 Инна Чувычкина (ред.)
Экспортные нефте- и газопроводы
на постсоветском пространстве
Анализ трубопроводной политики в свете
теории международных отношений
ISBN 978-3-8382-0822-0

144 *Johann Zajaczkowski*
Russland – eine pragmatische
Großmacht?
Eine rollentheoretische Untersuchung
russischer Außenpolitik am Beispiel der
Zusammenarbeit mit den USA nach 9/11 und
des Georgienkrieges von 2008
Mit einem Vorwort von Siegfried Schieder
ISBN 978-3-8382-0837-4

145 *Boris Popivanov*
Changing Images of the Left in
Bulgaria
The Challenge of Post-Communism in the
Early 21st Century
ISBN 978-3-8382-0667-7

146  Lenka Krátká
    A History of the Czechoslovak Ocean
    Shipping Company 1948-1989
    How a Small, Landlocked Country Ran
    Maritime Business During the Cold War
    ISBN 978-3-8382-0666-0

147  Alexander Sergunin
    Explaining Russian Foreign Policy
    Behavior
    Theory and Practice
    ISBN 978-3-8382-0752-0

148  Darya Malyutina
    Migrant Friendships in
    a Super-Diverse City
    Russian-Speakers and their Social
    Relationships in London in the 21st Century
    With a foreword by Claire Dwyer
    ISBN 978-3-8382-0652-3

149  Alexander Sergunin, Valery Konyshev
    Russia in the Arctic
    Hard or Soft Power?
    ISBN 978-3-8382-0753-7

150  John J. Maresca
    Helsinki Revisited
    A Key U.S. Negotiator's Memoirs
    on the Development of the CSCE into the
    OSCE
    With a foreword by Hafiz Pashayev
    ISBN 978-3-8382-0852-7

151  Jardar Østbø
    The New Third Rome
    Readings of a Russian Nationalist Myth
    With a foreword by Pål Kolstø
    ISBN 978-3-8382-0870-1

152  Simon Kordonsky
    Socio-Economic Foundations of the
    Russian Post-Soviet Regime
    The Resource-Based Economy and Estate-
    Based Social Structure of Contemporary
    Russia
    With a foreword by Svetlana Barsukova
    ISBN 978-3-8382-0775-9

153  Duncan Leitch
    Assisting Reform in Post-Communist
    Ukraine 2000–2012
    The Illusions of Donors and the Disillusion of
    Beneficiaries
    With a foreword by Kataryna Wolczuk
    ISBN 978-3-8382-0844-2

154  Abel Polese
    Limits of a Post-Soviet State
    How Informality Replaces, Renegotiates, and
    Reshapes Governance in Contemporary
    Ukraine
    With a foreword by Colin Williams
    ISBN 978-3-8382-0845-9

155  Mikhail Suslov (ed.)
    Digital Orthodoxy in the Post-Soviet
    World
    The Russian Orthodox Church and Web 2.0
    ISBN 978-3-8382-0871-8

*ibidem*-Verlag
Melchiorstr. 15
D-70439 Stuttgart
info@ibidem-verlag.de

www.ibidem-verlag.de
www.ibidem.eu
www.edition-noema.de
www.autorenbetreuung.de